Priscilla and Ch
A Story of Alter

Frank Frankfort Moore

Alpha Editions

This edition published in 2024

ISBN 9789362511263

Design and Setting By
Alpha Editions
www.alphaedis.com
Email - info@alphaedis.com

As per information held with us this book is in Public Domain.
This book is a reproduction of an important historical work.
Alpha Editions uses the best technology to reproduce historical work
in the same manner it was first published to preserve its original nature.
Any marks or number seen are left intentionally to preserve.

Contents

CHAPTER I	- 1 -
CHAPTER II	- 9 -
CHAPTER III	- 18 -
CHAPTER IV	- 22 -
CHAPTER V	- 31 -
CHAPTER VI	- 39 -
CHAPTER VII	- 49 -
CHAPTER VIII	- 58 -
CHAPTER IX	- 68 -
CHAPTER X	- 75 -
CHAPTER XI	- 81 -
CHAPTER XII	- 90 -
CHAPTER XIII	- 97 -
CHAPTER XIV	- 103 -
CHAPTER XV	- 109 -
CHAPTER XVI	- 115 -
CHAPTER XVII	- 122 -
CHAPTER XVIII	- 130 -
CHAPTER XIX	- 137 -
CHAPTER XX	- 145 -
CHAPTER XXI	- 152 -
CHAPTER XXII	- 161 -
CHAPTER XXIII	- 170 -
CHAPTER XXIV	- 175 -

CHAPTER XXV	- 184 -
CHAPTER XXVI	- 194 -
CHAPTER XXVII	- 202 -
CHAPTER XXVIII	- 208 -
CHAPTER XXIX	- 216 -
CHAPTER XXX	- 224 -
CHAPTER XXXI	- 232 -
CHAPTER XXXII	- 240 -
CHAPTER XXXIII	- 249 -
CHAPTER XXXIV	- 260 -
CHAPTER XXXV	- 266 -
THE END.	- 273 -

CHAPTER I

WHAT Morley Quorn could not understand was why people made such a fuss over that fellow Kelton. Who was Kelton anyway that he should give himself airs, he enquired with some insistence of the five "bassi"—they were labelled "bassi" in the programme—who were lounging about the door of the schoolroom where the rehearsal for the concert was being held.

"He does give himself airs, doesn't he?" growled another of the same division of the chorus.

The rest shook their heads gloomily. It was denied to them to express themselves adequately on this point, the fact being that the Reverend Edwin Tucknott, the curate of St. Joan of Arc, was standing hard by with his flute. The proximity of the clergyman checked complete freedom of speech, including "language," among the young men, for they failed to recollect that in the due performance of that portion of his sacred office known as the Commination Service he went much further than the most highly qualified basso could go even when he found it necessary to describe the absurdities of another and more popular vocalist.

Mr. Tucknott smiled his olive branch smile in the direction of the "bassi."

"I suppose it is natural for a tenor to give himself airs," he remarked. The instant he had spoken he glanced around in rather a shaky way. He had a feeling that he had gone a little too far. He hoped that no one would fancy he had been unable to resist a play upon the words. He had no need, however, to have any misgiving on this point. It was plain that his daring had hurt the susceptibilities of none.

"Oh, I don't say that we're not prepared for a good bit of side from a—a chap that fancies he sings tenor," said Morley Quorn; "but that fellow Kelton goes just too far. Now what is he up to this time? Cheeking Mozart Tutt! I wonder that Mr. Tutt stands his impudence."

But in a second it became plain that Mr. Mozart Tutt was doing nothing of the sort. He had been playing the pianoforte accompaniment to Mr.

Kelton's song, but not in a way that was met with the unqualified approval of Mr. Kelton.

"I must ask you to try to play *pianissimo* when I am doing my shake on the high note," said he; and Mr. Tutt had accordingly played *pianissimo* when the thing was repeated.

But Mr. Kelton did not attempt to ascend to the high notes. He stopped short, and let his page of music flap down in a movement suggestive of a disappointment that was practically hopeless.

"If you don't throw some life into the passage you had better let me sing without any accompaniment," he said in a pained way.

"I will play in any way you suggest, Mr. Kelton," said Mr. Tutt. "Will you kindly sit down to the piano and play the accompaniment as you wish it to be played?"

But this invitation the tenor felt it to be his duty to decline. He was no musician. He could not play a passage from the musical score to save his life, and of this fact Mr. Tutt was well aware.

"I don't ask very much—only that you should give me a little support," said Mr. Kelton with a suggestion of long-suffering in his voice. "I take it that the accompaniment to a song—a tenor song—should be played as if it were nothing more than a background, so to speak, and the vocalization supplies the colour. I don't wish to discourage you, Mr. Tutt; you play quite well sometimes—quite well enough for the people about here; but we must have light and shade, Mr. Tutt. Now let us try again."

If Mr. Kelton sang with expression, Mr. Tutt played with expressions—he was almost audible at the door. But still he attacked the air with spirit. He was a very competent man; he had composed a *Magnificat* which Miss Caffyn, the Rector's daughter, said took a deal of beating, like a dusty carpet.

Down went Mr. Kelton's page of music once more, after he had strained up to a very shaky G, and up jumped Mr. Mozart Tutt, before the vocalist had time to formulate his latest complaint.

"I've done my best, and if that isn't good enough for Mr. Kelton he would do well to play his own accompaniment, or get some one to play it who will submit to his insults," said the musician.

He walked with dignity to the door leading off the platform, and was enthusiastically greeted by the five "bassi." Mr. Tucknott, flute and all, ran away; he was fearful lest some people should associate him with the intrepid step taken by Mr. Tutt.

It was the Rector's wife who took command of the situation. She knew that the singing of Mr. Kelton increased to an appreciable extent the attractiveness of the concert, inasmuch as the Honourable Mrs. Bowlby-Sutherst had a passion for listening to tenor music, and Mrs. Bowlby-Sutherst lived at the Hall, and, her husband being patron of the living, she duly patronized the people who lived by it. It would never do, Mrs. Caffyn, the Rector's wife, perceived, to induce the patroness to attend the concert and then find that there was no tenor solo. That was why she approached Mr. Kelton with a smile that was meant to suggest a great deal, and that certainly assured Mr. Kelton that the Church was on his side.

"We mustn't be too hard on poor Mr. Tutt," she said soothingly.

"I'm not," cried the tenor quickly. "But it's a little too bad that a man in my position should be subjected to the caprice of such a person. I have a great mind to throw up the whole business."

He had turned a cold shoulder to the lady, as if he meant to leave the platform that very instant.

"Oh, no, Mr. Kelton, you would never desert us in such a fashion; it would not be like you to do so," said Mrs. Cafifyn. "Mrs. Bowlby-Sutherst is, I know, coming to our concert solely to hear you sing 'In the Land of Sleep.'"

"I cannot help that, Mrs. Cafifyn. I do not expect a great deal when I come to sing at a country concert, but I look for common civility, Mrs. Cafifyn—common civility."

"We are all so sorry. I would not for anything that this—this little difference should arise. You will make allowance for the strain upon poor Mr. Tutt—I know you will."

"Not unless he apologizes—I have a certain amount of self-respect, Mrs. Caffyn. I have no idea of allowing a person in the position of Mr. Tutt to presume——"

"Oh, mother, I have just been talking to Priscilla, and she says she will be delighted to play the accompaniment to 'The Land of Sleep,'" said Rosa Caffyn, who came up hastily to the platform at that moment. She was a girl who was alluded to in a friendly spirit as healthy—in an unhealthy spirit as blowsy. She had a good eye, critics of beauty affirmed, and a straightforward voice, Mr. Tutt had more than once announced to the schoolmistress.

"How sweet of Priscilla!" cried Mrs. Caffyn. "Oh, Mr. Kelton, you will, I know, be pleased with Priscilla's playing—Miss Wadhurst, you know," she added in an explanatory tone.

Mr. Kelton pursed out his lips slightly, assuming the air of a man who is being bandaged by the people in the motor that has knocked him down—an air of aggrieved submission.

"An amateur?" he said. "I am not familiar with the name as a professional."

"Oh, yes—strictly amateur," replied Miss Caffyn, who played golf and other things, and so knew all about the distinctions between performers.

"I'm not accustomed to be accompanied by amateurs," said the tenor, who was a bank clerk in the county town, "but I don't mind giving her a trial. Where is she?"

He put on his *pince-nez* and looked patronizingly around.

"Here she comes," said Rosa, beckoning to some one who was seated in the body of the school-house—a young woman with a good deal that might be called striking about her, besides her hair, which was rather marvellous, and made one think of a painter of the early Venetian school—there was too much of brown in it to allow of its ever being called golden, and too much of gold to admit of its being called coppery. People who knew where they stood compromised the matter by calling it marvellous. But whatever it was it suited her, though a girl or two had said positively that Priscilla Wadhurst would be nothing without her hair. They were wrong: she would still have been Priscilla—with a difference.

"It is so sweet of you, Priscilla," began Mrs Caffyn.

"Oh, no," said Priscilla; "I am not good enough—not nearly good enough."

She cast down her eyes for a tremulous moment, and then raised them coyly to Mr. Kelton's face; and she saw by the way he looked at her that he thought she would do.

"You will not find that I am such a terrible person after all, Miss—Miss——"

"Wadhurst," said Rosa. "I should have introduced you. Miss Wadhurst—Mr. Kelton."

"I heard you last year," murmured Miss Wadhurst. "I am not likely to forget it. I am not nearly good enough to be your accompanist, Mr. Kelton; but if you will make allowances——"

"Don't be afraid," said he with a condescending wave of the left hand—the right was engaged at the point of his moustache. "You will find me anything but the dreadful person you might imagine me to be. All that I ask is to have my instructions carried out to the letter. I am sure that I shall have no trouble with you, Miss Wadhurst."

"I can only do my best, Mr. Kelton," said Priscilla, sitting down at the piano.

"What a nice girl she is! and plays so prettily too," murmured Mrs. Cafifyn, resuming her seat and addressing the lady next to her, a Mrs. Musgrave.

"Pity she made such a fool of herself!" said Mrs. Musgrave, who, being a large subscriber to the Church and other charities, availed herself of the privilege of speaking out when she pleased; and it pleased her to speak rather more frequently than she pleased by speaking.

"Ah, yes, yes—a sad story—very sad!" assented the Rector's wife with a pleasant sigh.

And then Miss Wadhurst struck the first chords of "In the Land of Sleep" in no spirit of compromise. She played the accompaniment a great deal better than Mr. Tutt had played it—Mr. Tutt said so, and he knew. Mr. Kelton affirmed it, though he knew nothing about it. Miss Wadhurst knew a good deal about a piano, and within the past half-hour she had acquired more than an elementary knowledge of the vanity of an amateur tenor. She knew that she was at the piano not to do anything more artistic than to feed the vanity of the vocalist, and she found herself giving him a very generous meal. She never allowed the instrument to assert itself, and she wilfully rejected several chances that the music offered her of showing him what was the exact effect he should aim at achieving. She knew what the music meant and she knew what the man meant, and she let him do what he pleased. She gave him plenty of rope and he made use of every fathom. She waited while he lingered lovingly on the high note that came into the setting of every stanza, and she smothered up his false quantities in his lower range. She prolonged the symphony which the composer had artfully introduced between one stanza and the next—this was the great feature of the song, for it enabled the tenor to burst in with startling effect just when people were getting thoughtful—and, above all, she allowed the vocalist to have the last word, though the composer meant this to be the perquisite of the piano.

Mr. Kelton professed himself delighted. He was patronizingly polite in his reference to Miss Wadhurst's "touch"—it was quite creditable, he said; occasionally it had reminded him of Wallace Clarke—it really had. Wallace Clarke was the very prince of accompanists; it was a pleasure to sing to his playing. But lest Miss Wadhurst should allow her head to be turned by his encomiums, Mr. Kelton very discreetly expressed the hope that she would spend the evening with the music, so that when the time came for her to accompany him in public she should be able to give all her attention to his singing, and not have to glance at the pages of the music before her.

"Keep your eye on me," he said. "I never bind myself down to sing a song twice in the same way—I trust to the inspiration of the moment. My accompanist must be prepared for anything."

"You must not be too hard on Miss Wadhurst," said Mrs. Caffyn, smiling.

"Oh, dear, no! you may trust me," he said heartily. "I know Miss Wadhurst will trust me. By the way, Miss Wadhurst, I think I shall sing 'The Message' for the *encore*. I hope you know the accompaniment."

"I think I can manage it," said Priscilla.

"It is so good of you to promise us an *encore*," cried Mrs. Caffyn, "and I am sure that Mrs. Bowlby-Sutherst will be delighted."

"I am always ready to comply with an *encore*," said Mr. Kelton, "but I simply decline to respond when people *encore* my *encore*. Please bear that in mind, Mrs. Caffyn. I cannot in justice to myself do more than respond to one *encore*, let that be clearly understood. No matter how enthusiastic your friends may become———"

"I am going home. Are you coming, Priscilla?" cried Rosa Caffyn, breaking in on the cautionary remarks of the tenor with such abruptness as caused him to be startled, and put on his *pince-nez* for the purpose of giving her a rebuking stare. But she was off before he had fallen into the right pose to obtain the best results, and Priscilla was only a pace behind her.

"Did you ever hear such a bounder?" cried Rosa, before they were quite off the platform. "The idea of taking an *encore*—a double *encore*—for granted! Priscilla, I would give my second best hat to be sure that he did not get even the first *encore*."

"He knows that an *encore* is a foregone conclusion: every one *encores* the tenor," said Priscilla, smiling queerly. "Still, it wouldn't surprise me if for once—"

"What are you grinning about in that way? Do you mean to get up a *claque* to shout him down?" said Rosa, fancying that she saw some intelligence behind the smile of the other.

"Goodness! Do you think that it would be possible to import the tactics of Italian opera into our peaceful village?" cried Priscilla. "Besides, how could any one prevent an *encore* being given? It is easy enough to force one on, but how are you, short of hissing, to keep down the applause?"

Rosa looked at her searchingly.

"I don't know, but I believe that you do," she said.

"Oh, Laura Mercy!" exclaimed Priscilla, and laughed.

Before Rosa could demand an explanation of the laugh, they came face to face with Mr. Mozart Tutt. He was smiling, but not quite easily; it was plain that he was not sure how his behaviour in regard to the accompaniment would be regarded by the young women; he had a great respect for their point of view, and so his smile was a little blurred. Its outlines were fluctuating.

He raised a playful forefinger to Priscilla.

"I am ashamed of you," he said in a low voice.

"You need not be, Mr. Tutt. You know that I played the accompaniment quite well," said she.

"You played it artfully, not artistically," he replied. "The composer would be ready to tear his hair at the way you pandered at his expense to that fellow. Did you mean to teach me a lesson in manners?"

"I mean to teach him a lesson in manners, and music," said Priscilla confidentially.

"What do you say?" cried Rosa, who had failed to hear every word.

"I only mean that in my opinion Mr. Tutt showed himself singularly lacking in tact as well as tactics," said Priscilla. "The idea of a capable musician standing on his dignity with a man who sings without any knowledge of music! You should be ashamed of yourself, Mr. Tutt. You a master, and yet incapable of teaching him a lesson!"

"I think that you were quite right, Mr. Tutt," said Rosa. "You showed the most marvellous patience with that bounder, and you were fully justified in throwing him over. If he were Caruso himself he could not have behaved more insolently."

"I am so glad that you take my part, Miss Caffyn," said Mr. Tutt. "I am sorry that you have not been able to persuade Miss Wadhurst to take your view of the incident. I assure you that in all my experience I never found it necessary to act as I did to-day. It was very painful to me. I wish I understood you better, Miss Wadhurst."

"Didn't some one say that to be understood was to be found out?" said Priscilla. "Good-bye, Mr. Tutt. Mr. Kelton instructed me to spend the rest of the day in the company of—of the accompaniment, and I mean to obey him. I think I see my way to do a good deal with that accompaniment. Good-bye. I suppose you mean to wait for your mother, Rosa?"

"I wouldn't if you would make it worth my while not," said Rosa.

Priscilla shook her head and hurried off.

CHAPTER II

Attention was called to the fact that Mr. Kelton, the great tenor, who had come from Great Gagglington to sing at Mrs. Caffyn's concert, was walking about the streets—to be strictly accurate, the street—of Framsby in the morning, just as if he was an ordinary person. He was greatly looked at, and it was clearly understood that he was fully cognisant of this fact, for the self-conscious way in which he tried not to appear self-conscious could scarcely fail to strike even the young women of the Glee and Madrigal choir, who, it was understood, were devoted to him, not merely collectively, but individually.

It was a great gift, surely, that with which he was endowed, but at the same time, like other precious endowments of Nature, it carried with it a great responsibility—perhaps greater than any one man should be asked to sustain, was what Mr. Eggston, the Nonconformist draper of Framsby High Street, remarked to his two assistants (male) when he had returned to the low level of his shop work, after gazing out at Mr. Kelton, who went by with Clara Gibson, of the Bank. (Mr. Kelton was the guest of the Gibsons of the Bank—the Gibsons of the Bank were said to be "very musical.") Perhaps there was something in the Nonconformist judgment on this point, and perhaps there was also something in the view taken of the whole case of Mr. Kelton and his assumptions by the friends of Mr. Mozart Tutt, and crystallized into the one word "puppy!"

At any rate, during the day (the concert was to begin at eight o'clock in the evening) the topic of the town was the quarrel—perhaps it should rather be called an artistic misunderstanding—between Mr. Tutt and Mr. Kelton; and of course it was inevitable that the action of Miss Wadhurst in coming forward to play the accompaniment when Mr. Tutt had felt himself insulted and retired from the discharge of that duty, was widely commented on.

Some who took part in the discussion affirmed that it was rather extraordinary for a young woman, situated as she was, to place herself in a position of such prominence. Surely it would have shown better taste on her part if she had kept in the background. It was foolish for her to do anything that might have a tendency to attract attention to herself and to reawaken public interest in that other affair with which she had been connected. To be sure, it was not quite her fault, that other thing; but still, if she had made proper—even reasonable—enquiries before it happened she would not have been made a fool of. Oh, yes, it was a great pity that she had failed to learn her lesson at that time.

And then an impartial chronicler cannot neglect the criticisms of The Families—the important but not impartial families who surrounded Framsby with a cincture made up of ten generations of stupidity. The Palings, the Hamptsons, the Whiteleafifes—these represented the gems in the girdle that enclosed Framsby, and they agreed that that Wadhurst young woman was showing herself to be all that they had feared she must be. "Of course there never was a question of our looking on her as one of ourselves; but still we thought it might be possible, after a year or two, when the thing was not so fresh in people's minds... but the young woman has not shown herself to be duly penitent for having been made a fool of, and now she is actually going to appear on a platform—a public platform.... Oh, yes, it is quite as well that we made no move."

And all this discussion took place between Wednesday afternoon and Thursday evening. It was on Wednesday afternoon that the rehearsal of the music was held; the concert was to take place on the following evening. Rosa Caffyn heard a good deal of the talk that arose on all sides during this brief space of time, and she knew that, whatever surmises were made as to Priscilla's object in agreeing to play the accompaniment, not one of them got within measurable distance of the truth. What was the true object of Priscilla's ready compliance Rosa herself was at a loss to say; but she was quite convinced that good nature was not at the bottom of it—the suggestion made by Mrs. Caffyn and acquiesced in by the Rector—and she was equally certain that a desire to bring herself into prominence was not the impulse in the force of which she had acted. Good gracious! the prominence of the player of a pianoforte accompaniment to a single song! Good nature! the most weak-kneed of the virtues. Rosa knew perfectly well that Priscilla had too much character to be ever accused of being good-natured. Miss Caffyn was puzzled, and it was not for the first time that she was so in association with the affairs of Priscilla Wadhurst. There, for instance, was that other affair which gave Priscilla rather more than the prominence of an accompanist at a charity concert—that had puzzled Rosa. How could any girl——

But Rosa refused to allow herself to enter again into that tortuous question; all that she knew was that Priscilla Wadhurst remained before her eyes as an object worthy of admiration—a girl who could think out things beforehand, and who refused to allow herself to be got the better of by Fate; who refused to be submissive to the ways of Providence, but was always on the look-out for a by-way of her own—just what strong-minded persons are when they are busy making history. When any young woman like Rosa Caffyn has come to think of another in such a spirit, she has gone too far to be brought by much thinking into line with the rest of the world, who, though thinking they can see, are blind and incapable even of groping.

But the last criticism on Priscilla Wadhurst came from Morley Quorn and the company of "bassi." It took the form of a shaking of the head—a sad, disappointed shake taken at three-quarter time at first, but gradually quickening until it ceased in a quiver of quavers. The "bassi" were large-hearted fellows, and had always thought the best of Miss Wadhurst. They felt quite sad to think that she had consented to help that chap Kelton up to another step in that pyramid of self-conceit to the apex of which he had been toiling for years, since he had received his first *encore* on a platform in Framsby and had been asked to supper at the Bowlby-Sutherts. Yes, the "bassi" shook their heads, but they determined so far as the concert was concerned to remain neutral in respect of applause; they would not stoop so low as to refuse to applaud the singing of the song, if it was well sung, simply because the singer had insulted the musical conductor. At the same time they would certainly not applaud an incompetent rendering of the song simply because a young lady who had wonderful hair and who had been rather unfortunate in other ways was playing the accompaniment.

And thus, with criticism and comment and innuendo, the hours passed until the doors of the hall were opened and the public crushed into their places, the Bowlby-Sutherts arriving a little late. Priscilla sat in the third row of the front seats by the side of her friend Rosa Caffyn and her young brother Clifford Caffyn. The Rector and his wife had, of course, seats in the front row; it was necessary that they should be in that position, so that they might welcome their patrons the Bowlby-Sutherts, and this division of the family deprived people of the power of saying that Mrs. Caffyn wholly approved of Priscilla. Mrs. Caffyn had long ago perceived that it would be dangerous if not actually detrimental to her position—well, not exactly her position, for the position of the wife of a clergyman of the Church of England is not jeopardized even by a display of Christianity—no, but still—well, Mrs. Caffyn had no notion of allowing her name to be mixed up with that of Priscilla Wadhurst, especially when any of the Bowlby-Sutherts were at hand. And the consequence was that people said that Mrs. Caffyn had acted very well in this delicate matter, and that when her daughter Rosa got a year or two older she would find that it did not pay to foster close intimacies with people who showed a tendency to be unlucky in life.

Mr. Morley Quorn got a great reception when he came forward to sing "Honour and Arms," and when he got his second wind for one of the runs, and then went ahead of the piano through a feeling of terror lest he might not have enough breath to complete the run of "glo-ho-ho-ho-ho-ho-ho-ho-ho-ho-ho-ho-ho-ho-ho-horay," in one of those braggadocio flights of the great master, Mr. Kelton, who was among the performers on the platform, bowed his head and laughed gently to himself, but with the face of the man who laughs so that no one could fail to notice what he was about.

But although Morley Quorn saw him out of the corner of his eye, and longed to do for him all that Harapha looked forward to do for Samson, still he managed to pull himself together and make a distinct impression by his low note at the finish. He held on to that low note, and every one knew that he meant it to be a sort of challenge to that fellow Kelton. But Mr. Kelton, feeling the same thing, was more offensive than before, for he joined in the applause that greeted the singing of the *aria*; only he ceased clapping his hands long before the rest of the audience had ceased clapping theirs, and then he glanced around with a look of pained enquiry in his eyes, as if he were the conductor of an orchestra asking his kettledrums what they meant by continuing their noise after he had given the signal that the thing was over.

He made a little motion with his hands when an *encore* was insisted on, as though he felt that such an absence of discrimination made him quite hopeless of such an audience.

Mr. Morley Quorn, however, took his call, but not too easily, and when Mr. Tutt struck the first notes of "The Wolf" there were loud tokens of approval heard on all sides; for Morley's treatment of the panoramic effects of this song was well known to Framsby. While the horrors of the situation were being dealt with vocally, Kelton was wise enough to contain himself, and the basso went off the platform with an air of triumph.

Rosa looked into Priscilla's face and smiled; but Priscilla did not return her smile. She could not think that the fact of Morley Quorn's having come brilliantly out of the ordeal in any way exculpated Mr. Kelton for that sneering laugh of his.

But Mr. Kelton had not yet exhausted his resources of irritation, for when Mr. Mozart Tutt sat down to the piano to play the "Moonlight Sonata," instead of joining heartily in the greeting that the conductor received, as any one with any sense would have done, in order to give the audience to understand that, however he might differ from Mr. Tutt on certain points in playing an accompaniment, he was still generous enough to recognize the man's merit when displayed in other channels—instead of doing this, with emphasis, he yawned ostentatiously, tilting back his chair, with his hand over his mouth. Then he began to talk to the man beside him, and a little later he smiled down upon Priscilla in the third row and signalled something to her, afterwards lying back and laughing up to the ceiling, and, on recovering himself, assuming a bored look, and taking out his watch and putting it to his ear as if to satisfy his doubts as to the accuracy of its registration of an inexpressibly dull five minutes.

Mrs. Caffyn was not a very observant woman, but she made up her mind that she would never again write a letter of entreaty to Mr. Kelton concerning her concert. Even though the patronage of the Bowlby-Suthersts were reserved, still she would not bore him again.

The tenor's two songs had no place in the first part of the programme, and he did not resume his seat on the platform after the interval between the parts. He always took care that his entrance was made at the effective moment—when the audience had become warmed up, but not weary; and of course Priscilla had to leave her place in the body of the hall to await his moment in the little room where tea was brewed upon the occasion of some festivity involving the brewing of tea and the distribution of buns. Here she sat with Mr. Kelton and a couple of "soprani," as they were styled in the programme, whom Mr. Kelton made laugh by his clever imitation of Mr. Morley Quorn's "Wolf." He was under the impression, he said, that no concert direction was in so bad a way but that they could keep "The Wolf" from the door. But then Framsby was a funny place altogether. Fancy "Honour and Arms," "The Wolf," and that blessed "Moonlight Sonata" all in one evening! There was no other town known to him where so old-fashioned a programme would be tolerated.

Then he cleared his throat, and ran up the scale once or twice as he had heard artists do while waiting for their turn.

"Are you in good voice, Mr. Kelton?" enquired Priscilla. "Your song is the next."

He smiled.

"My dear young lady," he said, "I am not like one of those tenors of long ago who could never be depended on from one day to another—Sims Reeves, you know—people of that stamp. No, I am always to be depended on. I am always at my best."

"And never nervous?" she suggested.

"I don't know what nerves are," he replied.

And then they heard the sound of the applause that marked the finish of the duet which, in the programme, preceded "In the Land of Sleep." Priscilla jumped up from her seat. Mr. Kelton rose with the smile of a man of leisure and gave a self-satisfied glance at the little mirror. He improved the set of his collar by a deft little push and then saw to his cuffs.

"Don't be in a hurry; there's plenty of time," he remarked to Priscilla. He had no idea of falling into line with the ordinary amateurs who aimed at expedition. He knew the importance of making an audience slightly impatient for his appearance. He even knew the value of opening the door leading on to the platform and allowing it to close again—giving them a false alarm or two after a prolonged delay. He smiled at Priscilla g it when, after that trick of opening the door and closing it on a blank, there was a movement among the people in the hall. But this was just where Priscilla drew the line. She detested being associated with such trickery. She pulled open the door and walked on to the platform alone, making a straight line to the piano, and acknowledging in no way the warm greeting of the audience.

She had spoiled his *entree*, and he was well aware of this fact. The audience had wasted their applause upon her; he only came in for the tail end of it. And he was not artist enough to be able at a moment's notice to hide his discomfiture under the ingratiating smile of the professional, which is supposed to make the most critical audience become genial. His smile was the leer of a Cherokee when his successful opponent is removing his scalp.

Priscilla spread out the paper of the music and struck the first chord of the accompaniment. At the right moment the singer's voice came in, and he meandered through the stanza, reaching up for his high note in the repetition of the refrain and taking it easily. There was a considerable amount of applause at this point, and upon that applause Priscilla the pianist had counted, when she ran pleasantly into that very expressive "symphony" which every one knows makes so effective a link from stanza to stanza of "In the Land of Sleep." The accompaniment was still running along soothingly and dreamily when the vocalist once more took up the theme, and was perfectly well satisfied with his treatment of it until he got to the refrain. Then he became aware of the fact that his voice was rather strained. He felt that he must make an effort to do that high note, and when the moment came, he strained. He did not quite achieve it; every one that had ears to hear knew that he was flat; and he knew it himself. He found it necessary to resist the temptation—for the first time—of holding the note, and he finished the refrain in a hurry. Led by the Bowlby-Suthersts, however, the audience gave some applause to the second stanza; and once again Priscilla was grateful for it. She flashed into the introduction to the third stanza—the showy one, with the high A introduced twice, the second time with a grace-note that adds to its effect.

But it soon became plain that the vocalist, if he had never before known what nervousness meant, was quickly learning something of this mystery. It seemed as if his voice was becoming tired, and once there was actually a suggestion of breaking down. But then Mr. Kelton pulled himself together, lifted up his chin, and boldly attacked the refrain. In an instant it became certain that he would never be able to touch the high notes. For some reason or other, which was plain only to Mr. Mozart Tutt and a few other musicians who were present, Mr. Kelton's voice had lost some notes out of its range. He slurred over the lower notes on the principle of an aeronaut throwing out a sandbag or two, in order that he might get up higher. He went up and up and then made a bold attempt to squeeze out the A by some means. The result sounded like the quivering shriek of a leaky steam whistle. No one, however, knew exactly what it was like, the fact being that its vibrations were drowned by the shrieks of laughter of the school girls in the gallery, and in another instant these infectious sounds had spread to the body of the hall, and there was a whole minute of irrepressible merriment; even the honest attempt made by some of the boys from the grammar school to suggest a natural parallel to Mr. Kelton's note, failed to restore order; but this was only to be expected, considering that there was a serious difference of opinion among these authorities as to the direction in which the equivalent was to be found, a large and important section maintaining sturdily that the farmyard at the break of day provided a variety of such notes (examples given); while the lower forms rather more than hinted at their impression that not dawn but moonlight was made vocal with such sounds—moonlight and tiles, or perhaps a garden wall.

Mr. Kelton was unable to profit by this purely academical discussion, or to give his casting vote to decide which of the theories—equally well supported by the disputants—was the more plausible. His weird shriek had struck terror even to his own soul—the ravening howl of Morley Quorn's old "Wolf" sounded domestic by comparison—and with a gasp he had crumpled up the pages of his music and dashed the parcel at his feet, making a rush for the door, through which he went, closing it with an echoing bang that deprived the scene of the last shred of seriousness, and Mr. Kelton of the last shred of sympathy which his misfortune may have tended to excite among the audience.

Miss Wadhurst, every one agreed, had behaved nobly under the ordeal to which she, as (to some extent) a participant in the fiasco, had been subjected. She showed that she was doing her best to mask the retreat of the tenor by limbering up and bringing into action all the heavy artillery within the compass of her piano, and she was smiling so good-naturedly all the time that soon the cat-calls and cock-crowing merged into applause. When she rose from the instrument with a laugh, and took her call, nodding to the boys in the distance, she received an ovation, and made a graceful retreat to a chair just below the altos of the chorus.

In another minute Mr. Mozart Tutt was tapping with his *bâton* on the music stand, the members of the chorus sprang to their feet, and order came about quite naturally while "When the Wind Bloweth in from the Sea" was being charmingly sung by the choir; and the remaining details of an admirably selected programme were tastefully performed.

The performing members of the choir seemed extremely well satisfied with themselves, especially the "bassi"; but Mr. Morley Quorn wore a solemn look, while his friends were inclined to be jocular. He was wondering if, in spite of the verdict of science and the agnostic trend of modern thought, there was not such a thing as retributive justice. He felt strongly on the vexed question of "lessons." Surely the downfall of Mr. Kelton the tenor should convey to the most careless of amateurs the necessity for the maintenance of a spirit of meekness even though he may be able (upon ordinary occasions) to produce the high A. Mr. Quorn tried to feel subdued; so that when young Titmus assured him that he had never sung "The Wolf" with greater effect, he only shook his head.

He had no notion that the administration of the valuable "lesson" was due solely to the cleverness of Miss Wadhurst, who had seen great possibilities in that picturesque "symphony" in the accompaniment. It was very daring of her to run the chance of such applause greeting the finish of each stanza as should enable her to raise the key in which the song was set, without being detected. She knew that Mr. Kelton would be too greatly absorbed in himself to notice the modulation until it should be too late; but she was not so sure of some other people on the platform. It seemed, however, that no one had detected her manouvre except Mr. Tutt. She caught his eye when she was in the act of rising from the piano, and she perceived that he knew all.

That was why she tried to avoid him when she was leaving the platform, letting her steps drag behind the choir. She failed in her object this time, for he waited for her.

"I was lost in admiration," he murmured. "It never occurred to me. Anyhow, I never should have had the courage to try it on. You must have worked pretty hard at the thing last night. You have been well grounded. I couldn't have worked out the double transposition in the time. And then you had to trust to your memory."

"I meant to teach him a lesson," murmured Priscilla.

"And you have done it! My word, you have done it. He caught the last train to Sherningham, starting just as he was. His suit case is to be sent after him. I could hear him shaking off the dust of Framsby from his feet. He did it very soundly in the vestibule—a regular cloud of it. A lesson! My word! a lesson!"

CHAPTER III

Of course Priscilla confessed to her friend Rosa by what means she had encompassed the downfall of Mr. Kelton. Rosa was not much of a musician, and it seemed to her quite wonderful that any one could perform such a feat as the transposition of a song within the space of twenty-four hours, and then not shrink from playing the modulated version from memory.

"It had to be done," said Priscilla firmly. "How could I stand by and hear that conceited man—but there was a clever man—a Frenchman of course—who said 'a tenor is not a man but a disease.' I wonder why it is that so many girls simply worship a tenor. Dr. Needham says it dates back to primeval man and primeval woman, All singing, he says, is simply primeval man calling to primeval woman to come out for a walk in the moonlight. And that's why the most favourite songs nowadays are love-songs—tenor love-songs—languishing things—I hate them!"

"It served that horrid man right," said Rosa. She did not show herself to be greatly interested in the theories of Dr. Needham; but she was intensely interested in the humiliation of a man who was horrid. "I should like to be able to do just what you did. Men want to be taken down dreadfully; but if a girl ever rises to do it she is looked on as horrid herself."

"And she usually is," said Priscilla. "I have sometimes felt that it was very horrid of me to play that trick upon that odious Mr. Kelton. Who am I that I should set myself up to avenge his insults in regard to Mr. Tutt? I have heard a little voice whispering in my ear."

"You were quite right. Besides—" here Rosa made a little pause—"besides, haven't you very good reason to—to—well, I meant that you were very badly treated by men, Priscilla dear."

"Only by one man," said Priscilla quickly. "Only by one."

"And isn't that enough? It's a shame that one man should have it in his power to wreck the life of a girl."

"It does seem to be a shame. But what's the good of complaining? A woman has always been the bearer of burdens, and if she complains she is treated worse than ever. I'm not sure that in the old days—before there was any thought of convention or religion, which is only another form of convention—a woman was much better off than she is now. To be sure, when she found that she had married the wrong man she had it in her power to run away with the right one, or the nearest approach to the right one that she could find. I have now and again wondered during the past year why I shouldn't run away to another man and try to patch up this wrecked life of mine."

"Why shouldn't you? It would only be fair and just; but you never would do it, Priscilla."

"Why should I not? I believe that I would do it if only the right man turned up."

"If he would let you do it he would not be the-right man."

"I'm not so sure of that. The best men—the greatest men—the bravest—the cleverest—the most devout men have never been over-particular when it came to a question of women. I believe if I were really to fall in love with a man I would do as so many of the best women in the world have done—I would go to him, and let convention and religion go hang."

"Don't tell me. You would do nothing of the sort. But do you really feel so strongly about being married? I think, you know, that since you worked out your plan of teaching Mr. Kelton a lesson you seem to be a different girl, but still——"

"My dear Rosa, don't let any one try to tell you that there's any life for a woman in this world apart from a man. There's not. And don't let any one try to convince you that there's any life for a man without a woman by his side. There's not."

"To play his accompaniments?"

"Yes, in the right key, mind. That's just what a woman is placed in the world to do—to play a man's accompaniments in the right key. If Mr. Kelton had a wife by his side he would not now have a sense of being made a fool of."

"He's probably as conceited as ever by this time. Now how was it that we went on to talk of men and women when really our topic was Mr. Kelton?"

"I know. You were about to say that no one should think hardly of me for making a fool of any man, considering how great a fool I was made by a man. That was what was in your mind; but you were wrong, Rosie dear, for I don't think at all bitterly of men. On the contrary, I tell you that you must be prepared for the worst—what your father and other professional moralists would call the worst—from me. I'm only an amateur moralist. In fact, I'm not quite sure that I should even call myself an amateur. I don't really know that I have any morals whatever."

"You have no need for any. What do girls like you or me know of morals?"

"Nothing, except those we got hold of when we read Fontaine's Fables at school."

"And then we always skipped or slurred over the 'morals'—they spoilt the story."

"They did, and that is what they do every day; they spoil our stories. Oh, what idiots we are—a couple of girls who have seen nothing in the world and know nothing in the world, moralizing on morals! I'm not sure that it isn't immoral to discuss morality, Rosa. I should like to have the opinion of a specialist on this point."

"Try Miss Southover."

"A maiden schoolmistress who makes a thousand a year by teaching girls how to be at once dignified and dunces! She would be too shocked to be able to give an opinion. No, I should apply to a man of the world—a bishop, or at least a rural dean. Now I have done with this subject. I didn't go very far, did I? A year ago I'm pretty sure I wouldn't have gone even so far."

"Poor old Pris!"

"You may say that. I feel to-day as old as your grandmother. And I have been thinking—oh, what thinking! I know what there is in me, Rosa. If ever any girl was made to be a help to a man, that girl was me. And am I, because I allowed myself to be made a fool of—am I therefore bound to do nothing with my life—nothing, only to live it—to live my life apart from all that makes life life?"

"Poor old Pris! There never was any one who had half your bad luck!"

"You may say that. But you needn't think that I have done with life yet. I haven't."

"That's what I love about you, Priscilla. You are so rebellious! You are not one of the tame ones who submit to what they call the will of Providence."

"I think too highly of Providence to believe that its will is that my life should be wrecked by no fault of my own—no fault except obedience. It was my obedience that made me what I am to-day, and upon my word I don't believe that my punishment is out of proportion to my offence."

"Your offence? But you never———"

"I did. I ceased to be myself. I put myself behind myself and allowed myself to be led like a lamb to the slaughter—the slaughter of that womanhood which I should have upheld—my womanhood, which meant the right to think for myself—the right to be a woman to love a man, and help him in his life and be loved by him and to give him children. That is how love is immortal—our children live after us, and our children's children!... No more obedience for me, thanks; I mean to live my life. That's all!"

"I'll tell you what I think, Priscilla———" Rosa allowed a considerable interval to elapse before she spoke. "I'll tell you what I think, and that is, that the awfulness of the past year has made a woman of you in this way."

Priscilla seemed a little startled by the enunciation of this theory. She looked quickly at her companion, and then laughed queerly.

"God is too busy making worlds, universes and that, to have a moment to spare to a woman," said she. "No, it is the man who makes the woman; and be sure that if the woman is made by the man, the man is made by the woman—by the woman and by the children that she gives him. And yet—here we are."

"Yes," said Rosa, "here we are. Oh, there is one thing certain: God made primroses."

CHAPTER IV

They had been walking along the narrow hilly road that branched off from the broad highway between the little town of Framsby and the villages of Dean Grange, Beastlington, and Elfrisleigh, and now they were standing on the ridge of the Down that overlooked the lovely valley of the Wadron. The day was one toward the end of April, when everything in nature, including men and women and healthy girls, feels stirred with the impulses of the Spring, and while all fancy they are living only in the joy of the present, they are yet giving their thoughts to the future. Everything in nature was showing signs of thinking of the future. The early flowers were looking after themselves, doing their best to offer allurements to the insects which they trusted to carry their love tokens for them from stamen to pistil; and the pale butterflies became messenger Cupids all unconsciously. But the birds were doing their own love-making. Every bough was vocal, every brake quivered in harmony. In that green lane there was the furtive flutter of wings. Some nests had been built and padded for the eggs, and here and there a stranger looking carefully through the interspaces among the glossy leaves could see the glitter of the beady eye of a hiding blackbird, and, with greater pains, the mottling of a thrush's throat. Love-making and home-making on all sides—this is what the Spring meant, and it was probably because she was so closely in touch with the season and its instincts that one of the girls had spoken out some of the thoughts that made her warm as though her thoughts were infants of the Spring, to be cherished very close to her body.

They stood at that part of the road which bridged one of the tributary streams that went down to the Wadron, losing itself for many yards where it crept among the bosky slopes nearest to the road, but making its course apparent by many a twinkle of quick water, and now and again by a crystal pool, overflowing among mossy stones and cascading where there was a broad steep rock. Again it disappeared among the wilderness of bramble, but when one looked for its continuation, its glistening, not directly downward, but many yards to one side, gave one a glad surprise.

And all its course was marked by primroses. The park through which it flowed was carpeted with primroses, and all the distance of the valley was tinted with ten thousand tufts. Only on one of the high banks of the parkland, where the pines stood in groups, was the brown earth covered with a haze of bluebells. Close though this bank was to the road, it was picked over with rabbit burrows, and when the girls came near there was a scurrying of brown and a flicker of white among the bluebells and the ferns.

"It is getting wilder and wilder," said Rosa.

"Thank goodness!" added Priscilla. "It was the wisest thing that ever the owner did, to die and keep every one out of it for all these years."

"Yes, so far as we are concerned," said Rosa. "We have got more out of the place than any one else."

"You would have been a visitor to the Manor in any case," said Priscilla; "but what chance would I have had? Well, I might have come in under the shelter of your wing, not otherwise."

"Perhaps the son's wife might not have been so stuck up as the rest of the people in our neighbourhood," remarked Rosa, consolingly.

Priscilla laughed.

"I think I should take their—their—standoffishness more to heart if you were not here, Rosa," said Priscilla, thoughtfully "What shall I do when you go away?"

"Go away? I heard nothing about my going away."

"I hear a good deal about it to-day from the birds, and the sheep, and all the other voices of the Spring. They have talked about nothing else all the morning."

Rosa looked at her anxiously for some moments. Then she gave a sound that had something of contempt in it, crying, "What rot! My dear girl, you know as well as I do that I have no intention of going away—that I do not bother my head with any notion of—of that sort of thing. I am quite content to remain here. It would take a lot of coaxing to carry me away. Come along now, I don't trust strangers, and I certainly don't trust April weather, and I certainly don't trust that cloud that puts a black cap on Beacon Hill. If we are to get our baskets full in time we would do well not to wait here sentimentalizing."

She led the way on the road by the park fence, and Priscilla was still behind her when they went round the curve, where the road had been widened in front of the pillars that supported a pair of well-worn entrance gates. Lodges were on each side, picturesque sexagonal cottages, their shape almost undiscernible through the straggling mass of the creepers that covered them.

"Do you remember the pheasants' eggs?" whispered Rosa, when they had gone through the gates and had just passed the lodges.

"I am trying my best to forget them," replied Priscilla. "How awful it would be if I accidentally spoke of that omelette in the hearing of some one who would mention it to Mr. Dunning!"

"It would be awful!" acquiesced Rosa.

Their exchange of confidences related to the hospitality of the wife of one of the keepers, who occupied the lodge on the right. One day during the previous year the girls had been drenched in the park, and while they were drying their clothes the good woman, who had been a cook at the Manor, made them an omelette, using pheasants' eggs, of which quite a number were in her larder awaiting consumption.

"It was a nice omelette," said Priscilla, "but it made me feel that old Mr. Wingfield mightn't have been so wise after all in allowing the place to remain unoccupied for so long."

Signs of neglect were to be observed on all sides—not by any means the neglect that suggests the Court of Chancery or an impoverished owner; merely the neglect that is the result of the absence of any one interested in the maintenance of tidiness. The broad carriage drive was a trifle green, where fresh gravel was needed, and the grass borders had become irregular. The enormous bough that had broken away from the trunk of one of the elms of the avenue was lying just where it had fallen, sprawling halfway across the drive, and much of the timber shielding of a sapling had been broken down by some animal and remained unmended, so that the bark of the young tree had been injured. These tokens that some one had been saying "What does it matter?" a good many times within the year, were not the only ones to be seen within the grounds; and when Priscilla pointed them out to Rosa, she too said, "What does it matter? Who is there to make a row? You don't expect them to keep the place tidy for us?"

Priscilla said that nothing was further from her expectations, but still she thought—but of course beggars can't be choosers, and after all a primrose by the river's brim was still a yellow primrose, and a joy to the cottage hospital.

"And a black cloud is a beast of a thing when it bursts," added Rosa, pointing to the menace in the distance, above the balloon-like foliage of the immemorial elms.

Priscilla shook her head.

"We'll do it," she cried; "yes, if we hurry. I don't want to get this frock wet, so we'll rush for the primroses and shelter at the house. It will be an April shower, but we'll dodge it."

"No fear," acquiesced Rosa.

Down they plunged among the trees of the long slope, at the bottom of which the trout stream curled among the mossy stones, spreading its delicate white floss over some, and threading the narrows with a cord of silk, and then spattering the ferns on each side of a rock that met its advance too abruptly.

In a few minutes the girls were among the primroses. They were like the yellow pattern upon a green carpet at this place, only one could not see the carpet for the pattern. When the two serviceable baskets were packed with primroses there did not seem to be a clump the less in this garden that appeared to be the very throne of Spring itself—the throne and the golden treasury of the millionaire Spring.

And all the time that they were filling their baskets the blackbirds were making music among the bracken on the opposite slope, and once a great thrush came down with a wild winnowing of wings to a bramble that swung above the ripples of the water. It sounded its cackling note of alarm, and before it had ceased a cuckoo was heard as it flew from among a clump of chestnuts, gorgeous in drapery, to where a solitary ash, not yet green, stood far away from the billowy foliage of the slope.

And then the sunlit land became aware of a shadow sweeping up the valley. The rumble of thunder came from the distance.

"We're in for it!" cried Rosa, springing up from the carpet where she had been kneeling.

"We'll be in for it, as fast as we make ourselves—in the porch at least," shouted Priscilla, catching up her basket and making a run for the zig-zag track up the bank. She was followed by Rosa with all speed, but before they got to the carriage drive at the top the first drops were making kettledrums of the crowns of their straw hats, and once again the organ of the orchestra was beginning to peal.

They gathered up their print skirts and ran like young does for the shelter of the house. It was an example of dignified Georgian, with a pillared porch and square windows. People said there was no nonsense about Overdean Manor; and others remarked that that was a pity. The front was masked by trees from the carriage drive. Some people said that it was just as well that this was so; it gave the horses a chance. No horse could maintain a trot in view of so dignified a front.

But it had an ample porch, and into its sheltering embrace the two girls plunged with only breath enough left for their laughter.

"Not a dozen drops," they gasped, pinching each other's blouses at their arms. "Actually not a dozen drops—practically dry—but hot—oh, goodness, wasn't it hot!" And now they were going to have it in earnest.

They had it in earnest, but only as a spectacle. They were glowing after their race, but the porch contained no seats, and so they leant against the pillars and looked out at the rollicking Spring storm. It came with all the overdone vehemence of a practical jester—a comical bellow and a swirl and a swish; the topmost branches began complaining of their ill-treatment, bending and waving at first gracefully, then wildly—panic-stricken. Then the rain came—a comical flood suggesting the flinging of buckets of water—the rough play of grooms in the stable yard. The air became dark where the first swish of the rain swept by—dark and silent among the trees, while that madcap wind rushed on and made its fun on the fringe of the plantation. Out of the darkness a flash, and out of the distance a bombastic roar of thunder, but not the thunder of a storm that meant devastation; it was more like the laughter of good-humoured gods over some boy's joke—something that had to do with the bursting of a cistern, or the turning on of a standpipe in the centre of a score of unsuspecting gentlemen wearing tall hats. The girls joined in the laughter of that boisterous thunder; but only for a moment. They became aware of an extraordinary pause—the suspicious silence of a room where the schoolboys are in hiding and ready to jump out on you. Then came the sound of a mighty rushing in the air that was not the rushing of the wind. Half-a-dozen rooks whirled in a badly-balanced flight across the tops of the nearest trees, cawing frantically; and the next instant they were seen by the girls like fish in the tanks of an aquarium. The world had become a world of waters. They were looking out upon a solid wall of water, and a hurricane of hail made up the plate glass in front of the tank.

They watched its changes for the five minutes that it lasted, and the lightning became more real and the thunder more in earnest. Then it went slamming away into the distance, leaving the big sweep of the carriage drive in front of the house the glistening lake of a minute, and transforming the Georgian mansion into an Alpine mountain of innumerable rushing torrents. It seemed as if a thousand secret springs of water had been set free in a moment, and all rushing down through their runnels to the valley.

"It will all be over in a few minutes, now; but wasn't it a squelcher while it lasted!" cried Rosa, taking a cautious step outside to look round for the rainbow.

"I knew that we could just dodge it if we were slippy," said Priscilla. "I wish we had some place to sit down."

"Not worth while. We'll be off in a minute."

But it soon became plain that they would not be off quite so soon. When the thunderstorm with its wild blustering had departed, it left behind it, not the blue sky that might reasonably have been expected, but a tame flock of clouds that lumbered onward, discharging their contents upon the earth beneath with no great show of spirit, but with the depressing persistency of the mediocre.

"Hopeless!" sighed Priscilla.

"Horrid!" exclaimed Rosa.

After a few more minutes of waiting, the word "hungry" followed in alliterative sequence from both of them.

"If we could get round to Mrs. Pearce we might have some bread and butter," suggested Rosa. (Mrs. Pearce was the name of the caretaker, and her premises were naturally at the other side of the Georgian mansion.)

"If we made a rush for the lodge we might have some plovers' eggs," said Priscilla.

Rendered desperate and, consequently, courageous by the thought of such dainties, one of the pair suggested the possibility of attracting the attention of the caretaker by ringing the door bell. The idea was a daring one, but they felt that their situation was so desperate as to make a desperate remedy pardonable, if reasonably formulated.

Hallo! there was no need to pull the bell; looking about for the handle, they found that the hall door was ajar to the extent of four or five inches.

"Careless of Mrs. Pearce! We must speak seriously to her about this," said Rosa.

"When we have eaten her bread and butter," whispered Priscilla, with a sagacious nod.

They passed into the great square hall, with its imposing pillars supporting the beams of the ceiling, and then they stopped abruptly, for they found themselves confronted by a vivid smell of tobacco smoke.

"Has Mother Pearce been indulging?" whispered Rosa.

"Oh, dear, no; it's not that sort of tobacco," replied the sagacious Priscilla. "No; it only means that Mr. Dunning has been paying a visit of inspection."

(Mr. Dunning was the agent of the estate.)

They passed without further hesitation through the tobacco barrier, and seeing one of the doors open just beyond, they pushed through it and entered the room which they knew to be the library. They had been in the house more than once, before the days of its emptiness, and so knew their way about it.

"Hallo! we're in luck," said Rosa, pointing to where the table was laid with a cloth and plates, bread, cheese, biscuits, lettuce, and actually plovers' eggs. There was, however, only one knife and fork, only one glass, and only one bottle—it was a bottle of hock, and Rosa hastened to read its label—Liebfraumilch.

"Mr. Dunning is here on business and is having a scratch lunch," said Priscilla. "Liebfraumilch is a lovely wine, taking it year in and year out. Of course there are exceptionally good years of Liebfraumilch; but taking it all round it is a good sound wine."

"*Vide* auctioneer's catalogue," said Rosa. "But I decline to touch it, highly recommended though it is by a distinguished canootzer. I'll have of that bread, however, une trauche, s'il vous plait, and I'll poach a couple of those eggs, if I do get three months for it. How funny! Didn't I say something about plovers' eggs just now?"

"I'd be afraid to meddle with the eggs, but I'll back you up in the matter of the bread and cheese; I'm fairly starving. On the whole, perhaps we would do well to hunt up Mrs. Pearce first. It's as well to be ceremonial even in a house that you have broken into by stealth. If you take so much as a bite of that egg before we can start level, I'll cut you up into such small slices."

The knife which Priscilla had picked up for the purpose which she had but partly defined, fell from her hand. A sound had come from the big hooded chair in the shadow of the screen at the fireplace, and she had glanced round and seen, looking round the side of the chair at her, a man's face.

The knife fell from her grasp at the startling sight. Rosa, following the direction of her gaze, turned round and saw the apparition; but she did not let fall the egg which she had taken up for critical inspection.

There was an awkward silence, but an effective tableau, had any one been present to see it. There was the large square room, with bookcases of the loveliest Chippendale design hiding all its walls, and at one side of the table stood a young woman, with a face beautifully rosy, and a mouth slightly open to complete the expression of astonishment that looked forth from her eyes; at the end of the table nearest the fireplace, another girl glancing over her shoulder at the man's face that protruded beyond the line of downward slope at one side of the chair.

Perhaps the expression of astonishment on the man's face was the strongest of the three. His mouth was quite wide open, and his eyes were staring curiously, with a look within them that suggested that he had not quite succeeded in taking in the details of the picture before him—that he had not succeeded in reconciling all that he saw with the actualities of life.

Both the girls perceived in a moment that he had just awakened; but this fact did not prevent their being paralysed for the moment—for several moments. The moments went on into minutes, until the whole thing had the note of the child's game of "Who speaks first?"

It was this broadening of an impressive silence into a child's comedy that was the saving of the situation. A smile, to which his open mouth lent itself quite readily, came over the young man's face—he was a young man, and his face was still younger—and, after a maidenly hesitancy of a few seconds, the girls also smiled. His smile broadened into a grin, and both girls broke into a peal of laughter.

He pulled himself round in his chair and got upon his feet, still grinning, and then they saw that he was just what girls accustomed to tall men would call short, or what girls accustomed to short men would call medium-sized. He had very short hair of an indefinite shade of brown, and his mouth, when he grinned, was well proportioned, if it was designed to make a gap touching the lobe of each ear.

He stood up before them and shook himself out, as it seemed, after the manner of a newly awakened dog. Then he took in a reef or two (also speaking figuratively) of his mouth, and it became quite ordinary. He bowed as awkwardly as most men do in ordinary circumstances, and this fact was pleasing to the girls; no girl who is worth anything tolerates a man who makes a graceful bow.

"This is an unexpected pleasure," he said. "That is—for me; it can't be the same for you—that is, of course it's unexpected, but little enough of the pleasure. Only if I had known—you didn't say you were coming, you know—maybe you are in the habit of coming every day."

The girls shook their heads; both glanced toward the window. He followed their example.

"Gloriana!" he said, "it has been raining after all."

"Yes," said Priscilla. "It has been a thunderstorm—a terrible thunderstorm!"

"You don't say so! Long ago?"

"Half an hour ago. You must have heard it—the hail was terrific!" continued Priscilla.

"Gloriana! I'm afraid I've given myself away. If I said I wasn't asleep I suppose you wouldn't believe me."

He looked from one to the other as if to guess whether of the twain was the more charitable or the more likely to make a fool of herself by telling a lie that would take in no one. He could not make up his mind on either point; and so he illuminated the silence by another grin. The girls looked at each other; they could hardly be blamed; and they certainly were not blamed by him.

He became quite serious in a moment, and his mouth seemed actually normal.

"I think that I'm rather lucky, do you know, in awaking to find such visitors—my first visitors—the first people to give me a welcome in my house. Before I have slept a single night under its roof—only for a matter of half an hour, and that in the day—I have two visitors. I hope that you will let me bid you welcome and that you will welcome me. May we exchange cards? My name is Wingfield—Jack Wingfield. I am the grandson, you know. You didn't take me for the grandfather, did you?"

CHAPTER V

"WE never heard that you were coming—not a word," said Rosa.

"Not a word," echoed Priscilla. "We have enjoyed permission from Mr. Dunning to walk in the park and to pluck the wild flowers and blackberries and things like that. That was why we came to-day."

"Let me see; isn't it a bit too early for blackberries?" said he.

"Yes; but not for primroses," said Rosa.

"Nor for lunch," said he. "Did I dream that I heard one of you—if not both—say that this house should be called Starvation Hall?"

They both laughed.

"Not exactly," said Priscilla.

"Well, words to that effect," he cried. "Anyhow, whether you did or not, you'll never say it again. Here comes Mrs. Pearce—of course you know Mrs. Pearce. I needn't introduce her to you."

"Oh, we all know Mrs. Pearce," cried Rosa, as the caretaker entered, bearing a tray and a smell of a grill.

"Then she can introduce you to me," said he.

Mrs. Pearce, red of face and opulent of bust, stood for a moment as one amazed, looking from the young women to the young man.

"Good morning, Mrs. Pearce," cried Rosa.

"Good morning, Miss Rosa—Miss Caffyn," said the woman, nearly dropping the tray in her attempt to drop a curtsey—the curtsey of the charity school girl to a member of the Rector's family.

"Good morning," said Priscilla.

"Good morning, Miss Wadhurst."

"Thank you, Mrs. Pearce," said the man, as she laid down her tray on the table. "Do you think you could add to your favours by hunting out a couple more plates and knives and forks, and, above all, glasses? I quite forgot to tell you that I had sent out invitations to lunch. My first guests have arrived."

"Please do not trouble; bread and cheese for us," cried Priscilla.

"What about that plover's egg that you were trifling with—oh, I see you have laid it quietly back on the dish," he remarked, with an ingratiating smile in the direction of Rosa.

"I'm afraid," murmured Mrs. Pearce—"I'm afraid that—that——"

She was looking in the direction of the covered dish on the tray.

"I'm not," cried he. He lifted off the cover and displayed the twin halves of a chicken beautifully grilled. "She's afraid that there isn't enough to go round!" He pointed to the dish. "Gloriana! as if I could eat all that off my own bat! Do hurry about those plates—and, above all, don't forget the glasses. Can you guess what the name of this hock is?" he added, turning to Rosa.

"It's Liebfraumilch, and you were not asleep after all," cried the girl, rosy and smiling.

"Not after all, but just before," he said reassuringly, placing chairs at the table also with a good deal of assurance. But he was not so engrossed by the occupation as to fail to see the glances exchanged between the girls—glances of doubt, shot through with the enquiry, "Should we?"

"What a day it is turning out, and the morning looked so fine," said he, not gloomily, but cheerfully. "Won't you sit down? The spatchcock's all right, only it takes offence if it isn't eaten at once."

"I don't see why we shouldn't," said Rosa boldly to her friend. The man turned his head away to enable her to do so—a movement that displayed tact and not tactics.

"You are extremely kind, Mr. Wingfield," said Priscilla very formally. "I don't suppose that we are quite in line with the precepts of the book of etiquette; and, besides, we have no business to deprive you of your lunch and——"

"And sleep," murmured Rosa.

That finished the formally-worded apology. Before their triolet of laughter had passed away they were all seated at the table, and Mrs. Pearce had brought in the requisite crockery and cutlery. She did not forget the glasses. She beamed confidently upon the girls as if she was endeavouring to assure them that she was a mother herself, and that she would be at hand in case she should hear screams.

He showed some dexterity in carving his spatchcock. They kept their eyes on him, with a protest ready if he should leave nothing for himself; but they had no need of such vigilance, and their protest was uncalled for. He was quite fair to them and to himself, and witnessing his tact once more they became still more at their ease.

"The day doesn't seem quite so hopeless now as it did a quarter of an hour ago," he remarked, when they had all praised the cooking of Mrs. Pearce. "Nothing seems the same when a chap has done himself well in the eating and drinking line—especially the drinking. I don't wonder that crimes are committed when people haven't enough to eat."

"I wonder if having too little to eat or too much to drink is most responsible," said Priscilla.

"Meaning that it's about time I opened that bottle?" said he. "Now, I can't think that either of you is under the influence of a temperance lecturer; but if you are, you'll drink all the same to my homecoming."

"Delighted, I'm sure," cried Rosa. "There's no nicer thing to drink than Liebfraumilch, when it's of the right year."

"I was under the impression," said he, scrutinizing the bottom of the cork, "that taking the bad years with the good, a chap has a better chance with Liebfraumilch than anything in that line."

"I got it all from a catalogue—I have a good memory," confessed Priscilla. "I hope it's true."

"A wine merchant's catalogue? Gospel—absolute gospel," said he solemnly.

He poured out half a glass and became more solemn still while he examined it in breathless silence. He held it up to the light, and the girls saw that it was a pale flame smouldering in the glass. He gave it a shake and it became a glorious topaz.

"A very fair colour indeed," said he on the completion of these mysteries, and the girls breathed again. "Yes, I don't know who laid it down, but I know who'll take it up, and every time it will be with a hope that his grandsire's halo is as good a colour. The occasion is an extremely interesting one, and the wine is almost equal to the occasion. If not, we are. Ladies and gentlemen, it is with feelings of etcetera, etcetera, that I bring to your notice the toast of the young heir now come into his inheritance. Long may he reign—I mean long may it rain, when it was the means of bringing so charming a company round his table, and so say all of us; with a—I'm extremely obliged to you, and I'll respond later on."

He had the aspect and the manner of a merry boy. About him there was a complete absence of self-consciousness. He treated the girls in the spirit of comradeship, and Priscilla at least felt that he must have been possessed of a certain gift of intuition to perceive that this spirit and no other was the one that was appropriate to the occasion; and moreover that he must have had other gifts that enabled him to perceive that they were the very girls to appreciate such a form of unconventional courtesy. He was in no way breezy or free-and-easy in his manner. He made fun like a schoolboy, never forcing the note; and these young women knew that he was perfectly natural from the ease with which they remained natural and with no oppression of self-consciousness in his company, in spite of the fact that the situation was not merely unconventional, but within the prohibited degrees of consanguinity, to indiscreetness, as indiscreetness would be defined by the district visitor or her relative, Mrs. Grundy.

These young women, who found themselves taking lunch and drinking wine—actually hock of a brand that was habitually highly spoken of in the catalogues—at the invitation and in the house of a young man to whom they had never been presented, were beginning to feel as if they had been acquainted with him all their life, and they made an extremely good meal. The plovers' eggs vanished when the spatchcock had been despatched, and the cream cheese and lettuce were still occupying them when Mrs. Pearce came from the kitchen to find out if all was well, and if she should serve the coffee in the library or in the drawing-room.

"Oh, the drawing-room by all means," cried Mr. Wingfield; and when she disappeared he whispered, "The good creature has just been to the drawing-room to take off the covers, I'm sure, and she would never forgive us if we didn't go to see how careful she has been of everything. The only thing about it is that I couldn't find my way from here to the drawing-room."

"You may depend on us," said Rosa.

"I may? Then I place myself unreservedly in your hands," said he. "I'll tell you what we'll do. You shall show me through the house and tell me the story of all the rooms—who was killed in which, and where the celebrated duel was fought—you may, by the aid of a reasonable amount of imagination, still see the marks of the bullets in the wainscot."

"I never heard anything of that," said Rosa. "A duel? When did it happen?"

"What, do you mean to say that there's no room in this house where the celebrated duel was fought?" cried he. "And you can assure me that there's no picture of an old reprobate who went in the county by the name of Butcher Wingfield—or was it old Black Jack Wingfield—maybe Five-bottle Wingfield?"

"I really can't tell. All that I can say is that I never heard of any of them," said Rosa.

"This is a nice thing to confront a chap who has just entered into possession of an old house and, as he hoped, a lot of ready-made ancestors," said he mournfully. "Not one of them with any of the regulation tokens of the old and crusted ancestor about him! But you'll at least show me the room that Nell Gwyn slept in—or was it the Young Pretender?—you'll show me his initials, Y. P., that he carved on the eighteenth century panelling of the Priest's Room with the sliding panel—you know?"

"Oh, yes, I know," laughed Priscilla. "And the ghost of Lady Barbara that appears to the stranger who has been inadvertently put to sleep in the Blue Room, and the old chest where the bones were found, and the tiny pink shoes with genuine Liberty buckles."

"You give me hope—the ghost of a hope—I mean the hope of a ghost. I expected half a dozen at least; but one sees, on reflection, that that would be unreasonable. I'll be content with one if you throw the tiny shoes into the bargain."

"I'm afraid that you'll have to be contented with comfort and a surveyor's certificate," said Priscilla.

"What I am thinking is, who will give us a certificate that we have been reasonably engaged when we return home," remarked Rosa, when they were rising from the table—he did not offer them cigarettes.

"Do you really think it possible that your people will be uneasy?" said he, with some concern in his voice. "It's still raining. Will they not be certain that you took shelter somewhere? If there's any doubt, I'll send a message by my motor."

"You have brought a motor, and yet you looked for ghosts and things?" said Priscilla.

"I came from Barwellstone in it this morning. A nice run. I tried a railway guide for trains, and found that with luck I could do the journey in eight hours."

"And you did it in twenty minutes by motor?"

"Twenty-five, in addition to three hours. It's just ninety-two miles. So this is the drawing-room? Very nice, I'm sure."

They had walked across the hall and had passed through a very fine mahogany door into another big square room, with exquisite plaster decorations on the walls and ceiling and mantelpieces, of which there were two. The eighteenth century furniture was mahogany and upholstered in faded red damask. The chairs were all uncovered, though the curtains remained tied up in such a way as caused each to reproduce with extraordinary clearness the figure of Mrs. Pearce. The transparent cabinets all round the room were filled with specimens of the art of Josiah Wedgwood—blue and green and buff and black—beautiful things.

"This is the Wedgwood drawing-room," said Priscilla. "It is considered one of the most perfect things of its kind in the country."

"Why the Wedgwood room? Was there a Mr. Wedgwood who planned it?" asked the owner.

"There was a Mr. Wedgwood who supplied the china," said Priscilla.

"Local—a local man, I suppose—Framsby, or is it Southam?"

"Oh, no, Wedgwood was not a local man by any means," replied Priscilla, wondering in what circles this young man had spent the earlier years of his life that he had never heard of Wedgwood.

"Anyhow, it's quite nice to look at; and here comes the coffee," said he. "It's a queer room—gives even an ignorant chap like me a feeling that it's all right—furnished throughout, and not on the hire-purchase system."

Then he drank his coffee and looked about him, and then at his visitors—first at one and then at the other. They were standing together at one of the oval windows looking out upon a flagged terrace with a balustrade and piers and great stone vases of classical design.

"A really nice room," he said, as if he were summing up the result of his survey of the young women. "I think, you know, that I make its acquaintance in rather happy circumstances," he added. "I hope I may consider that you have left cards on me so that I may ask you to dinner or something. I went into the dining-room the first thing, and then down to the cellar. I don't think that the dining-room looks so finished as this room. I felt a bit uneasy, you know, to see all those frames with hand-painted ancestors grinning down at me. They seemed to be winking at one another and whispering, 'Lord, what a mug!' I didn't feel at all at home among them—pretty bounders they were to make their remarks—silk coats and satin embroidered waistcoats and powdered hair worn long! Bounders to a man! I felt a bit lonely among them, and that's why I told the woman I should have my plate laid in the library. I didn't want any of their cheek. I was thinking what a rather dismal homecoming it was for me—not a soul to say a word of welcome to a chap. I felt a bit down on my luck, and I suppose that's why I fell into that doze. Only five minutes I could have slept, and when I opened my eyes—I give you my word I had a feeling—

that halfwaking feeling, you know—that it was the ghosts of two of the nicest of my ancestors come back to say a word of encouragement to me to make up for the bad manners of those satin-upholstered ones. I do hate the kind of chap that gets painted in fancy dress!"

The notion of the Georgian portraits being in fancy dress sent the young women into a peal of laughter; and then he laughed too.

"That's like coming home," he said a minute later. "That's what I looked for, and if I didn't feel grateful to you both——"

"Grateful to the rain, the thunder and lightning," suggested Rosa.

"All right, thunder and lightning and rain and all the rest. I'll have a greater respect for them in the future; but all the same the gratitude will go to you. You have turned a failure into a success, and no other girls would have been able to do so much. They would have giggled and gone the moment they caught sight of me. Yes, I'm grateful."

"And we are glad," said Priscilla, gently. "And we're quite sorry that the rain is over so that we have no excuse for—for—oh, yes, trespassing on your hospitality."

"But you have only shown me one of the rooms, and there are about forty others, I believe. Think of me getting lost in a rabbit warren of bedrooms and dressing-rooms and still rooms and sparkling! Wouldn't it be on your conscience if you heard of that happening?"

"Our conscience—Mr. Wingfield takes it for granted that we have only one conscience between us," said Priscilla.

"And perhaps he thinks that he's generous," said Rosa.

They did it very nicely, he thought. They were really very charming—not a bit like any other girls he had ever met.

"You don't need a conscience, I'll bet," he said. "What do you ever do to keep it up to its work?"

"If we stay here another five minutes it will be working overtime," laughed Priscilla. "Good-bye, Mr. Wingfield, and receive our thanks for shelter, and a—a—most unusual afternoon."

"Good-bye. You have done a particularly good turn to a chap to-day, and don't you forget it. I'll go to the door with you."

He walked with them to the pillared porch and said another good-bye in a different key.

They heard him close the hall door, and they knew that he would have to go to a window of the dining-room if he wished to watch them departing on the carriage drive.

They wondered—each of them on her own account—if he had hurried to that particular window.

"He is not so silly as he promised to be the first five minutes we came upon him," said Rosa, when they were approaching the entrance gates.

"Not nearly. As a matter of fact I found him entertaining."

"Not intellectually."

"Perhaps not. I'm not sure that I am entertained by intellectual entertainment. He is a man in the clay stage. I'm not sure that that isn't the most interesting—it certainly is the most natural. He might be anything that a woman might choose to make him."

"Of course we'll tell them at home what happened," said Rosa, after a long pause.

"Why should we not? We would do well to be an hour or two in advance of Mrs. Pearce," said Priscilla.

They got upon the road, and were forced to pay attention to its condition of muddiness rather than to the delight of breathing the sweet scents of the rain-drenched hedges on each side. They parted at the cross-roads, and only at that moment remembered that they had left their primroses in the porch.

Rosa went in the direction of the town, and Priscilla set her face toward the slope of the Down in front of her. Before she had gone for more than half a mile on her way to the farm, she saw a man approaching her—a middle-aged man in a black coat and leggings rather the worse for wear. He held up his hand to her while they were still far apart.

"Something has happened," she said. "It cannot be that he became uneasy at my absence." Then they met. "What is it, father?" she asked quickly.

"Dead—he is dead—the man is dead!" he said in a low voice.

"Dead—Marcus Blaydon—dead—are you sure?"

"Quite sure," he replied.

"Thank God!" she said, speaking her words as though she were breathing a sigh of great relief.

And so she was; she was speaking of her husband.

CHAPTER VI

There came a dreadful misgiving to her. She clutched her father's arm as they stood together on the road.

"You are sure?" she said in a low voice, with her eyes looking at him with something of fierceness in their expression. "There is no mistake—no possibility of a mistake? Remember what the man was—a trickster—unscrupulous—you are sure? Is that a letter—a paper?"

"A paper," he said—"several papers. There can be no doubt about it. And don't speak ill of him now, Priscilla. You will be sorry for it. He died the death of a man. However bad his life may have been, he made up for it in his death."

"A hero?" she said, and she was smiling so that her father was angered.

"I would not have believed it of you; it is unnatural," he said. "Have you no sense of what's proper—what's decent?"

"I have no sense that makes me be a hypocrite," she said. "The man cheated me—he was within an hour or two of making me the most pitiful creature. As it was he made me the laughing-stock of the world. No one thought of my misfortune in being married to an impostor, a criminal, and having my life ruined by him. Every one took it for granted that I was a poor weak creature, on the look-out for a husband and ready to jump at the first suitor who turned up. What could I long for but his death? What chance should I have of doing anything in the world so long as he was alive and married to me? What could I long for but his death? At first it was mine that I longed for; but then I saw that to long for his was more sensible—more in keeping with the will of Heaven."

"The will of Heaven! How can you talk like that, Priscilla?"

"If God has any idea of justice—of right and wrong—as we have been taught to regard right and wrong by those who assure us that they have been let into some of His secrets—it could not be His will that I should have my life wrecked by that man. I felt that I was born for something better, and so I hoped that he would die. Now that by the goodness of God he is dead, shall I not be grateful? Oh, what fools! standing here on the roadside discussing a delicate point in theology instead of talking over the good news!"

He looked at her for a few stern moments, and then thrust into her hand a bundle of papers.

"Read them for yourself," he said. "I am going into the town. I don't want to be by while you are chuckling over the death of a man—a man who died as the noblest man might be proud to die—trying to save his fellow creatures from destruction. Read those papers for yourself, and then ask God to forgive you for your dreadful words."

"He died like a hero," she murmured, taking the papers; and then she smiled again.

Her father was striding down the hill; the self-respecting gait of the churchwarden was his—the uncompromising stride of the man who worshipped the Conventional, and never failed to go to church for this purpose, returning to eat a one o'clock dinner of roast sirloin and Yorkshire pudding.

She watched him for some time, and the smile had never left her face. Then she looked strangely at the bundle of papers which he had flung at her—his action had suggested flinging them—in his wrath at her utterance of all that had been in his own heart for more than a year.

She glanced at the papers. They were Canadian, she saw, and they were profuse in the display of strong lettering in the headlines of the columns that met her eyes. It seemed as if the half-column of headlines was designed to exhibit the resources of the typefounders. She saw, without unfolding the papers, that they referred to a wreck that had taken place off the coast of Nova Scotia, great stress being laid on the fact that sixteen lives were lost, and that a man who had tried to carry a line ashore from the wreck had been swept away to destruction. "A Hero's Death!" was the headline that called attention to this detail.

She folded the papers back into their creases. She felt that she could not do full justice on the open road to the matter with which they dealt. She must hurry home and read every line in the seclusion of her own room. In the same spirit she had occasionally hurried to her home with a new novel by a favourite author under her arm. Nothing must disturb her. She must be allowed to gloat over every line—to dwell lovingly upon the bold lettering of the headings, "A Hero's Death!"

She almost ran along the road in her eagerness; and now her elation had increased so greatly that she felt it to be indecent—almost disgraceful—all that her father had suggested that it was. It was all very well for her to be conscious of a certain amount of satisfaction on learning that she was released from the dreadful bondage which compelled her to be the wife of a convict, but it was quite another matter to feel herself lilting that comic opera air, "I'll kiss you and die like a 'ero"; and, when she succeeded in banishing that ridiculous melody from buzzing in her ears, to be conscious of the rattle of the drum and the trumpet call of the cornet introducing Don César's singing of "Let me like a soldier fall" in the opera of "Maritana." But there they went on in her ears—the banjo-bosh of the one and the swashbuckler's swagger of the other, accepting the beat of her hastening feet for their *tempo*. The more she hurried, the more rapidly the horrid tuney things went on; and she had a dreadful feeling of never being able to escape from them.

She was doomed for her wickedness to be haunted by those jingles for evermore.

Of course she had no idea that she was on the verge of hysteria; but her father would have known, if he had had any experience of the range of human emotion outside the profitable working of a large farm, that hysteria must be the sequel to that unnatural calm which his daughter had shown on learning that the man to whom she had bound herself was dead.

It was not, however, until she had reached her home and had gone very slowly upstairs to her room, that the buzzing and the lilting and the tinkling of tunes in her ears rushed together in a horrible terrifying jingle, and she cried out, flinging herself upon her bed in a paroxysm of wild tears and falsetto sobs. The reaction had come, and borne her down beneath its mad rush upon her.

When she became calm once more she had a sense of having been absurdly weak in failing to keep herself well in hand. She could not understand how it was that she had let herself behave so foolishly. If the man had been her lover she could not have been more upset by the news of his death, she thought.

But the thing had happened, however, and she felt that she might rest confident that it would never happen again. So she bathed her face and brushed her hair and set herself down to her newspapers on the seat at her open window. The sky was blue above the Downs, and the rain had left in the air a clean taste. In the meadow there were countless daffodils, and the afternoon sun was glistening upon the rain drops in their bells and on the blades of the emerald grasses of the slope. From the great brown field that was being ploughed came the rich smell of moist earth and the varying notes of the ploughman's words to his team. When he got to the end of the furrow nearest to the farmhouse she heard his words clearly; then he turned, and his voice became indistinct as he plodded slowly on in the other direction. From the clumps of larch in the paddock came the cawing of innumerable rooks, but the song of the lark fell to her ears from the blue sky itself.

She sat for a long time with the newspapers in her lap. She had not for many months felt so restful as she did now. It seemed to her that she had been in prison for more than a year. She had heard through iron bars all the sounds that were now coming from the earth and the air and the sky, but she had not been able to enjoy them; on the contrary, they had irritated her, reminding her of the liberty which had once been hers, but which (she had felt) she was never again to know.

And now...

She sat there living in the luxury of that sense of freedom which had come to her—that sense of restfulness—of exquisite peace—the peace of God that passeth understanding. It had come to her straight from God, she felt. Although she had shown but little faith in the goodness of God, still He had not forgotten her. The words of the hymn came to her memory:—

> "God moves in a mysterious way
>
> His wonders to perform,
>
> He plants His footsteps in the sea
>
> And rides upon the storm."

Ah! yes, it was His hand that had passed through the air, and that storm had rushed down upon that ship; it was His footsteps that had stirred up the seas to engulf it and that wretch who had tried to wreck her life—ah! it was he who had been the first to suffer wreck! Poor wretch! Poor wretch! In the course of her large thoughts of the mercy and justice of God she could even feel a passing current of pity for the wretch; but it was one of very low voltage: it would not have caused more than the merest deflection of the most sensitive patho-meter. When she had sighed "Poor wretch!" it was gone. Still she knew that she was no longer the hard woman that she had been ever since she had stood by the church porch and had watched the policeman putting the handcuffs on the man whom she had just married, and had heard his saturnine jest about having put a ring on her finger and then having bracelets put on his wrists. It was that hardness which had then come into her nature that caused her to speak to her father with such bitterness when he had met her with his news on the road.

But now she was changed. She would ask her father's forgiveness, and perhaps he would understand her, though she did not altogether understand herself.

And still the newspapers lay folded in her lap; and her memory began to review in order the incidents that had led up to that catastrophe of fourteen months ago. It was when she was visiting her aunt Emily that she had met him.

But her memory seemed determined to show itself a more complete recorder than she had meant it to be of everything connected with this matter. It carried her back to the earlier days when her hair had been hanging down her back, and her aunt had had long consultations with her mother on the subject of her education. "Befitting for a lady"—that had been her aunt's phrase—she, Priscilla, was to be educated in such a way as was befitting for a lady. Aunt Emily was herself a lady; she had done much better than her sister, Priscilla's mother, who had only become a farmer's wife. To be sure Phineas Wadhurst was not to be classed among the ordinary farmers of the neighbourhood, who barely succeeded in getting a living out of the land. The Wadhursts had been on their farm for some hundreds of years, and their names were to be read on a big square tablet in the church with 1581 figuring as the first date upon it. Some of them had made the land pay, but others had spent upon it the money that these had bequeathed to them, without prospering. It was old Phineas Wadhurst that had done best out of it, and when he died he had left to his son a small fortune in addition to a well-stocked farm.

But before many years had passed young Phineas, who had the reputation of being the longest-headed man that had ever been a Wadhurst, perceived that the conditions under which agriculture was carried on with a profit had changed considerably. He saw that the day of English wheat was pretty nearly over, but that if the day of wheat was over, the day of other things was dawning, and it was because he became the pioneer of profits that people called him long-headed. While his neighbours grumbled he experimented. The result was that in the course of five years he was making money more rapidly than it had ever been made out of the wheat. "Golden grain," it had been called long ago. Phineas Wadhurst smiled. Golden butter was what he had his eye on—golden swedes which he grew for his cattle, so that every bullock became bullion and every heifer a mint.

And then he did a foolish thing. He got married.

The woman he chose was a "lady." The English agriculturist's ideal lady is some one who has had nothing to do with farming all her life; just as his ideal gentleman is a retired English shopkeeper. Eleanor Glynde was one of the daughters of a hardworking doctor in general practice in the little town of Limborough.

She was an austere woman of thirty, of a pale complexion, which in the eyes of every agricultural community is the stamp of gentility in a lady. Mrs.

Wadhurst took no interest in the cultivation of anything except her own pallor. She had once been known as the Lily of Limborough, and she lived in the perpetual remembrance of this tradition. She did not annoy her husband very much; and though there were a good many people who said that Phineas Wadhurst would have shown himself to be longer-headed if he had married a woman in his own station in life, who would have looked after the dairy and kept all the "hands" busy, yet the man felt secretly proud of his wife's idleness and of her attention to her complexion. She read her novels and worked in crewels, and after five years became the mother of a girl, who grew up to be an extremely attractive creature, but a creature of whom her mother found great difficulty in making a lady.

Mrs. Wadhurst's ideal lady did not differ greatly from the ideal of the agriculturists; only she added to their definition a rider that she was to be one who should be visited by Framsby. To be on visiting terms with Framsby represented the height of her social ambition.

But Framsby is a queer place. It has eight thousand inhabitants and three distinct "sets" of gentility. The aristocracy of the town is made up of the family of a land agent, the family of a retired physician, the family of a solicitor still in practice, the family of a clergyman's widow, whose grandfather once "had the hounds," as she tells you before you have quite made up your mind whether the day is quite wonderful for this time of the year, or if you mean to attend the forthcoming Sale of Work. These and the elderly wife of a retired colonial civil servant made up the ruling "set" at Framsby. They were on golfing terms with the other sets, but socially they declined to look on them as their equals. The other sets consisted of the bank managers, two of the three doctors and their families—for some reason or other the third doctor, with a foolish talkative wife and a couple of exceedingly plain daughters, had *entrée* at the aristocratic gatherings—a couple of retired officers of Sappers and their families, and some officials, the county surveyor, the master of the grammar school, and the manager of the brewery, each with his *entourage*.

Of course the clergymen of the Established Church and their families were, *ex officio*, members of all sets, but it was clearly understood by the ruling party that they were only admitted on sufferance—they must at all times recollect that they were only honorary members, without any power of voting or vetoing on any of the great questions of leaving cards on strangers, or of the membership of the Badminton Club.

And the funny part of the matter was that while the members of the best set were neither people of good family nor people who were in the least degree interesting in themselves, whereas several of the other set were both well born and educated, no one was found to dispute the fact that the one was the right set and the other the wrong set.

When a girl in the wrong set was spoken to or patronized by a frump in the other, she showed herself to be greatly pleased, and became quite cool and "distant" with her own associates; and when one of the frumps snubbed the ambitions of a girl in the wrong set, all the other girls in the wrong set became chilling in their attitude to that girl; and a knowledge of these facts may perhaps account for the impression which was very general in other parts of the county that Framsby was a queer place, and that its precious "sets" might be roughly classified as toads and toadies. It was clearly understood that Framsby was an awful place for strangers to come to. No matter how clever they were—no matter how greatly distinguished in the world outside Framsby—they were not visited, except by the tradesmen, until they had been resident for at least two years. This circumstance, however, by no means raised an insurmountable barrier between them and the people who were hunting up subscribers for some of their numerous "objects." The newcomers were invariably called on for subscriptions by the very cream of the aristocracy of Framsby— subscriptions to the Hospital, to the Maternity Home, to the School Treats, to the Decayed Gardeners' Fund, the Decayed Gentlewomen's Fund, the Poor Brave Things' Fund, the Zenana Missions Fund, the Guild of St. Michael and All Angels Fund, the Guild of Repentant Motherhood (affiliated with the Guild of St. Salome), and the Guild of Aimless Idlers. These and a score of equally excellent "objects" were without any delay brought under the notice of all newcomers; so that if the old inhabitants showed themselves to be extremely discourteous and inhospitable in regard to strangers, it must be acknowledged that they made up for their neglect of social "calls" by the frequency and the persistence of their visitations when they thought there was anything to be got out of them.

And these were the people for whose patronage Phineas Wadhurst's wife pined all her life, and it was solely that her daughter might one day be received by some of the best set in Framsby that she agreed with her sister that Priscilla should be "finished" at a school the fees of which were notoriously exorbitant.

This was the point at which Priscilla's review of the past began while she sat on her chair that afternoon, when for the first time for a year she had a sense of peace—a sense of her life being cleansed from some impurity that had been clinging to it. It was the sense of the rain-washed air that induced this feeling; and she smiled while she remembered how, even so long ago as the time of which she was thinking, she had been amused by the seriousness with which her pale mother and her aunt Emily discussed the likelihood there was that when the fact of her being "finished" at that expensive school should be reasonably presented to the right people at Framsby, it would prove irresistible as a claim upon their compassion, so that they would come to visit her in flocks.

Alas! she had gone to the expensive school and had learned when there a great number of things—some of them not even charged for in the long list of extras; but still she was only regarded by the great people of Framsby as a farmer's daughter. Nay, several of the wrong set who had been on visiting terms with Mrs. Wadhurst took umbrage at the girl's being sent to a school to which they could not afford to send their daughters; and they talked of the great evils that frequently resulted from a girl being educated "above her station"—Priscilla remembered the ridiculous phrase for many days. But whatever their ideas on proportionate education may have been, Priscilla was educated. She took good care that she had everything that her father's money was paid for her to acquire. She did not mean to be over-exacting, but the truth was that she had a passion for learning everything that could be taught to her; and she easily took every prize that it was possible for her to take at the school.

But still the best set showed no signs of taking her up; and whatever chance she had of this form of rapture vanished on that day when, at a local bazaar, a young Austrian prince who spoke no English, was a visitor. He had been brought by Mrs. Bowlby-Sutherst, but that lady, having another engagement in the town, had asked one of the best set to lead him to some person who could speak German. But a full parade of all the members of the best set failed to yield even one person who could speak one word of that language. They were all smiling profusely, but they smiled in English, and the prince knew no English. Mrs. Bowlby-Sutherst was in despair, when suddenly Miss Caffyn, the daughter of the Rector of St. Mary's in the Meadows, brought up, without a word of warning, Priscilla Wadhurst, offering the great lady a personal guarantee that she would have no difficulty with the prince.

Of course Mrs. Bowlby-Sutherst was delighted. She saw that Miss Wadhurst was the most presentable girl in the hall, and she made no enquiry respecting her lineage or the armorial bearings of her father, but at once presented her to the young man, and noticed with great interest that she was not in the least fluttered at the honour; she was as much at her ease with him as if she had been in the habit of meeting princes all her life. She chattered to Prince Alex in his own language quite briskly, and for an hour and a half she had him all to herself, and delivered him up at the end of that time safe and sound to Mrs. Bowlby-Sutherst, on that lady's return.

This incident, taken in connection with its illustration in a London paper through the medium of an enterprising snap-shottist on the staff of the local *Gazette*, in which Priscilla "came out" extremely well, ruined whatever chance she might once have had of being visited by Framsby's best. They ignored her existence upon every occasion when they might reasonably have been expected to notice her; and the failure of her plans was too much for her mother. The lingering Lily of Limborough took to her bed—she had taken to her sofa the year before—and never held up her head afterwards.

And all the time that she was complaining of the want of appreciation of Framsby for all those accomplishments which constitute a "lady," she was imploring her daughter to make her a promise that she would not spend her future in so uncongenial a neighbourhood. Her aunt Emily, the wife of a prosperous brewer in a minor way in one of the largest cities in the Midlands, had joined her voice with that of Mrs. Wadhurst in this imploration; and with a view of giving her a chance of forming a permanent connection far away from the detestable place, had insisted on her paying several visits of some months' duration to her own house, and had presented to her favourable consideration more than one eligible man.

Somehow nothing came of these attentions, and Mrs. Wadhurst became gradually more feeble. Then all at once there appeared on the scene a gentleman named Blaydon, who occupied a good position in one of the great mercantile firms of the Midland city, having come there some years before from his home in Canada. He was greatly "smitten"—the expression was to be found in one of Aunt Emily's letters—with Priscilla, and there could be no doubt as to his intentions. There was none when he proposed to her, and was rejected.

He went away, sunk into the depths of an abyss of disappointment. And then it was that Aunt Emily threw up her hands in amazement. She wished to know whom the girl expected to marry—she, the daughter of a farmer—a wealthy and well-to-do farmer, to be sure, but still nothing more than a farmer. Did she look for a peer of the realm—a duke—or maybe a baronet or a prince? And Mr. Blaydon had eight hundred a year and a good situation. Moreover he had been told that her father was a farmer, and yet he had behaved as a gentleman!

What, in the face of all this impetuosity, was Priscilla's plaint that she had no affection for the man—that she felt she could not be happy with him—that she was not the sort of wife that such a man wanted?

Aunt Emily ridiculed her protests. They were artificial, she affirmed. They were the result of reading foolish novels in foreign languages; and in a year or two she would find out the mistake she was making—yes, when it would be too late—too late!

Priscilla fled to her home, but only to find that the story of her folly, of her flying in the face of Providence—the phrase was Aunt Emily's—had got there before her.

Within a week she had written accepting Mr. Blaydon. Her mother—her dying mother—backed up by her father, had brought this about. She had implored Priscilla to accept the man.

"My last words to you, my child—think of that," she had said. "The last request of a dying mother anxious for her child's happiness. I tell you, Priscilla, that I shall die happy if I can see you safely married to a man who will take you away from this neighbourhood. If you refuse, what will be your reflections so long as you live? You will have it on your soul that you refused to listen to the last prayer of your dying mother."

The girl made a rush for the writing-table with her heart full of anger and her eyes full of tears. But she wrote the letter, and the ardent and eligible Mr. Blaydon came down to Framsby, and they were married one February morning in Athalsdean Church, and he was arrested on a charge of embezzlement when they were in the act of leaving the sacred building. The police officers had arrived ten minutes too late.

It was the sentiment of the young and innocent wife, dwelt on so pathetically by his counsel—"Was it right that she, that guileless girl, should be made to suffer for a crime of which she was as innocent as an infant unborn?" he enquired—it was this sentiment that caused the jury to recommend him to mercy and the judge to sentence him to one year's imprisonment only, from the date of his committal.

He went to prison, and Priscilla went home, and continued to call herself by her maiden name—was she not as a maiden entitled to it? she asked. Six weeks later her mother died; and now...

CHAPTER VII

Every incident in this year of dreadful unrest passed through the mind of the girl sitting at the window, breathing of the clear air of this April afternoon, and feeling that rest had come to her at last. In the force of that review of the bitter past fresh upon her she wondered how she had ever had the courage to do all that she had done since. How had she ever been able to hold up her head walking through the streets of Framsby? How had it been possible for her, within three months of her marriage, to go about as if the only event that had made a mark upon her life was the funeral of her mother? She remembered how she had felt when, on going into Framsby for the first time in her black dress, she saw the interested expression that came over the faces of all the people whom she knew by sight. Every one gazed at her with that same look of curiosity that came to them when a celebrity chanced to visit the town. And upon that very first day she had met one of the ladies of the best set walking with her two daughters. She had seen them nudge one another and pass on a whisper, and then a little curious smile while she was still a good way off. The smile—and it was a very detestable one—lasted until she had walked past them. Another of the same set was with a stranger on the opposite side of the street, and Priscilla saw her point her out furtively to the stranger, and then over the back of her hand, explain what was the exact nature of the interest that attached to her.

A third lady—she was the wife of the retired colonial civil servant—had shown worse taste still; for although she had never spoken a word to Priscilla in all her life, yet now she stopped her and expressed her deep sympathy for her in "that sad affair," asking her what her plans were for the future, and saying, "Of course you will leave this neighbourhood as soon as you can."

How had she borne it all, she now asked herself. How had she the courage to face those people who seemed to think that that blow which had fallen on her had somehow brought Framsby within measurable distance of being thought disreputable by the world at large? But she had not merely borne it all, she had nerved herself to appear in public more frequently than she had ever done, and she went to help her friend Rosa Caffyn at the entertainment the wife of the Rector of St. Mary's in the Meadows was getting up in the Rectory grounds for the new Nurses' Home.

It was on account of her unbending attitude under the burden that she had to bear, that Rosa had talked with admiration of her confronting Fate and her splendid rebellion against what the Rector had claimed to be the heavy hand of a Power to whose mandates we should all be cheerfully resigned. Rosa was resolute in declining to accept the theories of the pulpit on the subject of cheerful resignation. How could she accept them, she asked, when her father refused to be either cheerful or resigned in such comparatively small dispensations of Providence as a cook with a heavy hand in the peppering of soups, or a parlourmaid with a passion for arranging the papers in his study?

But if Priscilla now found difficulty in understanding how she had had the resolution to face the world of Framsby as if nothing had happened, she did not fail to feel that her attitude was worthy of admiration, and she knew that it had received the admiration of Framsby in general, though the best set had felt scandalized by it. She had received many tokens of what she felt to be the true sympathy of the ordinary people of the town. A solicitor in the second set had offered to make an application to the courts of law—he was justifiably vague in their definition—to have her marriage rendered null and void, assuring her that he would do everything at his own expense. (He was well known to be an enterprising young man.) Many other and even more gracefully suggested evidences of the sympathy which was felt for her outside the jealously-guarded portals of the "right set" were given to her. In the eyes of the young men she had always been something of a heroine, and this matrimonial adventure of hers had not only established her claims to be looked on as a heroine, it had endowed her with the halo of a saint as well. And thus it was that, when she had appeared on the platform so fearlessly, and with a complete ignoring of the head-shakings and lip-pursings of the front rows, she had been received with the heartiest applause, very disconcerting to Mr. Kelton, who had never before in the whole course of his amateur experience known of an ordinary accompanist so "blanketing" a singer.

Her recollections of the various conflicting incidents and interests in her experiences of the year were quickly followed by some reflections upon her freedom and what she was to do with it. Thus she was led far into a bright if mysterious future; but presently she found her imagination becoming dazzled and dizzy, and down toppled the castle which she was building for herself after the most approved style affected by the architects of such structures in Spain—down toppled the castle, and she awoke from her vision, as one does from a dream of falling masonry, with a start.

What had she been thinking of? Was it all indeed a dream—this sense of Spring in the air—the rain-washed air—this sense of the peace of God?

She looked about her vaguely. Her hands fell on her lap, and came upon the still folded newspapers which remained there. She had forgotten all about the newspapers. (So the prisoner just released from gaol takes but the smallest amount of interest in the certificate of discharge.)

She read the account given in every one of the three of the wreck of the steel-built barque *Kingsdale* on the coast of Nova Scotia, in the neighbourhood of Yarmouth. The vessel had lost her rudder and become unmanageable, and she had been driven between the low headland and a sunken rock in the darkness. Boats had been stove in on an attempt being made to launch them; and then it was that the passenger whose name was Blaydon—"an unfortunate but well connected gentleman and a friend of Captain Lyman, of the ill-fated vessel"—had nobly volunteered to carry a line ashore. He was a powerful swimmer, and it was believed for some time by the wretched mariners whom he meant to save that his heroic attempt was crowned with success. Unhappily, however, this was not to be. On hauling upon the line after a long interval it had come all too easily. There was no resistance even of the man's body at the end. It was plain that the brave fellow, about whose shoulders it had been looped, had been dragged out of the bight and engulfed in the boiling surge, perishing in his heroic efforts on behalf of the crew. Through the night's exposure no fewer than eleven of the crew died within half an hour of being brought ashore by a fishing smack from St. John's. The survivors, twelve in number, included Captain Lyman, the master, and the second and third mates; also an apprentice named Jarvis, of Hull.

"From information supplied by Captain Lyman, we are able to state that the heroic man who perished in his attempt to provide the crew with the means of saving themselves, had but recently been released from an English prison, having worked out his sentence for a fraud committed by another man whom he was too high-minded to implicate. He had, it was said, a young wife in England, for whom the deepest sympathy will be felt."

Practically the same account appeared in all the papers; one, however, went more deeply into the past history of the man, giving—evidently by reference to some back files of an English paper—the date and particulars of the trial of Marcus Blaydon; but it did not introduce these details at the cost of the expression of sympathy with the young widow—all the accounts referred to the pathetic incident of the young widow and offered her the tribute of their deep sympathy.

And there the young widow sat at the open window, conscious of no impression beyond that which she had frequently acquired from reading a novel at the same window. She felt that she had been reading an account of a wreck in a novel, in which the hero lost his life in a forlorn hope to rescue his fellow creatures, and the hero had been a black sheep; the object of the writer being to show that even the worst man may have in his nature the elements of the heroic.

The man Blaydon seemed as legendary to her as Jim Bludso in Hay's ballad. He seemed quite as remote from her life. She took no more than a novel-reader's interest in the story. She was harder than the newspaper men, for she could not bring herself up to a point of sympathizing with the young widow.

"Good heavens!" she cried, getting to her feet so quickly that the papers fluttered down to the carpet. "Good heavens! have I allowed myself to be made miserable for so long by a person who was no more than a character out of a novel—one of the black sheep hero novels? Oh, what a fool I was—as foolish as the girls who cry copiously when their fustian hero gets into trouble."

Then she leant up against the side of the window and was lost in a maze of thought. Several minutes had passed before she found herself, so to speak; and she found herself with a smile on her face.

"Good heavens!" she said again. "Good heavens! After all I was not miserable, but glad. I allowed myself to be driven into marrying him when all the time I did not even like him. I had a sense of committing suicide—of annihilating myself—when I married him, and I now know that it was a relief to me when we were separated. And now the final relief has come—relief and release; and my life is once more in my own hands. Thank God for that! Thank God for that!"

And then, strange though it was, she began to recall, apparently without any connection with her previous reflections, something that she had said to Rosa when on their way to the primrose park in the forenoon—something about immorality—it was certainly a very foolish thing—some hint that if she were to set her mind—no, her heart—upon some object, she would not allow any considerations that were generally called moral considerations to interfere with her achievement of that object.

That was in substance what she had said in her foolishness, and now, thinking upon it, she felt that it was not merely a very foolish thing to say, but a very shocking thing as well. The very idea at which she had hinted was revolting to her now, so that she could not understand what was the origin of the impulse in the force of which she had talked so wildly. This was what she now felt, illustrating with some amount of emphasis how a slight change in the conditions which govern a young woman's life may cause her to lose a sense of the right perspective in a fancy picture that she is drawing, as she believes, direct from Nature.

It was with a blushing conscience that she now remembered how for some weeks she had been thinking that if the only obstacle that prevented her living her life as she felt that her life should be lived, was what would generally be regarded as a moral one, she would not hesitate for a moment to kick that obstacle out of her way, and live her life in accordance with the dictates of the heart of a woman:—a true woman, quivering with those true instincts which make up the life of a real woman.

That had actually been the substance of her thoughts for several weeks past. She shuddered at the recollection now. She thanked God that she could look at such matters very differently now; and this meant that she thanked God for having removed temptation from her.

The young widow bathed her face and smoothed her hair and looked at herself in the glass, and was quite satisfied with the reflection. She had emerged from an ordeal by fire, and she found that not a hair of her head was singed. The three young men who had passed through the seven times heated furnace must have felt pretty well satisfied with themselves when they found that they had not suffered. Only a few hours earlier this young woman had had her gloomy moments. She was an intelligent girl, and so was perfectly well aware of the fact that a girl's supreme chance in life comes to her by marriage, and she had thrown this chance away, and it might never return to her. It was the force of this reflection that had caused her to begin experimenting with her maimed life, with a view of making the most of it. The trick which she had played upon the bumptious tenor represented only one of her experiments. All the people around her, men as well as women, had been unable to stem the current of his insolence. They were all ready to lie down before him and allow him to achieve the triumph of the hero of a bas-relief, at their expense: they had permitted him to put his feet on their necks, as it were. She had wondered if it would not be possible for her to trip up this blatant alabaster hero when he was stalking about from neck to neck of better people than himself. Her experiment had succeeded, and she had gone home with a feeling that if she had been made a fool of by a man, she had shown herself capable of making a man look very like a fool even in his own eyes.

This was some encouragement to her; and she had thus been led to wonder if it might not be possible for her to employ her intelligence and her looks to such good purpose as should at least minimize her folly in throwing away her best chance of making a great thing out of her life. She knew that this question demanded some earnest thinking out, considering her position, but she had already attacked it, when lo! in a single moment all the conditions of the contest—it would be a contest, she knew—had changed.

Not once had she thought of the man's death as a possible factor in the solution of the problem of her life. Death was something between man and his God only, and she had so come to feel that the All-Powerful was leagued against her, that she had never thought of His making a move in her favour. Well, she had been wrong—she had done God an injustice, and she had apologized for it on her knees. And now she felt that if Providence were really and seriously to be on her side, or at least, as the man who met the grizzly in the open prayed, not on the side of the bear, her future might be all that she could hope it would be.

Having asked the forgiveness of God, it was a simple thing now to ask her father to pardon her for the extravagant way in which she had spoken when he had brought to her the news of the man's death. Mr. Wadhurst was one of those plain-spoken, straightforward men, who think it right and proper to be hypocritical over such matters as death and bankruptcy. He had joined solemnly in the complaints of his unprosperous neighbours over the bad times, and had shaken his head when one of them, who had been going to the wall for years, at last reached that impenetrable boundary of his incapacity; though Mr. Wadhurst did not fail to perceive that he would now be able to join the derelict farm on to his own and obtain the live stock at his own valuation—a chance for which he had been waiting for years. And he had never failed to be deeply shocked when he heard of the death of a drunken wife, or a ne'er-do-weel son, or a consumptive daughter on the eve of her marriage with a scorbutic man; and thus he hoped that God would look upon him as a man with a profound sense of decency. He certainly looked upon himself as such; and he never felt his position stronger in this respect than he did when his daughter met him in a contrite spirit for having spoken with so great a want of delicacy in regard to her rascally husband.

"I'm glad that you have come to see that—that vengeance is God's, not man's," said he, with great solemnity.

She replied substantially that she was glad it was in such capable hands, though the words that she employed were of conventional acquiescence in the conventionally Divine.

"Whatever the man may have been, he died like a man," resumed her father, repeating the phrase that he had used before. "You must respect his memory for that deed."

She could not help feeling that she would respect his memory more on this account if he had done the deed before she had met him. But she did not express this view. She only bent her head; she was no longer a rebellious child, only a hypocritical one.

"It's a shocking thing—an awful thing!" continued her father. "To think that within a year your mother and your husband have gone. Have you yet grasped the fact that you are a widow, Priscilla?"

She certainly had not grasped this fact. The notion of her being a widow seemed to her supremely funny. But for the sake of practice in the career of duplicity which he was marking out for her, she took out her handkerchief and averted her head.

He put a strong arm about her, saying, "My poor child—my poor motherless child! I did not forget you when I was in the town just now. I called at Grindley's and told them to send one of their hands out here with samples, so as to save you from the ordeal of appearing in public in your ordinary dress."

She moved away from his sheltering embrace.

"Samples—samples—of what?" she said.

"Of the cap—the—Ah! that I should live to see my child wearing widow's weeds!"

"You were very thoughtful, father," she murmured; "but I am not sure that I should think of myself as really a widow."

"You are a widow," he said, with some measure of asperity.

She shook her head in a way that suggested she felt that she was not worthy of such an honour.

"You are a widow, and I hope that you will remember that," he repeated. "Your marriage was quite regular. There was no flaw in it."

"I suppose, then——"

"You may not merely suppose, you may be sure of it. Do you fancy that there would be a flaw in any business, that I had to do with?"

"I do not, indeed. This was, however, a bad bit of business for me, father. However, we need say no more about it. I don't wish ever again to hear that wretched business alluded to. It has passed out of my life altogether, thanks be to God, and now it only remains in my mind as a horrid nightmare."

"It was a legal marriage, and marriage is a holy thing."

He spoke with the finality of the Vicar's churchwarden—as if he were withstanding the onslaught of a professed freethinker. His last statement was, however, too much for the patience of his daughter—to be more exact, it was too much for her mask of humility which she had put on to save the trouble of discussion with him.

She turned upon him, speaking with a definiteness and finality quite equal in force to his display of the same qualities.

"Look here, father," she said. "We may as well understand each other at once. You know as well as I do that there was nothing sacred about that marriage of mine. You know that the—the—no, I will not give him his true name, I will call him for once a man—he behaved like a man—*once*—you know, I say, that he married me simply because that foolish woman, Aunt Emily, gave him to understand that you would endow me handsomely on my wedding day, and he wanted the money to pay back all that he had embezzled. You also know that I never had the least feeling of affection, or even of regard, for the man—that I only agreed to marry him because my mother forced me to do so."

"Do not speak a word against your mother, girl."

"I am not speaking against her. She, I am sure, was convinced that she was urging me to take a step for my own good; she had always bowed down before the superior judgment of Aunt Emily. No matter about that; I married the man caring nothing for him, but believing that he cared something for me. It was proved at the church door that he never cared a scrap for me. That is the marriage which you tell me was sacred!"

"Marriage is a sacred ordinance. You can't get over that; and every marriage celebrated in the church——"

"Sacred ordinance! You might as well talk of any Stock Exchange transaction being sacred because it is made in what I believe they call the House. Sacred! A sacred farce! I remember feeling when I was in the church that day how dreadful was the mockery of the whole thing—how the curate talked about the mystic union between Christ and the Church being symbolized by marriage—dreadful!... Never mind, what you know as well as I know is that that marriage of mine was not made by God, but by the Power of Evil; it was the severance of that marriage that came from God, and the coming of it so quickly makes me feel such gratitude to God as I cannot express in words. That is all I have to say just now; only if you fancy that I shall be hypocrite enough to pretend that I am mourning for that man who did his best to wreck my life, you are mistaken. You know that all rightminded people will say 'What a happy release for the poor girl!' and they will be right. It is exactly what the poor girl herself is saying, and what the father of the poor girl is saying in his heart, however he may talk about the sacredness of marriage."

He looked at her for some moments, and the frown upon his face became more marked every moment. He seemed more than once about to make some answer to her impetuous speech, but he made none. When she had said her last word, he looked at her as though he meant to box her ears. Then he turned suddenly round and walked straight out of the room.

So that, after all, it may be said that he had answered her accusations.

She felt a great pity for him; she knew that she had treated him badly; but with the memory of the past year fresh upon her—the sense of having escaped from a noisome prison by the grace of God—she could no longer play the part which he was encouraging her to play.

She felt that, though a girl might marry a man whom she detested, solely to please, her mother, it was too much to expect that she should become a hypocrite solely to please her father.

She was aroused from a reverie by the unfamiliar sound of the throbbing of the passionate heart of a motor up the steep lane leading to the farm. The car appeared round the side of the house when she had got upon her feet to find out who the visitor was that had dared that tyre-rending track.

The car was a very fine one, but it carried only a chauffeur and a basket of primroses. They parted company at the door. Priscilla heard the man speaking a word or two to the maid at the hall door, and the machine was backed slowly in the segment of a circle away from the house to put it into position for taking the hill properly.

"Mrs. Pearce has told him who we were, and he found the baskets in the porch," were the words that came to her mind at that moment.

And then she gave a little start, and it was followed by a little laugh, and then a little frown.

It had suddenly occurred to her that here was a basket of flowers sent by a kindly hand as a conventional tribute of respect; only it was impossible that any such sentiment should be pinned to it, written on paper with a black border.

Still, there was the obituary notice in that newspaper on the table, and there was the basket of flowers—they could easily be worked into a wreath.

The maid brought them into the room and laid them on a chair.

CHAPTER VIII

Of course the next day some of the London newspapers contained ample, though by no means extravagant, reports of the wreck of the barque on the coast of Yarmouth, Nova Scotia. They had previously published cables to the same effect, but only to the extent of a hundred words. At that time no more interest was attached to the incident than would be associated with the wreck of an ordinary vessel. It was not until the arrival of the Canadian papers that it was found that there was a popular feature in the transaction. The public mind, always deeply stirred by an account of a black-sheep hero, could not be ignored by the newspapers; and in recognition of this fact, several columns in the aggregate and a few sub-leaders appeared dealing with the attempt—a successful attempt too—made by Marcus Blaydon to make up for the errors of his past by an act of heroism that had cost him his life. Posthumous honour in this form is always administered with a generous hand; and the consequence was that, by the time the country papers had, on account of the local interest attaching to the loss of the barque *Kingsdale*, filled to overflowing the cup of effervescent incident in this connection, and offered it to their readers, Mr. Wadhurst had come to think of himself as the father-in-law of a hero. He actually had a feeling of pride when he saw his name in the bracketed paragraphs at the foot of the spirited account of the wreck: "It will be remembered that the heroic if unfortunate man, Marcus Blaydon, married on the morning of his arrest, the only daughter of a much-respected practical agriculturist, Mr. Phineas Wadhurst, of Athalsdean, near Framsby."

He felt very bitterly on the subject of his daughter's refusal to wear mourning; and now that the local papers had dealt so fully with the leading incident of the wreck, recognizing the popular element that it contained, he was angrier than ever. He asked her if she had any idea what the people would think of her if she were to appear among them without even a hint at the "weeds"; and when she replied that she had never thought of the people of Framsby and did not intend to begin now, he expressed himself as being ready to accept a compromise from her on this point. He tried to suggest to her the possibility of adopting such a costume as would make it plain that, while she deplored the past errors of her husband, she fully appreciated the elements of distinction associated with his last act.

That was what he had in his mind, but he did not quite succeed in giving definition to it with sufficient clearness to enforce its appeal to her sense of proportion; and when she told him so, he stalked away from her.

And that "romance of the sea," as one newspaper termed it, had apparently attracted the attention of the lady who had been responsible for Priscilla's meeting with the man, for the young widow received a long letter from her Aunt Emily the purport of which was to convince her that, in spite of what had been said at the time of her marriage, she, Aunt Emily, had been quite correct in the estimate she had formed of the character of Marcus Blaydon: he had shown himself to be a fine and noble gentleman—Aunt Emily harped on the word "gentleman," as usual. She ended her letter with a sentence which, reduced to the plainest English, was in effect: "Since I did so well for you once before, if you come to me now you may depend on my doing as much for you again."

Her father thought she should visit her aunt and give her another trial. (He wanted to get her as far away as possible from the observation of Framsby—to get her removed to some place where the absence of those distinguishing "weeds" would not arouse comment.)

Priscilla threw the letter, torn into shreds, out of the window, and some of the choicest paragraphs became the lining of a blackbird's nest that was being hastily papered and plastered for the coming of a new brood.

She did not hasten to show herself in the street of Framsby. What was Framsby to her that she should flaunt in its face her feeling in regard to her position? She had no occasion to go into the town, and she took care that she did not create an artificial necessity for the sake of displaying her unconventionality. Her friend Rosa paid her a visit, accompanied by her mother, who really liked Priscilla. Now Rosa's visit was one of congratulation, whereas her mother's was one of condolence, so that she had no reason to complain on any score. She did not complain. She took the congratulations with the condolences in the spirit in which they were offered, and so every one was satisfied.

At the end of a fortnight she began to have a longing for some traffic with the outer world. She was becoming as melancholy as the Lady of Shalott; and the *Daily Mirror*, in which she gazed every morning to find a reflection of the incidents of life, only caused her longings to be increased. The things of the farm, the incidents of the orchard, the promise of the crops, the "likely" calves, the multiplying of the lambs, now ceased to interest her. Neither her father nor her mother had encouraged her to take any interest in the great money-making farm; they gave her to understand that her part in connection with the farm was to spend the money that it made for the family. She was to be a "lady," and this involved laziness in all matters that mattered in connection with the farm. She was to give all her attention to her piano, to her painting, to her dressing, all these being accomplishments as essential to the development of a "lady" as an acquaintance with the methods of the farm was detrimental to the effecting of this end—the great end of life.

But Priscilla had, without any desire to go against the will of her parents, come to perceive how infinitely more interesting were the things of the farm than the working of tea cloths and the embroidering of teapot cosies—the eminently ladylike occupations which her mother encouraged her to pursue. The consequence was that, in the course of a year or two, she knew a great deal about the farm, and several times she had detected errors made by the men responsible for at least two of the departments; but having only communicated her knowledge to the men themselves, and not to her father, she had not hurt the susceptibilities of either the former or the latter.

But now, as the month of May went on, and she remained watching how all living things around her were full of the delights of companionship, she had a sense of loneliness—of isolation. She felt keenly just now the cruelty of her position in respect of the "sets" at Framsby. She knew that the Tennis and Croquet Club was in full swing, but she was not a member. Rosa Caffyn had been made to understand by Mrs. Gifford, the lady who practically ran the club, that she need not put up Miss Wadhurst's name, for she would have no chance of being admitted. Then there were two cricket matches being played on the county ground, but she had no one with whom she could go, though she took great interest in cricket, and all Framsby would be there.

She felt very lonely in her isolation on the Downs, and began to go for long walks in the company only of Douglas, her Scotch collie, keeping as remote as possible from the motor tracks, for the month was turning out dusty dry. But in spite of her intentions in this direction, she detected the aroma of burning petrol when she was on her way home through a rather steep brambly lane, the surface of which retained the cart ruts of the previous winter—perhaps of an earlier winter still. The scent seemed warm, so she was not surprised to come upon the *fons et origo* when she had followed the bend of the lane toward the old coach road. The machine was standing with one wheel up on the ditch, and its engine was silent. Two men were on their knees in front of the exposed machinery, but it was plain that their posture was not devotional—in fact, from the character of a word or two that strayed to her ears, she gathered that it was just the opposite.

He waited for her to smile first: he seemed uncertain and rather anxious to know what she would do and so give him the note for him to follow; and when she smiled quite happily and unconcernedly, his mouth widened visibly, and he gave her an excellent caricature of a jocose boy. He had no notion of letting her walk on after she had greeted him and said:

"Thank you so much for sending the primroses. That is your motor, is it not? Nothing material, I hope?"

"Sure to be nothing when it's found out," he said. "It's a bit pink-eyed to-day—had rather a lurid night."

"Oh, really?" she said. "I thought that those things had iron constitutions—stand any amount of racket."

"I suppose I should say something about the amount of spirit they consume and that," he remarked, still smiling.

"Too obvious," she said, shaking her head. "Still after the obviousness of my 'iron constitution' you might say anything. What a lovely day it is—just the sort of day for a breakdown!"

She had begun to walk on, saying her last sentence with a sort of good-bye nod and smile.

"Might I walk on a bit with you?" he asked, becoming solemn and pitching his voice half a tone lower. "The fact is"—his voice became lower still, almost confidential—"the chap knows more about the machine than I do, and he works best when let alone."

"Of course you may walk as far as you wish. I shall be only too glad, I can tell you," said she. "I have been having a lot of solitary walks of late, and I'm sick of them. I was longing for some one to talk to."

"I'm sorry you haven't come across some one who is better in that line than myself," said he. "I never was up to much as a talker."

"Why, you talked quite a lot that day when you gave us so nice a lunch."

"Oh, I always talk a lot—no mistake about that; but there's no brains behind it all—no, not even grammar," he added, after an anxious moment.

"You have plenty of brains," she said, looking at him as if her remark had reference to the size of his head and she was verifying it. "What makes you fancy that you've no brains?"

"I do the wrong things so often—things that no chap would do if he had brains enough to think whether he should do them or not."

"For instance?"

"Oh, for instance? Gloriana! I've instances enough. Well, go no further than this moment. I'm not sure that another chap—a chap that remembers things, and knows the decent thing to do—would have stopped you in the way I did."

"Why shouldn't you stop me if you wished? Why, you were excessively polite in asking me if you might walk with me to keep you from getting in the way of the chauffeur."

"Of course—that's all right the way you put it; but—but—well, I heard from Mrs. Pearce who you were, and then I read all that in the papers, so that I wasn't sure if—if—it was just the thing, you know."

"If it was quite in good taste to speak naturally to one who had suffered a recent bereavement?"

He nodded, his eyes brightening as if in recognition of the excellent way in which she expressed what was in his mind. He went further, seeming to feel quite pleased that he had in his mind something that could be so well expressed.

"Mr. Wingfield," she said, "you have the highest form of brain power, let me tell you—the power to see in a single glance what most other men would require to have explained to them, and even then not be able to grasp properly. You saw in a moment that I was not the sort of girl who would try to affect the part of the bereaved widow, taking all the circumstances of the bereavement into consideration."

He looked at her in frank admiration for some moments; then he said:

"It's you that have the brains, to see that that is just what I saw. I knew in a moment that you would not put on a woebegone air when you know what everybody else knows, that you have only cause to feel delighted."

"Not exactly——"

"I beg your pardon; of course not delighted—a man's a man—you couldn't feel delighted to hear of the death of any man, even though he was as great a rascal as the fellow who did his best to drag you down to hell with him. If he had cared the merest scrap for you he never would have asked you to marry him—he would have run away to the other end of the world or cut his throat first."

"Yes; but he's dead now."

"Yes, I know; *de mortuis* and the rest; and so no one should speak a word against Judas Iscariot. A kiss—a kiss was the sign of the betrayal."

There was a suggestion of fierceness in the way he spoke, but nothing that approached the passion with which she flared up, "He never kissed me—never once!" she cried, her face flushing and her hands trembling visibly. Her collie, who had been running ahead, turned and came back to her. He looked up at her and then glanced, enquiringly, at the man. She laid one trembling hand on the dog's head, and then seemed to calm herself.

"Pardon me," she said, "you really did not suggest—but you had every right to take it for granted that we had been lovers—that I had some regard for him. It is as great a crime for a woman to marry a man without caring for him in the least as it is for the man to marry her. I deserved all that I suffered; but I was spared, thank God, the memory of having had so much as one kiss from him. I never told him that I had any regard for him; but I did say that perhaps one day I might come to have some sort of feeling for him, but till then—I wonder if anything like this ever happened before. It's funny, isn't it?"

"Funny? No. If any one else told me of it, I would think it funny; but when I look at you, I don't think anything of the sort."

"It is funny, and what's funnier still is that you are the first person whom I have told this to. Now, why should I tell it to you?"

"I don't know why, I'm sure, only I can tell you that you have told it to the right man. And now will you go a step further and confide in me how it was that you ever did marry the fellow? and we'll drop the subject for ever and the day after. Don't tell me if you don't wish."

"I have gone so far that I may as well go further. I never knew until now how fascinating a thing is confession. I suppose that if it were not for women there would be no such thing as a confessional in any church."

"I should say not; but their secrets are sacred."

"I could never doubt you, and that is why I tell you now that I allowed myself to be persuaded by my poor mother into marrying that man. She believed that it would be for my own good."

"Of course. But why—why? Your father has heaps of money, I'm told, and the man's position was a poor one."

"It was my position in this neighbourhood that was a poor one. You see, I'm only the daughter of a farmer."

"What better could you be? The Wadhursts have been at Athalsdean for hundreds of years, and in the neighbourhood for maybe a thousand. The name is Saxon. I looked up the whole dynasty in the county history."

"Then you know all about that; but is there any county history that will tell you who are the sort of people at Framsby that have it in their power to decree who are to be visited and who are not?"

"A pack of idiots—old women—tabbies with their claws always out, and not prize tabbies at that. I've heard all about them. The family of the village sawbones—the village attorney—a colonial clerk whose ability was assessed at four or five hundred a year—I have been properly coached on the whole crew—all rotters. But it's the same way in every beggarly town like Framsby. It's in the hands of half-a-dozen tabbies, and their whole aim is to keep out the nicest people—the best-looking girls and the best educated."

"They kept me out, at any rate. Perhaps they were right; if they began admitting farmers' daughters into their sacred circle, where would its sacredness be? They kept me out as they had kept my poor mother out, and the very means that she had taken to have me recognized—the education that she insisted on my getting, the expensive frocks, the good furs— real sables, mind, not musquash sables at forty pounds or rabbit-skin sables at thirty shillings, but real sables—these only caused the door to be more tightly closed against me; and my dear mother took it all so much to heart that she never raised her head afterwards. That was why she made me accept the first offer I received from some one who would take me away from this neighbourhood."

"You should not have allowed yourself to be forced, mother or no mother. A girl like you!"

"She was dying. She said to me: 'Will you let me go down to the grave without having my one request granted? I have done everything for you— will you not do this one thing for me so that I may close my eyes in peace?'"

He shook his head. Then he looked at her, but he only saw the back of her head; she had turned away her face and her eyes were on the ground. He knew that they were full of tears. They walked on slowly for some time, and then he took his right hand out of the pocket of his jacket and let it drop till it was on a level with her left. Very gently his fingers closed over hers for a moment—only a moment.

"I was wrong," he said. "There was nothing else left for you to do; but it was rough on you. Well, well; you have had a bad year of it—that's all, but you might have had a bad fifty years. It's odd how the rights of a story do get about somehow, whatever people may say. Now that gossipy old woman, Mrs. Pearce, was only too glad to tell me all about you when you went away that day we met; and when I said that it was your own fault— that it was a shame, but you had made your own bed—she took your part and said that if duty to a mother was a fault, then you were to blame. She holds that a girl should do just what a mother tells her to do in all matters, but especially as regards marriage. I don't. But then I fancy I miss my gear pretty frequently when I try to express myself on most matters. I'm all for independence of thought and action. That's why they presented me with the Fellowship at the University."

"A Fellowship—and you said you had no brains?" She had recovered herself and was now looking at him with only the smallest trace of her former emotion in her face.

"A Fellowship—yes, the Fellowship of the Boot," he said with a grin.

"Oh, you were sent down?"

"If you wish to put it that way."

"It was your independence of thought that did it?"

"Beyond a doubt. You see, I never could see the humour in talking of the University as the Varsity; and I pretended not to understand one of the dons—the surliest and the most ignorant of the lot, if I knew anything——"

"But you don't. You confessed just now that you didn't"

"I know that—he was a chap with the mug and the pug of a pugilist. They've made him a bishop since—a sort of bishop."

"A sort of bishop, Mr. Wingfield?"

"This one was made Metropolitan of the Salamander Archipelago. His see was in the sea—that was the joke made at the time. Anyhow, I asked him on what philological grounds he called the University the Varsity. I added that I came to Oxford to be educated, but I didn't think that the people who shirked the correct pronunciation of the name of the very institution itself, but adopted the vulgarest that could be imagined and clung to it in spite of all correction, could say that they were earning their money honestly."

"You said that to a don?"

"To that effect. You see he had been cheeking me like ribbons about something else."

"And so they sent you down for your independence of thought?"

"Well, there was a bit of a scrap over the Varsity question. I got up a faction who had pledged themselves to call the place the University, and in our zeal for the truth we insulted the Varsity faction. They replied with counter-insults that took the form of pieces of brick aimed at our windows; we replied with pieces of stone and a few tins of ready-made paint that I had picked up seeing them go for next to nothing at a sale. It was that paint that did it. The paint was traced to me, and so I was the one to be sacrificed on the altar of pure pronunciation of the English language as opposed to the Oxford manner."

"Well, you have the satisfaction of knowing that you are a martyr to your own opinions, and that your opinions were right."

"Yes, but though we hear that a great cause has its foundations cemented by the blood of martyrs, yet it didn't turn out that way when I was the martyr; they went back to the old vulgarity of Varsity in a moment. There was not one there to pass on the blazing torch of pure English which I had lighted for them."

"You shouldn't have made the torch out of the old oak."

He gazed at her in amazement.

"Who told you that about the oak door?" he asked.

"No one; only it occurred to me that there must have been something of that sort going on in the course of the proceedings. I have heard that you may do anything you please at Oxford if you only keep good hours and respect the oak. Here comes your machine. The chauffeur quite bore out the character you gave him; but I shall feel that I did something to help him by taking you out of his way."

"Confound him! he's just a bit too quick," said Mr. Wingfield. "We've got a lot more to say, haven't we?"

"You must say it to the chauffeur," she said.

"No; I'll send him home with the machine and you'll let me walk up the hill with you."

"Not to-day, please. Good-bye. I am very glad that we met. I have got rid of my gloomiest thoughts. I knew that what I wanted was a chat with some one who was—was—like you—some one not just like the rest of the world—some one who was a rigid purist in the matter of pronunciation—some one who had gained distinction as a painter."

"Oh, I say; you must forget that business. I'm not proud of it now. As a matter of fact I can recollect very little that I have a reason to be proud of."

"Good-bye. You maybe proud of having pulled a poor girl out of the black depths of her own reflections."

"Not black depths, surely."

"Black, without relief. You pulled me out of the Slough of Despond, and the world appears with a rose-coloured ribbon or two fluttering about it before my eyes. Thank you again and again. Good-bye."

"Good-bye. We are pretty sure to meet again. I suppose it wouldn't be possible for you to suggest some place where you are likely to take your walks abroad?"

She shook her head.

"That would be to set oneself up as a sort of Providence, wouldn't it?"

"I like to make arrangements beforehand for coincidences," said he. "Never mind. When you feel gloomy, and want somebody to confess to, don't forget that I'm your man."

"You may be sure of that."

They had walked a dozen yards or so away from where the car had pulled up, and now he went back to it, and took the wheel from the chauffeur. She watched him start and gave him a little wave of her hand.

He was a mile away before she had turned her face homeward.

CHAPTER IX

Priscilla's father had a piece of news for her when they met at supper that night—the *menage* at the farm involved tea at six and supper at half-past nine.

"That young Wingfield, the grandson of the old man, has come to live at the Manor," he said. "I heard all about it from Mr. Hickman to-day. Hickman is not his solicitor, but he knows all about it. A young scamp who will simply walk through that fine property which has been nursed for him by the trustees all these years."

"I think you told us that the old man hoped that by preventing him from inheriting the property until he was twenty-seven he would give him a chance of gaining some sense to enable him to work it properly," remarked Priscilla.

"That was the old man's notion; but I don't suppose it will prove to have been worth anything. It's usually the case that an ill-conditioned puppy turns out an ill-conditioned dog. The young man is a wild young ass, kicking up his heels at all authority. He was turned out of Oxford in his third year. They couldn't stand his ways any longer."

"That must have happened several years ago if he is twenty-seven now. I wonder what he has been doing in the meantime."

"Wild—he has been very wild, I hear; knocking about the world—India, Australia, the South Sea Islands, with America to follow. He has been doing no good anywhere. He has no head, you see; his father had no head either—allowed himself to be imposed on right and left. The old man had to pay his debts half-a-dozen times over before he died. The boy seems ready to follow in his father's footsteps. It's very sad. Twelve thousand a year at the least."

"But are there not some farms still unlet?"

"There are three; but that would only make a difference of a thousand a year. I'm not sure that Dunning did his best in the matter of the big farm—Birchknowle. But the trustees thought no end of Dunning, and you may be sure that when they couldn't see through him the young man won't either. Dunning is a muddler if ever there was one. Wouldn't allow Brigstock the year's rent that he wanted when he was going in for market gardening. A man could make a fortune off a market garden at Birchknowle, since they brought the branch line there—a fortune. I told Dunning so; and I told

Brigstock the same. And so they've lost a couple of thousand pounds to the estate when the year's rent that Brigstock looked for only came to three hundred! Dunning's a muddler."

"I wonder will young Mr. Wingfield find that out for himself?"

Mr. Wadhurst looked up from his plate with a very grim smile.

"He's not the sort to find things out for himself—he has no head, I tell you," he replied. "Ducks and drakes—that's the sort of game that will be played by the young ass until every penny's gone."

"It's a pretty large poultry bill that will absorb twelve thousand a year, to say nothing of the accumulations," said Priscilla.

"Poultry bill? Pheasants, do you mean?" he said.

"Ducks and drakes—that was what you mentioned," said she.

He shook his head in reproof of his daughter's levity.

"When a young spendthrift makes spending the business of his life you may trust him to run through a million in a month. I wonder if he'll ever find out about the pheasants. Dunning did pretty well out of the pheasants."

"Perhaps he put down all that he made by them—put it down to the credit side of the estate," she suggested; and again he smiled that grim smile of his—the smile of the shrewd man who is conscious of his own shrewdness.

"If he was doing that he wouldn't have taken the trouble to bind Jenkins over to secrecy," said the farmer.

"But you found out all about it in spite of Jenkins being bound over," said she.

He smiled less grimly, accepting her compliment, and then rose from the table, having finished his supper, and went into the room that he used as his office. His business methods were admirable. For over thirty years he had spent an hour in his office every night before going to bed. This space out of every day was small, but it was quite enough to enable him to know exactly how he stood financially from one week to another. His system was admirable; but it had helped to kill his wife.

When Priscilla went to her own room and looked out upon that May night of pale starlight and clear sky she could not help feeling that an element of interest had come into her life, beyond any that had ever been associated with it. Here was a man who represented an estate of twelve thousand pounds a year, and the question was, "What is to be the result of his entering into possession of this splendid property? Is he to turn it to good account, or to dissipate it like the young fools of whom I have heard so much lately?"

Here there was a question of real interest beyond any that had ever risen above the somewhat restricted horizon of her life. What were all the questions that her father had to decide in connection with his farm compared with this? What were all the questions connected with the social life of Framsby, or even Birchleigh—proud of its ten thousand inhabitants—compared with this?

Was he a fool—the fool that her father believed him to be, forming his conclusion on the reports made to him by Mr. Hickman, the solicitor, at Framsby—the fool who, according to the proverb, is quickly parted from his money?

This was the question the answer to which was bound to influence the answer that should be given to the other question.

She could not bring herself to think of him as a fool. To be sure it could not be denied that his attitude in relation to certain matters was not at all that which the majority of people would think justifiable; and in the eyes of most persons, her father included, this fact was in itself strong presumptive evidence that he was inclined to be a young fool. A man who declines to fall into line with the prejudices and the conventionalities of the majority of his elders is looked on as a bit of a fool. Yes; unless he succeeds in becoming a leader of thought, in which case he becomes a hero, though as a rule he has been dead some time before this happens. Priscilla knew a good deal in a general way of the history of the world, and the men who made history, in action and by putting their thoughts on paper; but she could not remember one of these who had not begun life by being looked on as a bit of a fool.

Now, of all the institutions that have existed for the conservation of the conventional, Oxford University is the most notorious; and yet people were ready to call that undergraduate, Mr. Wingfield, a giddy young fool because he had refused to accede to one of the most cherished—one of the least worthily cherished—of its conventions!

Putting the matter in this way, she felt that she had every right to decline to accept the judgment of such people.

But what about his own confession to her? Had he not confessed quite frankly to her that he had no brains?

He certainly had done so; but what did this prove except that he had brains? It is only the empty-headed man who thinks that he is largely endowed with brains. She could recall several little things that Jack Wingfield had done—she left out of consideration altogether the things that he had said—which convinced her that he had some ability, and that he possessed something of the supreme gift of understanding how to make people do what he wanted them to do. If he had failed to exercise this valuable endowment of his upon the authorities at Oxford, he had succeeded in doing so upon the two young women who had paid him that remarkable visit on the day of his arrival at his home. By the exercise of extraordinary tact he had induced them to take lunch with him, and to sit with him afterwards in his drawing-room. If any one had said to her the day before this happened, "You will go boldly into a strange house, and you will there meet a young man whom you have never seen before; he will ask you to remain to lunch before you have even heard his name, or he yours, and you will accept his invitation without feeling—you who have been to a 'finishing school'—that you have done anything *outré*"—if any one had said this to her she would at once have denied the possibility of such an incident taking place. And yet it had taken place, and the tact shown by the young man had made it seem quite an ordinary matter.

Did not this show that he possessed the supreme talent of knowing how to deal with people—how to persuade them that the unique was the usual—nay, the inevitable?

And then, what about their coming together on the road? How had he, a man whom she had seen but once before, and that in no regular way—how had he succeeded in getting her to confess to him that—that—well, all that she had confessed?

She really could not understand how it was that she had been led to confide in this young Mr. Wingfield what she had not even confided to her one dear friend, Rosa Caffyn: it must only have been by the exercise on his part of an extraordinary ability—more than ability, intuition—that he had drawn from her that confession. And would any one succeed in persuading her, after this, that Jack Wingfield was a bit of a fool?

And what an effect her stroll and chat with him had had upon her! She had been, as she told him (more confession), plunged into the black depths of despondency; and yet within five minutes, owing to his sympathetic attitude—owing to her feeling that he understood her and sympathized with her and applauded her boldness in standing out against her father's prejudices in carrying out that form of hypocrisy known as mourning—she had been drawn out of the depths and made to feel that there might yet be a place for her in the world.

The result of her consideration of the whole of this question—the most interesting that had ever come within her ken—was to make her feel that she would like to have it in her power to do something for that man—something important—something that would make people see that he was not the brainless spendthrift which so many people, on quite insufficient evidence, assumed him to be.

She was perfectly well aware of the fact that she was not in love with him, and she felt that she understood him so well that she could not be mistaken in perceiving that neither was he in love with her. She had always been an observant girl, and she had had several opportunities of diagnosing—of subjecting to the interpretation of her mental spectroscope, so to speak—the various phases incidental to the progress of the phenomena of falling in love. She had never actually been in love herself, but several men had been in love with her, and with the exception of her music master at that finishing school, whose methods were very pronounced, all her incipient lovers had behaved alike, and she could see no difference between the way their love affected them and the way it affected some of the living things of the farm. The ingratiating tones of voice, the alternate little shynesses and boldnesses, the irritation at the approach of any others of the same sex, and the overweening desire to appear at their best before the object of their worship—all these foolish, pretty ways incidental to the condition known as being in love, she had observed in her incipient lovers, in common with other animals; and her observance of them enabled her to be always on her guard.

But he showed no sign of being even momentarily under such an influence as suggested its presence in some of the ways she knew so well. She felt that he was not in love with her, and she was glad that he was not. There is no such breaking up of friendship as love, and she felt that one suggestion of love on his part—one glance of love's admiration—would have been enough to prevent her from looking forward to a hard-and-fast friendship with this young man of great interests in life. He had treated her all along in exactly the right spirit of companionship. There had not been a false note in their interchange of words. Their sympathies were alike, and their sense of humour. But she had noticed that there had been a certain lack of enthusiasm in the tone of his voice when referring to some matters upon which she would have been disposed to speak with warmth; there was the shrug of a man who has seen a good deal, in some of the things that he had said; and she had felt that his experiences, whatever they had been, had tended to make him too tolerant, and toleration she had good reason to believe was mostly the result of laziness. He was the sort of man who underrated his own powers, and was therefore disinclined to be active in the exercise of such ability as he possessed.

And then this farseeing young woman perceived that his grandfather had made a mistake in his over-anxiety to avoid one. If Jack Wingfield had entered upon possession of his property when he was six years younger he might have set about its management with enthusiasm, but in the interregnum to which he was forced to submit he had lost (she believed) something of the sanguine nature of the very young, which often causes them to do better work than they feel inclined ever to set their hand to later on.

But then she reflected that, however tolerant he had shown himself to be in talking of things in general, he had been as warm as she could possibly have wished in his criticism of the "best set" in Framsby and the empty arrogance of its leaders. Possibly it was her recollection of this fact that caused her to feel that she had never yet met a man on whose behalf she would do all that it was possible for her to do—it was with regret that she reflected upon how little it was in her power to do for him. She hoped that he would before long show the people around him who thought him a fool, that he was very far removed from being a fool. She did not stop to think if her anxiety on his behalf might not possibly have its origin in the feeling that if he proved himself too sapient he could hardly be guilty of the folly of striking up a friendship with her.

She sat for a long time at her open window, breathing the sweet scents of that May night, and feeling better satisfied with the world than she had felt since she had last sat at that window, trying to realize the idea that the man who held her in bondage was dead. At that time all her thoughts had been of the past; but now they were all of the future. The idea of a sincere and far-reaching friendship with a man was very pleasing to her. It took away from her the sense of isolation. She recalled many cases of which she had read of the admirable operation of a true friendship between a man and a woman, and why might it not be possible, after all, for her to help the man of whom she was thinking in some way by which his interests in the world might be appreciably advanced?

The thought of this possibility was much more agreeable to her *amour propre* than any thought of the possibility of his loving her would have been upon this particular night.

And all the joy of the silver summer night was about her as she sat there. Her own garden was just beneath her window, and in its borders the groups of old-fashioned spring flowers could be dimly seen through the silver-shot air. From the meadow at the foot of the Downs came the barking of a dog, and the sound was faintly answered from the shepherd's hut higher up. There was the occasional lowing of one of the herd of Jerseys, only a short time sent out to the grass and not yet used to the change. Every now and again a bat flapped between her face and the sheen of the sky, and gave her the impression of the hand of some ghostly figure making a grasp at something close to her. At rarer intervals a still more spectral thing swooped by, and its passage was followed by the squeal of a rat, and later by a "tu-whit-tu-whoo" of the barn owl.

She leant out of the window so that she could see the dark, many-folded cloud spreading itself abroad halfway across the valley through which the Wadron wandered. That cloud represented the trees of Overdean Manor. The Manor House was hidden by the summer boskage of the Park, so that she saw nothing of it—not even a light in one of the windows.

She drew back into her room and, after another interval of thought, unfastened the clasps of her clothes and let them slip down to her feet; she had already loosened the coils of her hair, and now, by a shake of her head, her white shoulders and the exquisite full curves of roseate flesh were deluged with a thousand little cascades flowing and overflowing with the unevenness of a torrent on which a fitful moon is shining. She began her task of brushing, and went on with it for five minutes until her arms began to ache. Then she wove her plaits, and in crossing the room to get her nightdress she caught a glimpse of her figure passing the tall looking-glass. The glimpse did not interest her in the least. She did not cast a second glance at the glass. She slipped her nightdress over her head, blew out her candles, and went into bed.

No, she was not in the least in love with the man of whom she had been thinking.

CHAPTER X

The news that young Mr. Wingfield had come not only into possession of the property which he had inherited, after the interval made compulsory by the will, but into residence at the Manor House as well, did not take long to spread round Framsby. Framsby was ready to receive him to her great motherly heart. The fact of his being a prodigal did not interfere in the least with the warmth of the maternal embrace which Framsby was preparing for him; nay, it actually increased the enthusiasm with which the sentiment of his coming was hailed. Is it not well known that the prodigal son is the nearest to the mother's heart of all her family?

Now, nothing was known of the details of Jack Wingfield's prodigality; but the terms of his grandfather's will had assumed that his prodigality would be a matter of course, and all Framsby were ready to stand by the inference of so interesting a legal document. If there was any doubt in the matter, they were quite ready to give him the benefit of it by assuming that the piquancy of prodigality was attached to him. He would make the money fly, no fear! was the prediction of the men who winked at one another in the evening over the pewter measures of the "Field and Furrow"; and the tradesmen of Framsby hoped with all their heart and soul that he would. A prodigal during the first few years of his career is the idol of the tradesmen; later on they think of Jeroboam the son of Nebat first, and of the fate that befell his house, and of Pharaoh the monarch of Egypt afterwards. They turn away from the worship of idols and harden their hearts at the suggestion of credit.

But of course it was the representatives of the right set at Framsby who were most interested in the news that Jack Wingfield had come to the Manor House. The truth was that eligible men were not numerous in Framsby or the neighbourhood; and this was, socially speaking, rather a pity, considering what a number of eligible women there were. The worst of a country society, or, for the matter of that, the society in any community, is that every woman is "eligible," but only a man here and there. Every girl in Framsby considered herself eligible, and her mother agreed with her; but there the matter began and ended. The select set was not the set from which eligible men made their selection, and the consequence was that the number of unmarried young women of various ages between twenty and forty-six became oppressive to any statistician who was thinking with interest, increased by alarm, of the future generation.

But none of them gave up all hope. Some of them hunted a little and got themselves splashed thoroughly with the mud of many ditches, and torn woefully with the briars of many gaps, and the barbarities of numerous fences—they made themselves blowsy at hockey and brown at golf, hoping that they would be taken for young women still; but they would not have minded being taken for middle-aged women or elderly women, if only they would be taken. It seemed, however, as if no man would take them at any estimate. Their devotion to sport was keen, but, unhappily, keenness does not invariably mean proficiency. It means talk, and there was consequently plenty of talk at Framsby about golf and hockey and lawn tennis and croquet, but the examples of play given by the exponents of every one of these games were deplorable. The Tennis and Croquet Club, however, absorbed practically the whole time of the members of the right set throughout the summer; but when it became known that the Manor House was occupied by Mr. Wingfield and his mother, the civility of these representatives of Framsby society caused them to steal some hours from the courts to pay their respects to the newcomers; and within a week Mrs. Wingfield and her son received twenty-five visitors, and an equal number of offers to propose them as members of the Lawn Tennis and Croquet Club. Unfortunately, Mr. Wingfield had not an opportunity of making the acquaintance of any of those visitors, the fact being that he had slipped out upon that convenient terrace which went round the front and the side of the house, the moment that the approach of the visitors became imminent. In two cases he was just half a minute too late to be absolutely free from any charge of impoliteness: the French window of the drawing-room, by which he was escaping, was stiff and jerky in one case, and in the other the edge of one wing got caught in the curtains, thereby detaining him most awkwardly for several seconds. The back view of him which the callers obtained did not afford them sufficient data for a detailed description of young Mr. Wingfield, but they made the most of it in conversation with their less fortunate associates the next day.

"Have you called on the Manor people yet? What, not yet? We were there yesterday. My husband knew old Mr. Wingfield very well, you know. Mrs. Wingfield is a charming person—quite handsome still. She had been looking forward to seeing us. She feared that there were no families with whom she could make real friends in this neighbourhood."

"Was the son there? Did you see the son?"

"Ah, yes, we saw him—only for a short time, however; he had to hurry off to keep an appointment. What is he like? Oh, quite nice—rather retiring, I should say."

"We heard some rather dreadful stories about him. Did he seem wild?"

"Oh, nothing to speak of. It doesn't do to believe all that one hears about young men like that. I hear that the property, even allowing for the unlet farms, amounts to something close upon twenty thousand a year."

And then the audience raised interested eyebrows and smiled complete acquiescence in the obvious truth that one should be slow to believe anything to the discredit of an eligible bachelor with an income approaching twenty thousand pounds a year.

It so happened, however, that Jack Wingfield was something of a lawn tennis player, and he had already entered for an open tournament to be held on the Framsby ground the first week in June; and he was glad when his mother told him that she had accepted the offer of Mrs. Bowlby-Sutherst to put up his name and her own for the club. Jack Wingfield belonged to Ranelagh and Hurlingham and a couple of lawn tennis clubs, and he had snatched a second-class prize now and again at Cannes and Mentone. He had been told encouragingly by the men who had beaten him that he had in him the making of a first-class player; and perhaps he had, but he had also in him an inherited trait of self-depreciation which prevented him from working hard to attain anything. He thought very poorly of himself all round; and when urged by competent advisers to give himself a chance, he had invariably given his shrug, saying, "What's the good? I'll never be anything but a plater or an 'also ran.' I get some fun out of it as it is, but I'll never do more than I have done."

So it was with cricket and polo. He never took every ounce out of himself in fighting for anything.

Framsby's lawn tennis week begins on the first Monday in June, and the tournament being an open one, and several champions and ex-champions coming to take part in it, some good play was certain to be seen when the Framsby folk were got rid of, which was usually during the first day's play. Moreover, there was a "gate" during this week, so that the ground, sacred for the rest of the year to the members, was invaded by outsiders with shillings in their hands—five shillings for the week.

And that was how it came that Priscilla Wadhurst contrived to put in an appearance at the club from the membership of which she was excluded by the engineering of the select and the elect.

This was the first time she was seen by the Framsby people since her name had appeared in the local papers in brackets at the foot of the account of the loss of the barque *Kingsdale*; and there was a consensus of opinion in the pavilion that she showed rather more than doubtful taste in exhibiting herself to the public—the phrase was Mrs. Gifford's. Mrs. Gifford was the senior member of the select, the wife of the colonial gentleman with a pension. "But it was just what might be expected from her," another of the set whispered to her when Priscilla passed in front of the pavilion. The pair took good care to be so engrossed in conversation together that even an ambitious young woman like Priscilla could hardly have looked for a recognition from them. (She was on nodding terms with the most exclusive ladies in Framsby, but only when they met her in the street—not upon special occasions when important strangers were present, who might go away with the notion that they were intimate with her.)

But whatever bad taste Priscilla showed in appearing in a public place so soon after the death of the man who had tried to wreck her life, no one could suggest that any detail of her dress was not tasteful. All that people might have found fault with was her dress as a whole. And a good many of her own sex availed themselves of such a chance. She was undoubtedly a widow, and yet she bore no token of widowhood in her dress; and so the right set either turned their eyes toward each others' faces as she passed, or gazed at some point in space a considerable distance above her head. Thus they avoided hurting her feelings by letting her see how shocked they were.

But all the same she knew that they wished it to be known that they were shocked; and she also knew that they would not have been so greatly shocked if her dress had not fitted so extremely well. A chastened spirit and a misfit invariably go together in some people's minds.

Priscilla knew what it was to dress well, and she was quite aware of the difference there is between a garden party and a lawn tennis meeting. She wore the simplest hat and the simplest frock; both white, and neither relieved by the least touch of colour. But the hat and the frock and the shoes and the gloves and the sunshade were the best that money could buy. They were the sort of things that owed their distinction to the wearer, and only when she had served them in this way did they show their generosity by conferring distinction upon her.

"Who is that exquisite creature?" said one of the strangers in the front row of the pavilion seats, as Priscilla moved past without so much as casting a glance at the occupants of any of the seats.

"An exquisite creature, indeed!" said the one to whom the remark was addressed. "She walks like a goddess; and what hair!"

The two of the right set smiled each in the other's face, with the corners of their lips turned down. They could hardly resist giving the strangers the information that she was not an exquisite creature, but only a farmer's daughter.

But before they had straightened their lips once more the ladies in front of them, who had followed Priscilla with their eyes, were becoming excited.

"Dear me!" cried one. "Cynthia is speaking to her. I hope she will bring her here."

"How nice of Cynthia!" said the other.

The Framsby people, by putting their heads slightly forward, saw that a big girl in tennis costume and with a racket in her hand had sprung up from a seat where she had been resting between games, and flung herself upon Priscilla, kissing her impetuously and then roaring with laughter. Priscilla had received her onslaught only a trifle more sedately, and they stood together on the turf beside one of the courts, chatting like old friends who have not met for years.

And now the Framsby people saw that the young girl was pointing with her racket to the pavilion, and then leading Priscilla back by the way she had come. She led her, still chatting briskly, until they were both beside the two strangers in the front row.

"Mother," said the girl, "your chance has come at last;—this is Priscilla the Puritan maiden."

The lady got upon her feet.

"Not Miss Wadhurst?" she said. "But of course you are Miss Wadhurst. I should have known you from Cynthia's photograph, only you are older now—more—what shall I say?—no, not more—less, yes, you are less of a girl."

"That is charmingly put, Lady Gainsforth," said Priscilla.

The Framsby ones gasped. So that was the Countess of Gainsforth, and that girl was her daughter, Lady Cynthia Brooks, the great tennis player, who was waiting for the mixed doubles. They gasped together; and then each tried to outdo the other in an attempt to catch Priscilla's eye. One of them succeeded, but somehow Priscilla missed seeing her even with the eye that she caught, and the next moment Priscilla was being presented to the second lady, whose name was Mrs. Marlowe.

And then the four began to chat of matters far beyond the horizon of Framsby folk—of the old school where it seemed the girls had been together—of Lady Gainsforth's kindness in asking Priscilla to stay at Gainsforth Towers during the Cowes week, which Priscilla so greatly appreciated, only regretting that she had promised to go with the Von Hochmans to their villa at Honnef-on-Rhine; and after all the Count had been ill, so that they had nothing of him or his opera. Oh, yes, the opera was produced at Frankfort and afterwards at Nice.

"Why, did they not sing your old English song in it?" asked Lady Gainsforth.

"Oh, yes," replied Priscilla. "It was highly praised too in one of the papers. This is what they said about it"—here followed half-a-dozen phrases in French, which might have been Sanscrit to the listening Framsby folk—and Priscilla went on:

"Vanity, was it not, committing the criticism to memory?"

"Shocking vanity!" laughed Lady Cynthia, and when Lady Cynthia laughed the people in the furthest court looked round, and then they laughed also.

But the Framsby folk did not laugh, although they were closer to the cyclonic centre. They were, however, ready to smile should Priscilla give them the chance. But Priscilla was a hard woman; she could so easily have spoken to them; and after that it would have been a simple matter introducing them to Lady Gainsforth and Mrs. Marlowe as the leaders of society in Framsby; but Priscilla would not do it, just because they had taken some pains to cut her a quarter of an hour earlier. Oh, she was a hard woman for one so young!

Lady Cynthia had, however, betrayed her whereabouts by her laugh, and one of the officials of the Association sent her a message to the effect that the second of the Mixed Doubles would be played when the court would be vacant at the end of the Gentlemen's Singles.

"I must rush," she cried. "I have a good fighting chance for the M.D.s., though not a ghost of one for the L.S.s. Come round with me, Prissy."

Priscilla said *au revoir* to Lady Gainsforth and Mrs. Marlowe and strolled away with Lady Cynthia's arm through hers; but before she had turned the corner of the pavilion she found herself face to face with Mr. Wingfield, and he took off his cap and greeted her also as if he was an old friend—it seemed that he had been talking to Lady Cynthia earlier in the day.

Framsby gaped and then gasped.

CHAPTER XI

In a few minutes they were alone together, Lady Cynthia having hurried to the court which was now vacant. They were alone, with something like two hundred people about them.

"I have not seen her for two years," said she. "Funny, isn't it, that girls may be the closest of chums at school and yet never see each other again in life? Of course it is less funny in regard to Lady Cynthia and myself, because we move in what's called different spheres."

"Of course," he assented with a laugh. "I never thought of that. Yes, to be sure; you are the daughter of a farmer and her sire is an earl. Her grandfather was a working navvy, and no human being knows who his father was. Your grandfather and great-grandfather and great-great-great-grand-grand-grandfather was a Wad-hurst of Athalsdean on back to the time of William the Conqueror, a noted robber who flourished in the year ten hundred and something, and brought over a crowd of gaolbirds to England to turn out the Saxons. They didn't turn out the Wadhurst of the time, and so here you are moving in a different sphere from Lady Cynthia. And that brings us up to the present moment. Now maybe you'll tell me in what particular sphere you've been moving since I saw you last. That's ten days ago. I hoped to have the chance of coming across you at some place."

"I have not been very far beyond the boundaries of the farm," she said. "I have been fully occupied. You see, I'm very fond of two things—music and milk, and both are absorbing all my time."

"I could understand music absorbing you, but surely it's you who absorb the milk, if you like it," said he.

"It wasn't that sort of absorption," she said. "No one knows anything about milk by drinking it."

"And what on earth do you do with it?"

"Test it—analyse it; so that at a moment's notice you can say what it is."

"It's never anything but milk, is it—before it's wheeled off to the railway stations and sent up to the retailers who mix it with things—water and boracic acid?"

"That's the haphazard way in which a dairy was run until recently. My father used actually to run his on the same want of principle. It was I who got the laboratory built, and now he works it on a proper system. We got rid of over fifty cows in a fortnight—some of them were believed by the dairy manager to be the best on the farm. It was only after a number of tests that I found out that their milk contained only the most miserable proportion of the true component parts of good milk."

"And was it worth your while, may I ask?"

She looked at him in surprise.

"Worth our while? Why, the milk question is the most important that exists in England or anywhere else at the present moment. It is not going too far to say that the whole future of England depends upon the milk consumed by the people. Milk is the most marvellous thing in the world. It seems to me that it should be given a place in Nature all to itself. There is nothing so marvellous as milk, believe me."

"It's not so popular as beer in most localities. But now that I come to think of it, I fancy that you are right about it. It certainly is worth your while keeping your eye on it."

"Oh, everything is worth one's while if one does it properly."

"Everything—except farming, it would appear. Dunning, my agent, has a very bad account to give of our farms—three of them without tenants—the largest has had no tenant for over three years. That's not encouraging."

"What are you going to do?"

"What can I do?"

"Why is the largest farm unlet?"

"Bad times; the chap who had it last threw it up in despair. He wanted to get it rent free for a year and half-rent for the next two so that he might carry out some wild-cat scheme of market gardening on the French principle."

"And why didn't Mr. Dunning let him have it on his own terms?"

"I suppose Dunning knows. He saw that the market garden notion was all tommy rot."

"Did he go into the matter thoroughly—scientifically? Did he show you the basis of his calculations, and did you verify them?"

"Is it I? Great Gloriana! Where should I be by the side of Dunning?"

"You would be there—by the side of Dunning, and you would make Dunning look silly. Why should you accept any man's judgment without figures? Make him give you figures."

"He said it would be madness to give him the place rent free for a year."

"But you have given it over to Nature, rent free, for three years. The figures that Mr. Dunning has given you are £2,000 with a minus sign in front."

"That's a fact. You are beginning to wake me up, Miss Wadhurst. I wish I wasn't so lazy. But that market garden scheme—Dunning says the chap had been reading up a lot of stuff that was written about the French system, and that turned his head."

"It turned his head—yes, it turned it in the right direction, Mr. Wingfield; that farm would make a fortune for any one setting to work it solely for market produce."

"God bless my soul!" Jack Wingfield stopped dead when Priscilla had spoken—they had gone beyond the green limits of the furthest of the nets and were walking under the group of trees that had been allowed to remain standing when the ground had been deforested in order to make the tennis courts. "God bless my soul!" he repeated, in quite a reverent voice, which he assumed to counteract the suggested levity of his first utterance of the exclamation.

"Have I startled you?" she asked. "I meant to startle you. I used every art that I could think of to startle you. I should be horribly disappointed if you had remained unmoved."

"Unmoved," he said, in a slow way, moving from one syllable to the other. "Unmoved. I say, there's a seat in a reasonable place under those trees. Let us make for it. I want to hear more."

"I can't quite see that you are justified in practically leaving the courts when you may be called on at any moment to play your game."

"Oh, it doesn't matter; I've got no chance of anything. The people here are too good for me. I don't bother myself working up my game until the week before."

"You never will do anything in the world on that principle."

"I don't suppose I shall; but what's the odds? You can't turn out a Derby winner if you have only a humdrum roadster to go upon."

"And you are content to live the life of a humdrum roadster?"

"The roadster that looks to win the Derby is an ass—a fool! Now isn't he?"

"I'm not sure of that. He may become the fastes roadster of his day, and that's something. No, I'll not' encourage you to sit on that lazy man's seat under the trees. I want you to play every ounce you have in you in your game. I don't want the strangers to go away at the end of the week saying that there isn't a player in this neighbourhood."

"Oh, let the game go hang! I want you to tell me what you meant by startling me as you did just now. What did you mean when you said that about the market garden? Was it merely a ruse to draw me out?"

They were now standing on the low natural terrace with the trees at their back. She lowered her sunshade.

"I meant to startle you, but not at the sacrifice of the truth," she replied firmly. "We know all about that farm. My father, who is the best judge of land in the county, and who has made more by this knowledge than any man in the county, went over every inch of the farm, and he is absolutely certain that it would make the fortune of any man working it as a market garden."

"If I was startled a minute ago, I'm amazed just now," said he. "Does your father not believe in Dunning?"

"I can tell you nothing about that," she replied, shaking her head. "I can't say what his opinion of Mr. Dunning may be, but he knows something about men and farms and—cats and mice."

"If he has a working knowledge of parables he beats me," said Wingfield. "Cats and mice—what have cats and—Oh, Lord! maybe I do see it after all. When the cat's away——"

"Exactly. And you told me that you hadn't brains!"

"Your father thinks that Dunning is no exception to the rule that applies to cats and mice?"

"I'm sure he thinks that he could convince you in a day or two that that farm could be worked at a profit if the worker turned it into a market garden, and showed the railway that it would be greatly to their advantage to give him siding and a wagon all to himself. You could do that, Mr. Wingfield. What have you on your hands just now?"

"Time," he said mournfully. "I've time on my hands, and by the Lord Harry it hangs pretty heavy there. I was just thinking how on earth I was going to put in the summer in this place."

"And you haven't been here more than a month?"

"Even so. What is a chap to do when he has pottered about the place with a couple of fat dogs at his heels? I love summer and I love the place, but what is a chap to do to keep himself from dying by sheer boredom?"

"Good gracious!" she cried, lifting up her beautifully-fitting gloves so that he was as much impressed by the movement as he would have been if her arms had been bare. "Good gracious! You can talk of being bored at a place so full of possibilities as yours!"

"Possibilities? You see possibilities in the place as well as in me? You look through the eyes of an incorrigible optimist. Your generosity runs away with you. Possibilities? Should I learn how to test the quality of milk, for example? I believe there is a pretty good lot of beasts at the home farm. I wonder, by the way, what becomes of all the milk."

"Look into that. I don't want to be the means of depriving any deserving or undeserving family of their perquisites; but you take the first opportunity of placing the transaction—the benefaction—on a proper basis. And take the advice of one who knows, and get rid of that nice lot of beasts which you have heard are on the home farm."

"You mean to say that they are not a nice lot?"

"They were a nice lot ten years ago, my father told me; but instead of being kept up to the highest level, they have been allowed to degenerate to a frightful extent."

"How?"

"The same way as any first-class stock degenerates—by marrying beneath them. Now the matrimonial alliances among the beasts on that farm would make any matchmaking mother weep. There's not one in the family that did not make a *mesalliance* at some time of her life. And your grandfather was so careful in this respect. If you have any respect for his memory you will get rid of the lot."

He was greatly interested in her revelations, and said so, adding,

"What a juggins you must all think me! But I suppose that was because you worked on the same principle as Adam did when he was asked to give the fox a name. 'I'll call it a fox,' said he, 'and a better name you'll not get for it, because it's a fox, if I know anything about animals.' You couldn't find a better name for me than a juggins, because I am one."

"That's nonsense," she said. "There's nothing of the juggins about you if I know what a juggins is. If you were one would you be talking here to me on the most important topics that an owner of property can talk about, when you might be criticizing some of the play at the nets? And if I thought you a juggins would I talk to you for five minutes—for one single minute? I'm mistress of myself. I'm independent of the opinion of any of the people here. I see no reason to be bored for the sake of being polite. I told you the last time we met just what I thought of you, and since then I've thought more on precisely the same lines. Of course I feel flattered at your listening to all that I have to say; but I'm not so eager for flattery that I should bother myself talking to you for the pure joy of seeing you listen to me with one ear while I knew that all the time everything I said was trickling out by the other. Now the next word you say depreciating yourself will make me consider that you are trying to depreciate me, so I'll get up and walk away, or else say something about the weather."

He had turned his eyes slowly upon her in the course of her long speech—she had spoken her words so rapidly and with such animation it did not seem so very long—and by the time she had ended, which she had with a little flush, he was gazing at her with an expression that was bordering upon wonderment. In the pause that followed, his expression had become lighted up with admiration. Then he looked away from her, and rubbed the tip of his chin with the tip of one forefinger. He became very thoughtful, and the break in their conversation was so long as to assume the proportions of an irreparable rupture. It was, however, nothing of the sort. It was long only because he found it necessary to review and to revise some of the most highly cherished beliefs of his life, and the young woman beside him was fully aware that this was so. She had no mind to obtrude upon his course of thought.

At last he spoke.

"I wonder if you could tell me if I really did think myself a juggins," he said.

"Why do you ask me such a question, Mr. Wingfield?"

"Because you have opened my eyes to so many things. You have shown that you can read me like a book."

"Before I talk to you about reading you like a book, I will try to answer your question. I believe that from the first you have been in contact with very foolish people—as foolish as the people at Framsby—it has been called 'foolish Framsby' before now."

"If not, we'll call it so now. Go on."

"These people, I have an impression, assumed that because your grandfather so arranged things that you should not take over the property until you were twenty-seven, you were bound to be the sort of person your grandfather believed you would be, and they treated you accordingly, and you were content to accept yourself at their valuation."

He almost sprang out of his chair, making in the excitement of the moment a downward smash with his racket which, if it had taken place in the course of a set, would never have had a chance of being returned by an opponent.

"Great Gloriana! you have hit the nail on the head!" he said. "I don't know how you've come to know it, but you have come to know it; and now you've let me into the secret, and I'm hanged if it isn't the most important secret of my life—it's a revelation—that's what it is! I've been now and again at the point of finding it out, but I never got so far. I don't know how you came to make the discovery, but you have done it, and by the Lord Harry Augustus it has made a new man of me!"

Suddenly he appeared to recover himself. He had spoken so excitedly that he had not only startled her, he had also drawn the attention of some one who was standing by the nearest of the courts, and that person—a stranger—was smiling.

He dropped into his seat at once, saying, "I beg your pardon; I'm making rather a fool of myself; but—well, it can't be helped."

"Don't trouble yourself about him," she said—she saw that he had noticed that the stranger had noticed him. "He'll only fancy that we are quarrelling; but we're not, so it doesn't matter."

"Not a tinker's curse," he replied, with more than necessary emphasis. Then he turned to her and spoke, leaning forward, swinging his racket between his knees, so as to convince the observant stranger that he was not so excited after all. "I tell you that you have hit upon the mistake that I have made all my life and that everybody about me has made," he said. "From the first it was taken for granted that because my poor father was a fool I must be one too. I tell you that I took it for granted myself. Now, when a chap starts life in that way what chance has he, I should like to know? When a poor devil is told by every one around him that he has in him the seeds of an incurable disease—consumption, or cancer, or something—what chance has he? I never had a chance. That was why I made an ass of myself at Oxford. Oh, those blessed trustees! They told me when they were sending me to Oxford that they were perfectly certain I should make an ass of myself, and they somehow made me feel that it was inevitable that I should, and so I rode for a fall. I see it now. And it was the same when I went on my travels. They believed that I wanted to paint every place sealing-wax red that I came to, as I had painted the college oak navy blue, and they made that an excuse for cutting down my allowance to bedrock—they didn't let me have enough to buy turpentine even at wholesale price to mix my paint."

"And you didn't buy a can or two of distemper—distemper is what young dogs suffer from, and you were a sad young dog, you know," said she, laughing under her breath.

"I never did any painting at all after Oxford," he said. "I had really only now and again an inclination for it. I give you my word that I began to feel ashamed—actually ashamed—at my own tameness, and it was really because I did so that I now and again nerved myself to go on a bust. Gloriana! what poor busts they were. I never came in touch with the police but once, and nothing came of it; the judge—every magistrate is a judge out there—began to laugh at the business—it had something to do with a mule, of course—and then the *polis* began to laugh, and so the bust bust up, with every one grinning, and making me feel that I was pretty bit of a mug that couldn't even get up a row that would be taken seriously."

"What did you do to the poor mule?" she asked, for she had detected the note of despondency in his voice as he told her the story of his failure, and she wanted to cheer him up.

"Oh, it was some rot or other," he replied. "There was the old mule, with his ears going like the fans of a screw propeller, and his tail whisking mosquitoes into eternity by the thousand, and there was the basket with the eggs, and when the mule man went into the wineshop with the woman that had laid down the basket, what was there to be done?"

"You needn't ask me; you saw for yourself. But after all you only got the length of painting the pavement a nice yellow—not vermilion. It's no wonder that the judge laughed."

"I suppose it isn't. But you needn't. I'm sorry I said anything about the mule. You may begin to think that I'm not serious in all that I say."

"Are you serious?" she cried very seriously.

"I give you my word that I am. The scales have fallen from my eyes. I'll never think of myself as a juggins again. Oh, confound this fellow! He's looking for me. I think I'll scratch for the rest of the day. I've no chance against Glenister. Yes, I'll tell him——"

"Now's your chance," she said earnestly. "If you have made up your mind not to treat yourself in future as your trustees and the rest treated you in the past, you'll play every ounce that's in you in this tournament and ever afterwards."

He looked at her.

"What's a set or two—knocking a ball backwards and forwards across a net, when we're talking together on a vital matter?" he said peevishly. "I want to have my talk out with you and—here he comes, I'll tell him to go to———"

"To the court and wait for you," she said, rising. "Now's your chance. If there's anything in what I've said to you or you've said to me, you'll play as you never played before. Now just try the experiment."

He looked at her again—steadily—in a way that he had never looked at her before.

"By God I will!" he said, and marched off to meet the man who had come in search of him for the second of the singles.

The man was cross and confounded him properly for a dam skulker. He was, of course, a particular friend of Jack Wingfield's, or he would have frozen him with politeness.

CHAPTER XII

Priscilla watched him with a considerable amount of interest, for she was far enough away from the crowds at the courts to allow of her watching him without feeling that she was being watched. She saw how he was walking—swiftly—eagerly—a foot or two ahead of the man who had found him—his head slightly bent forward, his fingers clutching the grip of his racket as though he were ready to return with fury the ball that had been served to him with a smash—as if he had made up his mind that the man who sowed the wind (within an indiarubber sphere) should reap the whirlwind—if he could.

He never looked back—that she noticed with the greatest amount of interest. If he had looked back she would have felt that she had not succeeded in her endeavour to force him to take every ounce out of himself. But now she saw that she had been successful.

Was she just too successful? That was a dreadful question which suggested itself to her. Was that the proper spirit in which he should approach his task of getting one step near to the holder of the cup? Would he not have a better chance if he had gone to the court in the tranquil spirit that was usually his—the spirit of Horatio—the man that Fortune's buffets and awards had ta'en with equal thanks? She knew that the race is not always to the swift, nor the set to the smasher. The eager man with the racket is apt to become racketty and not precise; and she had sent him from her as full of enthusiasm as a schoolboy arriving in London with a sovereign in one pocket and in the other a ticket for the pavilion at the Oval for Surrey v. Sussex, and Ranji 75 not out the previous evening.

For a while she had a grave misgiving. She felt that after all she had misjudged the man. She had never believed that he would be capable of anything like this within half an hour of her beginning to speak to him. She had never believed in sudden conversions—the *tours de force* of the brilliant evangelist; and she had fancied that it would take her several days, extending over the whole summer, to convince that man that there was something in him. And yet there he was, profane—actually profane in his enthusiasm in less than half an hour!

And the worst of it was that she had been foolish enough to allow her action in this matter to suggest that she was staking her reputation as a prophetess upon the event. That was very foolish on her part. No sibil worthy of the name would have done this. The sibil made her book with wisdom and caution, a safe hedging and an ambiguous phrase being the note of her advice.

Priscilla felt that by laying so much emphasis upon the necessity for his throwing his whole soul into his game of tennis she had jeopardized the success of her counsel to him in the matters that mattered.

She felt angry with herself when this reflection came to her; but a few minutes later she felt far angrier at the thought that she had been angry over something that was no business of hers. What did it matter to her if Jack Wingfield made a fool of himself over his tennis or anything else or everything else? How could his success affect her one way or another?

She really could make no satisfactory reply to this question that suggested itself to her; for clever and all as she was, she was as imperfectly acquainted with her own character as most other women are of theirs. The eagerness with which she had carried out her scheme of adopting the *role* of a retributory Providence in respect of Mr. Kelton had not given her a hint as to what was the dominant impulse of her nature; nor had her enthusiasm in regard to the working of her father's farm and the reform of the dairy revealed it to her; though she had been on the brink of a discovery of the truth when she had had her conversation with her friend Rosa going a-primrosing, and had said that if a man sometimes was the means of a girl's sudden development into a woman, she was equally sure that it was a woman who made a man of a man.

She did not know that in herself was so strongly developed the instinct of woman to be a maker of men—to put forth her strength in order that they may be strong. To be the mother of a man child, to give him of the sustenance of her body, to have him by her side and to have command over him until he breaks away, as she thinks, from her control, leaving her in tears, but always ready to advise him in the taking of a wife and to advise the wife, when she is chosen, how to conduct her household—that is the best part of the nature of a woman. But the exercise of the power to influence a man, to make herself necessary to the happiness and the prosperity of a man, is the most irresistible joy that a woman can know, though she does not know it.

Priscilla Wadhurst had felt a certain satisfaction in the thought that she had the destiny of Mr. Kelton under her fingers, so far as Framsby's concerts were concerned; and she had been greatly gratified when her father had admitted that her reform of the dairy was a step in the right direction. But what were these triumphs compared to those that she longed to effect, though she might not have part or lot in the supreme tableaux in the procession of events?

And yet, in spite of the consciousness that she had exercised her influence upon another man for his benefit, she sat there asking herself why she should feel it as a personal matter whether Jack Wingfield made a fool of himself over his tennis or in any other way?

And then she saw once again the look that had appeared on his face for more than a moment when his eyes were upon her. It had startled her, and the recollection of it gave her a little fright. But her fright quickly subsided, and she sat there losing herself and all sense of her surroundings in the thoughts that came down upon her, not like a riotous throng of fantastic things, but like a silver mist shot through with a gleam of golden light here and there, but making everything about her seem blurred—indefinite as the future seems to any one landing on the shore of a strange land.

Suddenly she sprang to her feet—almost as suddenly as he had risen when in the midst of their little chat together; only the exclamation that she gave was not the same as his. Hers was derisive, contemptuous, impatient, and there was certainly something of impatience in her walk round the courts where play was going on. She had, however, recovered herself—she had walked herself outside the atmosphere, so to speak, of whatever thoughts had irritated her—before she had come opposite the court where Jack Wingfield was playing off the second set of the "Gentlemen's Singles"; but even if she had not done so, a few minutes of watching the game that was in progress would certainly have cleared away any wisp of mist that might have remained with her on emerging from that atmosphere of conjecture into which she had allowed herself to stray.

She slipped into the only unoccupied chair at this court. It was at the end of the third row of the seats at the side from which Jack Wingfield was serving. An elderly visitor, wearing a velvet hat built up like a pagoda, sat immediately in front of her, so that she ran no chance of being seen by him. This was what, she thought when she took the seat; but before being in it many seconds she could not help smiling at the thought of how ridiculous it was to fancy that her coming might divert his attention for a single moment from the game, to the detriment of his play. The scheme of Oriental architecture in front of her effectually hid every inch of the court and the players from her, but her seat being at the end of the row, she had only to move a few inches to one side to command a complete and perfect view of the whole; and she perceived in a moment that the man who was serving with his back to her and to the whole world and all that is therein, had become compressed into the spheroid which he held in his left hand preparatory to launching it like a thunderbolt with a twist over the net. She smiled. If the German Emperor or Mr. Roosevelt or some other commanding personality had suddenly appeared on the court, Jack Wingfield would have seen nothing of him. He had eyes only for the ball.

But for the ball he surpassed Shelley's night in the number of eyes that he had. He was playing against a very good man—a man who, according to some newspapers, had a very good chance of winning the cup that carried with it the title of Champion of South Saxony—but Priscilla saw in a moment how things were going. It seemed to her that it was not Jack Wingfield who was serving, but quite a different person. She could not imagine that desperately alert young man who served as if his whole future were dependent upon his placing the ball on the exact inch of ground at which he aimed—she could not imagine that this was the Jack Wingfield of the shrug—the Jack Wingfield who half an hour ago had been ready to scratch to the man whom he was now playing as if he had no object in life but his defeat.

He was playing with an enthusiasm which surprised every one who was acquainted with his form, and no one more than his antagonist and himself. Glenister was his antagonist—a brilliant man, not perhaps quite so brilliant as he believed himself to be, but still as far above the average in this respect as the sapphire excels the lapis lazuli. He was a man of resource and imagination, and these qualities often stood him in good stead; but it was to his brilliancy he trusted to win his games for him. Priscilla heard the remarks that were being made by competent critics sitting just behind her; and knowing what Glenister's play was, and seeing what Wingfield's was, she appreciated the accuracy of the criticisms.

"Glenny as usual underrated his man," some one remarked. "That was how he lost the first two."

"He could beat half a dozen Wingfields any day," was the counter. "How the mischief could he tell that Wingfield was going to play as he is now? How the——hallo! Did you see that?"

"No, what was it? (In a whisper) Confound that hat! What was it?"

"My aunt! Wingfield played the ball over his shoulder from the line, and placed it too."

"Luck!"

"I suppose so. No one could have a ghost of a chance of doing more than getting it over. Is that Wingfield's third?"

"His third. He won the first and Glenister pulled off the second. Now we'll see what Glenny's service is worth?"

And they did. They saw that its brilliancy was simply thrown away upon Wingfield. He declined to be intimidated by it. He made an attempt to return every ball, and succeeded in getting the third over; with the first and second that were served to him Glenister made fifteen and thirty. But he seemed so greatly surprised by Wingfield's success with the third as to be quite satisfied to send it back over the net right opposite to where Wingfield was standing. Wingfield took a long aim, and Glenister, watching his eye, ran to the extreme right of the line to meet the ball; but Wingfield changed his mind and sent it to the extreme left, making his first score. The next service no human being could have returned. Forty—fifteen. The next was an easy one, and there was some splendid play before Glenister got a downward smash which he planted obliquely not two feet from the net on the left side and got his game. 2—3.

"Getting into his form, hey?" said one of the critics behind Priscilla.

"It's the way with all of them; but Wingfield takes it out of him, all the same," was the reply.

"He does, by George! I didn't think that Wingfield had it in him; he always seemed to me a lazy sort of beggar—doesn't care whether he wins or loses—doesn't seem to know which he does. His partners in the doubles bless him unawares. That was a good serve. My aunt, it was a good serve! He's working. Has he something on the game, do you suppose?"

"If he had he wouldn't worry as he's doing. Most likely some pal of his put a shilling on him and told him. But his backer would do well to hedge. That's deuce. Glenny will take all the rest."

But this prediction, like the many prophecies of critics, was not realized. The play on both sides was quick, firm and commonplace, and Glenister got his vantage. By two more services Wingfield got deuce and vantage; Glenister returned the third ball, and Wingfield sent it back in a tight place; but Glenister managed to get under it; he did the same with Wingfield's return, only he placed the ball. Wingfield got at it, however, with his left, and when the other man was returning it to the bottom of the court far over his head, Wingfield jumped for it, and just managed to touch it over. His antagonist never even ran for it.

"Luck!" remarked one of the critics. "That was a lucky win for Wingfield. It might have gone anywhere."

Score 4—2.

From that moment Glenister seemed to go all to pieces. The next game realized "game—love," and the next "game—fifteen," and Wingfield walked out, examining with extraordinary attention what he seemed to think was a defect in the stringing of his racket. He went straight past Priscilla without seeing her. She meant to say "Well played!" as he was passing, but when the moment came she found herself speechless. She could scarcely rise from her chair. She had no notion that her excitement could have such an effect upon her; and what was strangest of all to her was the tears in her eyes. Why on earth had the tears come to her eyes the moment after he had gone past her?

This was incomprehensible to her. There seemed to her to be no sense in it. She did not take any exception to the feeling of pride of which she was conscious, or to the whisper that sounded in her ears: "You did it—it was you—you—you who made him win, and you have now linked yourself to his success in life, and you will have to stand by him."

That was all right; she had no idea of making any attempt to evade her responsibility. She had the instincts of a mother; was she one who would set a child on its feet in the middle of the roadway and then run away? She had talked to him so that his success in that match which he had just played had become something like the ordeal of drawing lots in the days when the Powers took care that there was no tomfoolery in the business; she had taken on her the *rôle* of the prophetess and had in effect said to him, "Lo! this shall be a sign unto thee"—and he had accepted the hazard which she suggested to him, and had won, though the odds, as he knew, were against him.

Well, the thing having worked out so, would he not follow up the dictation of the sign? Would he not allow himself to be subjugated by the logic of the lot and hasten to work out his own emancipation with a firm hand and in a confident spirit?

Of course he would. And what then?

"Then I shall have made a man of him," was the clarion sound that rang in her ears. That was to be her reward; the reflection that she had accomplished this—the sense of her own influence upon the life of a man. She felt at that moment that she wanted nothing more. Her woman's instinct to be a maker of men was satisfied.

She remained in her seat for several minutes, while the crowd who had been watching the set melted away, or hung about the chairs with their comments. She listened while some asked what on earth had come over Glenister, and others what the mischief had come over Wingfield. How did it come that Wingfield had just managed to nip his set away from Paisley, who was practically an outsider, and then had licked Glenister, who had been runner-up for the cup last year, into blue fits? That was what they all wanted badly to know; and that was just what the young woman with the lace sunshade and the beautifully made dress could have told them.

But they did not address their questions to her; and when the talk about the match that had just finished melted into talk about the two players who had just taken possession of the court, she got upon her feet and walked away—straight away from all the play and from the ground and from the man.

She drove to the farm, took off her beautiful dress and hung it up, and laid away the lace sunshade, and, putting on her working overall, spent the rest of the day in the dairy, among her lactometers and test tubes.

Yes, she found that she had been quite right: the four new Jerseys were more than justifying the records of the stud book.

She reflected with satisfaction upon the circumstance that her father had bought them on her advice. His judgment as to the look of the beasts bore out all that her scientific research had made plain.

CHAPTER XIII

His mother, though not an invalid, had need to be very careful as to her health. Undoubtedly she had been better since she had come to the Manor than she had been for years; but it so happened that she had not felt well enough to go with her son Jack to the opening day of the Lawn Tennis meeting. She easily submitted to his injunction to remain in her chair on the terrace. The great magnolia that would make the whole side of the house so glorious in another month, was not yet in bloom, but a couple of old-fashioned climbing roses had worked their way round the angle of the wall and laid out fantastic arms heavy with blooms over the trellis, and Mrs. Wingfield loved roses of all sorts, and nightingales and all the other old-fashioned things of the English garden. She was quite content with her surroundings and her canopy and her pavement on this June day, and felt confident that her son's assurance that she would enjoy her day very much more as he arranged it for her, than if she were to join the giddy throng in watching him knock the balls about, was well founded. He had settled her in her chair and exclaimed:

"Why was I such an idiot as to enter for the two events? The chances are that I'll scratch when I get on the ground and come straight back to you."

"You must do nothing of the sort, my dear," she said. "Play all your games; it will make a good impression upon the people."

"My aim in life is to impress Framsby," said he. "It strikes me that the only impression my play will produce upon the privileged beholders will be that whatever I may be in other respects I'm a thundering duffer at tennis."

"You can't tell what their form maybe. You may have to play a second or third class man who is worse even than you," said his mother, in the tone of the invalid who has been told by her doctor to be cheerful.

He laughed. "Bless you, my dear mother, for your kind intentions; but I feel that you are a sad flatterer," he said, going off, having lighted his pipe.

She watched him as the mother of an only son watches him; and when he had disappeared and she heard him start the engine of his motor, she laid down her magazine and sighed. She knew very well why she did so. She knew how large her hopes had been that his entering into possession of his property would mean a settling down for him. In the days of their poverty—comparative poverty—the settling up every now and again was what she had good reason to dread, and now that they were wealthy—

comparatively wealthy—the settling down occupied her thoughts quite as painfully.

She had seen, with a sinking of the heart, that he was beginning to lose a sense of the novelty of his position. He had become weary of it already. He had not fallen properly into the place which his grandfather had occupied; his grandfather had thought it the highest place to which a human being could aspire—the position of an English country gentleman. Jack Wingfield was beginning to be bored by it already, she could see. It was a life of pottering, she knew, and pottering, as a profession, must either be begun very early or very late in life if one is to attain to eminence in its practice. Jack had set about it too late for a young man and too early for an old one. He had had nearly six years of wandering—a little in Africa and a great deal in South America. They had been busy years, and certainly they had been restless years; but they had been years of life, not of vegetating. The rolling stone does not become associated with even so humble a form of vegetation as moss; but when it has done its rolling and finds itself in a position for such an accumulation, it is rather a pitiable object.

For more than a week Mrs. Wingfield had noted the approach of that cloud of *ennui* which she had always dreaded when she had thought of him as entering upon a career of pottering. She had made several suggestions to him with a view to its dispersal before it settled down upon him. She thought of the hounds—might it not be possible for him to take the hounds? Was the present master not tired of them yet? And then she thought of the pheasants—the pheasants had never been properly looked after, she knew, though she was quite unaware of how handy the gamekeeper's wife at the lodge had found their eggs when she had to make an omelette in a hurry.

Only when she had thought of these ways of anchoring a man to the county, the bower anchor of the hounds and the kedge anchor of the pheasant, did she think of the third way—The Girl. She had been thinking a great deal about the girl during the previous week; and already she was wondering if she might not pencil in some dates in her diary for mothers with nice—really nice, girls—they were getting scarcer and scarcer, she thought—to pay a visit to the Manor and so give Providence a chance of doing something for her son and incidentally for the girl: for would she not be a fortunate girl who should attract the attention of so eligible a man?

She had dreams of cosy house parties; and now, instead of making herself familiar with the stores of wisdom in the magazines on the table beside her, she was looking wistfully out from the terrace across the lawn to the water garden with its old stonework and its shrubberies and its many fascinating and secluded nooks. How happy she would be if she could but see her boy emerge from one of those romantic places with a charming roseate girl—if he would lead that girl to her side with a word or two to ask her to welcome a daughter!

And it was just when such a picture was presenting itself to her that the postbag arrived and was brought to her by a footman. She unlocked it, and found within half-a-dozen letters for herself, a large number of the inevitable tradesmen's circulars, offering coal at the lowest summer prices and a fine choice of grates in which to consume it. She threw them to one side; but she did not so treat the two long envelopes with evidently bulky enclosures which remained among the contents of the mail. One had its origin printed right across it—"The East Indian Steam Ship Company"; the other was floridly embossed with a tropical scene, and the strap that enclosed it was stamped "The Madagascar Direct Route." A sort of guidebook pamphlet entitled "Try Patagonia" had also come, addressed to her son, and a small volume purporting to be on "Tarpon, and How to Catch Them."

She looked at each of them a second time, and read all the reading there was on the covers. Then she laid them on her table, and kept her hand on the topmost as though she were anxious to hide it from every eye.

It had come—she had seen it coming—she had seen the restlessness in his eyes that told her that the call had come to him out of the distance of dreams—those dreams which had always been his—dreams of a sea that he had never sailed on—a land that his feet had never trodden. The end of their life together at this house which she hoped would be their home, had come before it had well begun.

The poor woman lay back on her chair and closed her eyes, thinking her thoughts—asking herself how it was that she, a woman who cared about nothing in the world so much as a home, should be denied one, just when she fancied that the gift for which she had always yearned had been given to her. She knew all that a home meant—that it was not merely a well-appointed dwelling, but a place the tenure of which should be secure to her so long as she lived. Such had been denied to her all her life; for her husband had been a wanderer with no certainty in his wanderings except of their continuance; and now, when she fancied that the desire of her life had been given to her, it was snatched away before she had taken more than a sip of its sweetness. He was preparing to go away from her once more. He could not help it; the travel lust had taken possession of him, and once more she would be left alone.

She sat there asking herself if she had failed in her duty toward her son. Had she too easily yielded to him, letting him have his own way in the matter of travel? What had she left undone that might have prepared him for the "settling down" which was bound to come, she thought, when he really had a home to return to? Even now it might not be too late to do something that would make him not merely endure the home that he had inherited, but enjoy it as well.

She could think of nothing that had not been in her thoughts long ago; and so the day wore on, but the pain which she had at her heart was not outworn.

Oh, who could leave this place that was meant for that repose which is the sweetest part of life—this gracious land of woodland and park and meadow and paddock—the songs of the blackbird and the thrush—the glimpse of the quick swallows athwart the lawn—the melodious murmur of innumerable bees—the scent of the roses: who would choose to leave such a place for the dread uncertainties of other lands? She knew something of Jack's travels; they had not been under the control of a personal conductor. He had slept with a rifle by his side and a revolver under his pillow, and when he was not suffering from a plague of mosquitoes he was having his toes cut open to expel the enterprising "jigger" that had made a burrow for itself and its progeny beneath his flesh.

That was a very fair synopsis of his travels, she thought—at any rate, those were the points that appealed most powerfully to her imagination; and yet she had imagination enough to perceive how, having once tasted of the excitement of living that wild life, he should feel the tameness of his new inheritance to be unendurable.

She had her invalid's lunch brought to her where she sat, and she was still in her chair when she heard the sound of his motor returning. He strolled round to her on the terrace at once, still wearing his flannels.

"Well, what sort of a day had you—rollicking, eh?" he cried. "I got away in good time to have tea with you. They had no use for me any more."

"Did you not play after all?" she asked; she felt sure that he had not troubled himself to play, or if he had played it was only one set. She knew his ways.

"Oh, yes, I played," he replied.

"But you did nothing? How could you expect to do anything? You left here not caring whether you played or not. I wish you wouldn't take it all so pleasantly. Why don't you rail against your luck?"

"I don't see why the mischief I should; I've nothing to complain of in the way of luck," said he.

"That's the way with you, Jack—it has always been the way with you; you will blame no one and nothing—only yourself."

"That shows how strongly developed is my sense of justice, dear mother. I should make a first-class judge, if I hadn't to debase myself by being a lawyer to start with. But you see I am just enough not to blame my luck."

"You had no luck, I suppose, all the same?"

"Not a scrap. I did it all by sheer good play, and a straight upper lip."

"You beat anybody?"

"I beat Paisley first and Glenister second."

"Glenister? But he is one of the best men! You never beat Glenister."

"Six—two. Poor Glenny never got the better of his surprise when I stole my first game from him. He tried to think that it was a dream; I don't believe that he has recovered yet. Nairne was my last man. He got a pain in his in'ards when the game stood four—love; and by the advice of an old prescription of the family doctor, he retired into the shade. Poor chap! he played very well in the M.D.s five minutes later. A splendid recovery! I know that there's nothing like taking a thing in time—especially the advice of the family medico."

"I can't understand how you did so well, considering that you have had no practice."

He was silent. He had picked up his post and was glancing at the covers. She watched him nervously. He read the steamship company's imprint on each, and then smiled queerly. She fancied that he was smiling at the thought of being once again away from such absurdities of civilization as lawn tennis. But suddenly his smile ceased. He allowed his eyes to stray in the direction that hers had taken a few hours earlier—over the green of the lawns, and the ballooning foliage on the outskirts of the park. He continued so for a long time, siffling an air between his lips, and tapping the large envelopes fitfully on his palm.

She watched him, waiting for what was to come—he was going to say something to her, she felt—something in the way of breaking the news of his departure to her.

She watched him.

Suddenly his soft whistling ceased. He drew a long breath, and smiled still more queerly than before.

At that instant he caught her eye. He gave a little start, saying with something of surprise in his voice:

"What's the matter? Why are you looking at me in that way?"

She continued gazing at him in silence. And then he saw that her eyes had filled with tears even while they were on his face.

"My dear girl, what's the matter? Who has been saying what to you, and why?" he asked.

She pointed to the envelopes in his hand. He glanced down at them, saying:

"What—what's the matter here?"

She shook her head and then turned away, and he knew that her tears had begun to fall.

In a moment he perceived all.

She heard him laugh, and raised her head, trying to disguise her tears.

She saw the smile that was on his face as he tore in two each unopened cover, and then tore the two in four, and the four into eight, tossing the fragments over the balustrade of the terrace on to the roof of a great pyramid bay below. The act was one of great untidiness, but she easily forgave him, garden worshipper and all though she was. She stretched a white hand across the table to him eagerly, and once again her eyes were moist.

"My dear boy! My dear boy! You mean to stay?" she whispered.

"Yes, I mean to stay," he replied.

CHAPTER XIV

She waited for something to follow—something that would let her into the secret of his flinging away the fragments of the circulars for which he had written to the officials of the steamship companies. She would have liked to know that it was on her account he had abandoned whatever project of travel he had in his mind; but dear as the reflection that he had done it for her sake would have been, it would have brought with it a certain pang to feel that she was a brake upon his enterprises.

She had a mother's instinct that there was something to be told to her—something that would suggest to her what were his reasons for making up his mind to give his new life a fair trial. So she waited. She could see that something had touched him and left its mark upon him, whether for good or bad she could not tell; but surely, she thought, it must be for good. She was not so simple as to fancy that his success in the tennis tournament was the incident that had been potent enough to cause him to change his plans. The very fact of his enlarging as he did upon his own play and the play of the other men was enough to convince her that the day's tennis had nothing to do with the matter. So she listened, and became animated in her commendation of his perseverance, and waited.

He drank tea with her, still talking of the tennis, with an occasional discursion in respect of the people who were on the ground; and then he lit a cigar, and fell into a train of thoughtfulness. She believed that he would now tell her something of what she wanted to, know; but he was still reticent, and before he had got halfway through his cigar he rose from his chair saying:

"I think that I shall take a stroll across the park to the farm. Funny, isn't it, that I only spent about half an hour there since I arrived?"

"I am sure that they will appreciate a visit," said his mother. "After so long an interregnum they will welcome the appearance of a new ruler."

"Especially if he doesn't rule," said he, grimly.

"I don't know that," she replied. "These people even in this democratic age like a little ruling. Where is Mr. Dunning? Would it not be well to take him with you, or get him to coach you on a few points?"

"I think I prefer to drive my own coach a bit," said he, and so he went off.

He returned about half an hour before it was time to dress for dinner, and during that comparatively short space of time he gave her a *resume* of the more prominent points which he had observed in the mismanagement of the farm. He could not have believed it possible, he declared, that such gross negligence could exist on any estate. Verrall, the manager, had not been on the premises, he said, and no one seemed to know exactly where he was to be found; and that gave the owner a chance of poking about the place himself, and thus seeing all that there was to be seen, without the assistance of a guide to prevent him from straying into corners which might be considered inconvenient to inspect. The owner had, it appeared, done a good deal of straying on his own account.

"The place is simply disgraceful," he said. "Dunning hasn't been near it for more than a year. I got so much out of one of the hands. He has been leaving everything in the hands of Verrall; and Verrall, it seems, is a great authority in coursing. He has quite a large kennel of greyhounds, which naturally he keeps and has been keeping at my expense. I will say that they looked first-rate dogs. But it seemed as if the kennel was kept up at the sacrifice of the dairy. The dairy is a disgrace. Unclean! That gives no idea of what it was like—absolutely filthy—sickening. The pump in the dairy is out of order. And when had it been in order? I asked. Seven months ago, I found out by crossexamining some of the slovenly hands who were loafing about. And the cattle! Dunning had told me that there were some fine beasts on the home farm. He knew nothing about it. There was not a single good point among the cows."

"And your grandfather was so proud of his herd!" said Mrs. Wingfield.

"He wouldn't see much to be proud of among their successors," said Jack. "I never felt so ashamed in all my life. Verrall drove up in a dogcart when I was in the dairy, and began bawling out for some one to come to the horse. He had brought a new greyhound with him, and he bawled out for some one to come and look after the dog. I saw the origin of all this bawling when he tried to get down. He wasn't over successful. He certainly wasn't over sober. I had a very brief interview with him. He was startled at first, and then he thought that the right way to get round me was by becoming jocular. I fancy that, fuddled and all as he was, he has come to the conclusion by this time that that was a strategical mistake."

"You gave him notice to quit?"

"Oh, no; I couldn't very well go so far as that on the spot; but I am to go over the books of the farm to-morrow—I had previously found out that no books were kept—and I'm inclined to think that Mr. Verrall will give me notice of his intention to take himself off before we get far in our investigation of how the books came to be accidentally burnt or drowned or eaten by the prize cattle—whatever story he may invent to account for their disappearance."

So he went on as they sat in the hall looking out upon the western sun that was sending his level beams over the great elms of the avenue. He had become quite heated in his account of the mismanagement of the farm. A few hours ago his mother would have refused to believe in the possibility of his being sufficiently interested in such an episode in the profession of a potterer as to become even warm over its narration. How on earth had the sudden change come about?

That was the question which she kept asking herself all the time her maid was dressing her for dinner, and her son Jack was splashing in his bath, trying to remove some of the memories of his visit to his farm. But it was not until the following afternoon that she got from him any suggestion that she could accept as a clue to the secret of the situation.

He had been at the home farm at six in the morning and had dismissed Farmer Verrall before breakfast. Farmer Verrall had looked for his coming about eleven or twelve, and having been up until pretty late the night before, he had not quite succeeded in his endeavour to do himself justice by "sleeping it off"—the phrase was Mrs. Verrall's—so that Mr. Wingfield had further opportunities for inspection before the man had got on even the most rudimentary clothing.

After the simultaneous discharge of his duty and his manager, Jack Wingfield had eaten a good breakfast and gone off to the tennis ground, where he succeeded in beating two more antagonists in the G.S.s, and had then got knocked out in the first set he played with a partner—a very wild young woman—in the M.D.s. After these excitements he returned to have tea with his mother.

It was after a long pause at the close of that meal that he remarked, so casually as to awaken the suspicions of his mother in a moment:

"Talking of the dairy—" he had been saying a word or two respecting the dairy—"I wonder if you have ever heard of a man named Wadhurst—a great authority on shorthorns—in fact, a great dairyman altogether."

"Of course I have heard of him, several times," she replied. "Why, I heard something of him only a few weeks ago—something in a newspaper. Something he had done in America, I think—something brave—not connected with a dairy. What nonsense! I remember now. It was another man—was it his son who tried to save some people on a wreck and got drowned himself?"

"Not exactly his son. The man who did that was a scheming rascal who had inveigled Mr. Wadhurst's daughter into a marriage with him and got arrested for a swindle on the steps of the church."

"Of course, that was it. Stupid of me to forget. But really, what between these Frenchwomen poisoning their husbands and Americans getting divorces, it is hard to remember the details of any one particular case. But I only need to be reminded and the whole thing comes back to me."

"Miss Wadhurst of course returned to her father's house. She is living there at present. She never had slept a night out of it."

"The detectives were just in time! How lucky for her! But she is not Miss Wadhurst: she must be Mrs. something or other. The ceremony was gone through with, wasn't it?"

"I believe it was, but it was only natural—only right—just—that she should revert to her maiden name. She had a right to her maiden name, hadn't she?"

"I suppose so; but a marriage is a marriage, and a sacred thing, whatever the Americans may say."

"A sacred swindle, this particular one was, my dear mother. Anyhow, the young woman is here and I have met her, and I don't think I ever met a more clearheaded young woman. She practically runs that big dairy of her father's off her own bat—they send a thousand gallons of milk to London every morning."

In a moment she perceived what was the origin of her son's zeal in the matter of dairy work; her heart sank. But she made no sign. She only remarked:

"A thousand gallons! Surely that is impossible, Jack! A thousand——"

"It's a fact. It's by far the biggest dairy in the county. I am going up the hill to see it one of these days; and meantime——"

He paused, and she looked up from the old lace that she was mending—she looked up interrogatively.

"Meantime I want her to give me a hint or two, and I should like, if you don't mind, to ask her to visit you."

"Is that necessary, do you think? Wouldn't she feel more at home if she looked in at the farm? She could then see in a moment at what end to begin to work as regards your improvements."

"I think that she would feel at home anywhere or in any society," said he. "You would agree with me if you saw her and had a chat. She is really a very clever girl." Jack Wingfield's mother had a natural antipathy to clever girls. She had met a few in the course of her life with a reputation for cleverness, and for some reason or other the impression that she had acquired of them and their ways was that a clever girl was another name for a scheming girl, and that whether she was called clever or scheming she was an unscrupulous girl. That was why she shook her head, saying:

"I'm not sure that clever girls are quite at home in my company, Jack. I know that I am never at home in theirs."

"And if you're not I'm sure that I'm not," said he. "But you'll not find that Miss Priscilla Wadhurst is that sort of a clever girl."

Mrs. Wingfield felt that if the young woman had impressed upon her son the fact that she was a clever girl, but not that sort of a clever girl, she was the cleverest girl of all; but she herself, being possessed of a certain share of this particular quality, knew perfectly well that in the way of a man with a maid there is nothing so stimulating as opposition, especially reasonable opposition, so she hastened to assure him that of course she should be greatly pleased if Mrs.—or, as she wished to be called, Miss Wadhurst—would call upon her; and the son, without being a clever man, had still no difficulty in perceiving that his mother was afraid to show any further opposition to his suggestion lest mischief might come of it. But he only said, "That's all right, then. I think she may come, though I'm not quite sure."

"I don't suppose that she would find a visit to an old woman who has lived away from everything in the world for so long very attractive," she remarked. "Have you asked this young person to advise you as to the dairy?"

"Not I. But I'm sure she'll do it. She wears no frills."

"You met her yesterday?"

"Well, I was going to speak to Lady Cynthia Brooks about the Mixed Doubles, when she rushed into the arms of Miss Wadhurst—there was kissing and all that; it seems that they had been at school together, and very chummy. Lady Gainsforth was tremendously taken with her."

He did not think that it was absolutely necessary for him to tell his mother that he first made the acquaintance of Miss Wadhurst in the room next to that in which they were sitting; and he saw no harm in introducing the name of a countess and her daughter in the course of his account of meeting Miss Wadhurst.

"Cynthia Brooks was always a nice girl," said Mrs. Wingfield. "I'm not sure that going about from one tennis meeting to another is very good for a girl; but if her mother doesn't mind—— Wasn't it at Biarritz we met them? That was three years ago—just before you went to South America."

"Yes; it was at Biarritz. We carried off the M.D.s; but we had a very shady lot against us. We should have no chance playing together at such a meeting as this."

Not another word passed between them on the subject of Miss Wadhurst, and Mrs. Wingfield went to her bed in a condition of great uncertainty on the subject of her son and the young woman who was to come to pay her a visit. A farmer's daughter, with views of dairy management; that was rather a curious sort of young person for Jack to take up—if he had taken her up. But Jack was, she knew, like many other young men of whom she had been hearing recently—ready to do the unexpected. It was shocking to hear of them marrying girls who danced and did things. She had not quite succeeded in determining whether dancing or a dairy was the worse. Hadn't some well-known man written a poem about a dairymaid?—or was it a musical comedy? But here was a dairymaid with a romantic story swirling round her like one of those gauzy robes in which some *premiere danseuse* was accustomed to make her gyrations. Mrs. Wingfield had a horror of being in anyway associated with a person who had had a romance in his or her life. She connected romance with unrespectability just as she did cleverness and scheming.

She sighed at the thought of her son's marrying a dairymaid; but if he had set his heart on marrying her and failed to do so, would he not forthwith start once again upon his wanderings?

Which of the two prospects was to be preferred? That was the question which she had to decide. It was a case of Scylla and Charybdis—*Priscilla and Charybdis*, she thought; but she went asleep before she had made up her mind on this question. After all, was there any reason for her to keep awake thinking if it was possible that her son, who had run the gauntlet of many young women in search of husbands, and many young women—these were the more dangerous—having husbands of their own already, during the previous four years, was now head and ears in love with a red-faced, brownarmed, blowsy dairymaid?

She hoped for the best.

CHAPTER XV

As for her son, he did not go to bed very soon. He had a good deal to think about apart from that grave step which he had taken in the morning—the first important step he had ever taken before breakfast. As a matter of fact, everything that he had to think about he thought about quite apart from his discharging the drowsy and thirsty Mr. Verrall, though to be sure there was a certain connection between the person whom he had in his mind and his recently-acquired zeal to set his household in order.

He had come upon her on the tennis ground when he was about to enter the court for the Mixed Doubles, and she had greeted him with smiles, but with no cry of "You see what I made you do yesterday!" He had asked her at what time she had left the ground the previous day, and she had said "Just after your match."

"You saw it, then?"

"Oh, yes, I saw it. You surprised poor Mr. Glenister."

"And anyone else?"

"Probably yourself."

"Probably everyone on the ground except you."

"I am glad you except me."

"I could swear by the horns of the altar that you were not a bit surprised."

"And you would not perjure yourself—I'm not sure if the horns of the altar are binding as a form of oath; but anyhow, you would have been right. I did not fancy for a moment that my judgment as a prophetess was in jeopardy when Mr. Glenister took two or three games from you."

"Then you watched it all?"

"Every stroke after the first couple of sets."

"That was very nice of you. I kicked out Farmer Verrall before breakfast this morning."

"What, the manager of your farm?"

"There was no help for it. I went over the place yesterday afternoon, and I saw with half an eye that he had allowed the whole farm to go to the dogs—to the greyhounds."

"The greyhounds? You are coming on, Mr. Wingfield. We shall have you running a dairy farm yourself and taking away our bread and butter—certainly the butter—if we don't look out."

That was the sum of their conversation before the alert official had separated them, dragging him off to play in the M.D.s and get ignominiously beaten, for which he had apologized most humbly to his partner, and she went away affirming that he was a very nice man, only it was a pity he didn't practise more. But she was careful not to let a whisper of this reach the ears of their successful opponents; she was not sure that they would not say that it was her silly play that had lost the game.

He had manoeuvred to get close to her at lunch, but in this he was not very successful. She was with the Gainsforth set, and they hadn't invited him to their table; but afterwards he had managed to beat to windward of the party and to sail down upon her at the right moment. Unfortunately it was only for a moment that he was allowed to be beside her. He had only time to say, "I want to have a long talk with you," and to hear her answer "You will find me a most appreciative listener, Mr. Wingfield," when Lady Cynthia carried her off in one direction and the alert official carried him off in another to play a single. When he had beaten his man and set out to look for her, he saw that she was between Lady Gainsforth and another watching a paltry match in which Lady Cynthia was doing some effective work with a partner who tried to poach every ball that came to her.

He had strolled away, and had passed a dim halfhour by the side of Rosa Caffyn, who presented him to her mother, and her mother had asked him if he did not think Miss Wadhurst was looking extremely well, considering all that she had come through, poor thing! and she feared that a good many people would say that it was in rather doubtful taste for her to appear in a public place and not in mourning, though her husband had been dead scarcely more than two months; and he had replied that she had the doubtful taste to refrain from that form of etiquette known as hypocrisy; and Rosa had clapped her hands, crying "Bravo! That's what I have said all along."

His thoughts went over all the ground that he traversed during the day. It was when he was motoring to the Manor that he had made up his mind to mention her name to his mother, and she had replied to him. And what then?

What then?

That was the question which remained to be answered by himself to himself.

Why was he taking so much trouble to bring her and his mother together? Was it in order to give his mother the privilege of another acquaintance? or was he anxious to show Priscilla how charming a mother was his?

He had gone out upon the terrace with his cigar when his mother had left him, and now he sat in the long chair among some very well-disposed cushions. It was a night that lent itself with all the seductiveness of an English June, not to thought, but to feeling. One could feel the earth throbbing with the sensuousness of the season, although the stars of that summer night were but feebly palpitating out of the faint mystery of their grey-blue canopy. He had started thinking, but he was soon compelled to relinquish it in favour of feeling.

"If she were but sitting in that other chair—nay, why the other chair? Why should there not be only one chair between us?" He fancied her sitting where he sat, her head among the cushions—oh, that perfect head, with its glory of hair, shining like some of the embroidery of that satin cushion at his shoulder! He pulled up the pillow and put his cheek close to it. Oh, if only she were there! He would sit on the rest for her feet, and hold them in his hands and put his face down upon the arch of their instep. He had seen her feet that day when she had been watching the game, by the side of her friends, and he knew what they would be like to kiss. And then he would kneel by the side of the chair and put his head down to the cushion that was below hers, so that their faces—their lips—should not be far apart— not further apart than a finger's breadth—sometimes not even so far.

And they would be silent together, drinking deep of the delight of each other's silence. For what would they have to talk about on such a night as this?

And while he sat there, abandoning himself to the abandonment of Nature—that glorious Nature whose passionate heart was beating in everything under the stars of this June night—a nightingale began to sing out of the darkness of the shrubbery. He listened to it, feeling that that singing was the most complete expression of the passion of June.

But the incompleteness of his life—sitting there alone, full of that longing which the nightingale could so interpret! Why was she not here beside him—in his arms?

A window was being opened in one of the rooms above where he sat. Why was not that the window of her room? Why was it not opened to let her speak out to him—to whisper to him that she was there—waiting for him—waiting for him? He was a sane man under the influence of a pure passion—a passion whose chief property it is to stimulate the imagination even of the unimaginative; and every sound that he heard breaking the silence of this exquisite summer night had this effect upon him. He felt that he could not live without her. He had fallen into such a condition of thinking about her as made it impossible for him to weigh in connection with her such considerations as prudence, propriety and Mrs. Grundy; all that he knew, or was capable of knowing, was that he loved her, and that he wanted her to be with him always—he loved her and nothing else in the world; he was incapable of loving anything else in the world. She absorbed all the love of which he was capable. He felt that he should be deserving of the fate of Ananias and Sapphira his wife if he had kept back any of his possessions of love from her to bestow upon some one else. He cared nothing for anything in the heaven above or the earth beneath, or the waters that are under the earth, apart from her; but with her he felt that he loved them all!

This was the condition of the man who had never in his life been involved in an affair in which love played any but the most subordinate part. He had had his chances, as most men who have lived for nearly thirty years with no recognized occupation usually have. If he had caused the worldly mothers of eligible daughters (and too many of them) who were aware of his prospects, to hold him in contempt, he had at the same time caused the husbands of uncertain wives no uneasiness whatever He had had his little episodes, of course—those patches of pattern which go so far to relieve the fabric of a man's life from monotony; but, to continue the simile, this pattern had not been printed in fast colours; it had not stood the test of time or cold water, but had faded out of his life, leaving scarcely a trace behind. He had never believed himself to be capable of rising to the dizzy heights of such a passion as this in whose grasp he felt himself, high above the earth and all earthly considerations. He was astonished at first when he found himself walking about the turf of the tennis ground in order to catch a glimpse of her—detesting the play, and so making it pretty hot for his opponents because it stood between her and himself; cursing the nice people who had found her so nice that they took care to keep her near themselves; and at last leaving the ground in sheer despair of being able to find her alone, so that he could sit beside her and watch her face, or the exquisite lines of her figure down to her fairy feet which he wanted to kiss.

He had driven to his home at something in excess of the legal maximum, hating her (as he thought—the most solid proof of his love for her) and hating himself for being such a fool as he felt himself to be.

The necessity for strategy in talking to his mother helped to bring him within the range of ordinary well-ordered life once more, and he had ridden his soul on the curb, so to speak, ever since; but now his mother had gone to bed, and here he was stretched at full length on his chair, having abandoned himself to his passion—thrown out every ounce of ballast in order that he might get a little nearer to the stars that were as soft as pearls above him.

He had ceased to be astonished at himself. He had reached that rarer atmosphere where the conditions of life are altogether different from those that prevail on lower levels, and where extravagance of thought is simply the result of breathing the air. His intoxication took the form of feeling that he was on the brink of a great happiness—that he was a king on the eve of a great victory—that he was so considerable a person in the world that he could carry out with a high hand every purpose in life. In his heart was all the swagger of those braggart warriors strutting about in armour and feathers on the walls of Troy or beneath them.

And in this condition of intoxication and its consequent hallucination he remained until the stars of the one hour of the summer night waxed paler than pearls in the exquisite dawn of the summer day.

The nightingale that had been singing in the early night had long ago become hushed. From a distant meadow there came the sound of the unmelodious corncrake. There was a little cheeping and rustling among the ivy of the walls, and then came a blackbird's syrupy contralto from among the laurels of the shrubbery, and far away the delicious liquid ripples of a lark—two larks—three—the pearly air was thrilling with the melody of larks and with the flutings of thrushes, and the cooings of the wood pigeons, long before the sultans of the farmyards sent forth their challenges to be passed on and on like the ripple on a lake, until the last could be but faintly heard coming from the height of the Downs.

He sat there listening to everything, and scarcely conscious of the melting of the night into the dawn. There had been no darkness at any time of that June night, and the dawn was only like all the pearls of the sky melting in the liquid air.

At last he got up from his seat and walked to the balustrade of the terrace, looking forth over the white mists that curled and rose from the lawns and the meadows beneath. He felt that his new day had arisen for him. He went upstairs to his room, and when he had got into bed, he was asleep within five minutes.

It so happened, however, that the room in which his mother slept was just opposite to his on the same corridor, and even the slight sound that he made closing his door was enough to awaken her. She could then hear the sound of his swinging back the curtains which the careful housemaids invariably drew across his windows when they were turning down the counterpane; and then she knew that he must just have come upstairs. Her room was quite light, so that she could see the hour shown by the little bracket clock. It was five minutes past two.

So he had passed the four hours that elapsed since they had parted, sitting alone in the empty room! (She knew nothing of his having gone out upon the terrace.)

Her knowledge of this circumstance told her a great deal more of his condition than she could have learned from his own lips had he felt inclined to confess to her all that was in his heart.

It was true, then—the inference that she had drawn from his guarded words respecting the young woman was correct. It was on her account he had made up his mind that there was no place like home.

The mother was in great distress for some time. She shed some tears, but not many, for she reflected that at least a year must elapse before this young widow—for she was a widow, whatever sophists might say—could make another matrimonial venture, and what may not happen within a year?

This reflection comforted her, and so did the thought:

"After all, I have not seen her yet."

CHAPTER XVI

He saw matters with rather more reasonable eyes when he awoke after six hours of very refreshing sleep—more than his poor mother had during the whole night. He saw that all that passionate longing for her which had taken possession of him in the early night was of no effect. He could not possibly have her with him inside twenty-four hours, as was his desire.

In the new light that came to him he saw a good many things. He saw that there were such elements as delicacy and decency which were highly respected by all respectable young women, and that in his case the amalgamation of the two meant delay. Was she a girl, he asked himself, who would be likely to fall in love with such a fellow as he? He could not bring himself to answer this question without a certain sinking at heart. All the conceit had been knocked out of him with the broadening of the light of day. He no longer felt himself to be a conqueror. The brazen bucklers of the Trojan heroes were not for him. He felt that he was not brave enough even to be a suitor. He feared her eyes—they were beautiful eyes, but they were capable of expressing a pretty fair amount of derision when occasion arose, and he could not imagine them wearing any other expression when he thought of his standing before her and asking her if she would consent to love him.

What chance would he or any other man have with that particular girl? Even if she were well disposed in regard to him, what would that amount to in the face of the experience which had been hers? Had she not had enough experience of men, and of marrying, to last her for some time at any rate, if not for the rest of her life? And was he, Jack Wingfield, the sort of man who would tempt that girl into a second adventure? In spite of his recent successes—at tennis and in his own Augean dairy—he had not got out of his old habit of thinking slightingly of himself and the possibility of his reaching to any high level of attainment. What he had achieved the day before he had achieved through her. He placed it to her credit without any reservation—he did not deduct even the customary commission which should have accrued to him as an agent.

And when she had shown herself to be strong enough to make him do all that he had done, was she likely to be weak enough to listen to his prayer?

All this form of reflection was very disheartening to him. He was a very different man indeed from the one who had taken part in those fancy flights on the terrace before the dawn, when he had put his cheek down to that cushion where he had pictured her head to be lying.

"Lord, what a bounder!" was the thought that came to him from that reflection now.

In the course of his reflections he did not even get so far as his mother had gone, when she had thought that, let the worst come to the worst—the best to the best was how he would have put it—a full year was bound to pass before he could have her with him. There was no need for him to draw upon so distant a source of uneasiness when there were so many others to supply him close at hand.

His mother never came down to breakfast, but he invariably went to her room to bid her good morning. He thought that now she looked at him narrowly, and he had an intuition that by some means she had come to know of his late hours on the terrace, so like a sensible man, who confesses when he knows he has been found out, he said cheerily:

"I had rather a bad night. I went out upon the terrace when you left me, and, by George! it was dawn—almost daylight—before I got to bed."

"That was very foolish of you, Jack," said she. "But I suppose you were thinking about—about—something of importance."

"That was it," he assented, with the glibness of the accomplished liar, though he was not a liar but only a lover. "That was it: I was wondering if I had not been a bit too hasty with Verrall. Perhaps I should give him another chance. Well, well; a chap doesn't like starting life at home by kicking out a man who has been about the place for so long as Verrall has been. Oh, yes; I had a lot to think over. Well, wish me luck."

"Wish you luck, dear—how?" said the mother.

"How? Don't you know that I am down to play some giants to-day, and won't you wish your little Jack—Jack the giant killer—the best of luck?"

"With all my heart—with all my heart—the best of good luck," said she, and he kissed her, and went away whistling like a successful dissembler.

And then there happened the best thing that could befall a man who is inclined to be weak-kneed and who stands in great need of a stiffening. Mr. Dunning, the agent whom he had taken over from the trustees when he had entered into possession of the estate, had had things his own way for something like eleven years; there had been no voice of authority but his own on the estate, and the result of two or three interviews which he had with Mr. Jack Wingfield had been of so pleasing a character that he felt that his voice would continue to give the word of command from the Dan of

Dington at one end of the property to the Beersheba of Little Gaddlingworth at the other. He had communicated his estimate of young Wingfield to his enquiring wife by a shrewd shake of the head and a smile. He thought precious little of this young Wingfield.

He was therefore all the more surprised when he received a visit the previous day from Farmer Verrall, whom he had installed at the home farm, to acquaint him with the fact that young Mr. Wingfield had practically kicked him out of the place. Mr. Dunning felt that it would never do for him to stand such an insult from a fellow who was nothing more than the owner of the property. He saw clearly that now was the time for him to strike. If he were to submit to such high-handed action without protest he should have no end of trouble in the future. The owner might even go so far as to exercise some authority over his estate. Yes, he would show this young man what was his place.

He scarcely waited for young Wingfield to bid him good morning.

"Good morning. What's this I hear about Verrall?" he said, all in a breath.

"What's what you hear about Verrall?" said young Wingfield, after a pause.

"This about his being turned out of his farm at a moment's notice?"

And then young Wingfield took the measure of his visitor, and saw with great clearness what was the object of his visit.

"Look here, Mr. Dunning," he said, "if you know all about the matter, it seems hardly necessary for you to bother yourself coming to ask me about it?"

"Mr. Wingfield, I'm not accustomed to be treated in this cavalier fashion," cried the agent. "I think an explanation is due to me."

"Of course an explanation is due to you, Mr. Dunning. I was about to send you a message asking you when it would be convenient for you to drop in on me."

"It would have been much better if you had sent for me in the first instance." Mr. Dunning's tone was now one of forgiveness, tempered by reproof. "So far as I can gather, you told Verrall to turn out of his farm, neck and crop. That was a bit high-handed, and not just the thing that one might expect, considering that you have scarcely found your feet on the property, Mr. Wingfield. The tenants are not accustomed to such high-handed treatment, and I must say that neither am I, Mr. Wingfield."

"I place myself in your hands, Mr. Dunning," said Jack. "You see, I'm new to this sort of thing, and you are not. What am I to do in the future?"

And then Mr. Dunning felt that his little plan had succeeded. Firmness—there was nothing like firmness with chaps like young Wingfield. Give them to understand at the outset that you'll stand no dam nonsense. That was what he felt, and he spoke in the spirit of his philosophy.

"You don't know the mischief you may do—the difficulties that you may place in my way," he said. "In future you must leave these things to me. In case you see anything that you think needs explanation, just acquaint me with what you think should be done, and I'll consider it."

"That will be very kind of you, Mr. Dunning," said young Wingfield. "Well, I may as well begin now. What I think should be done is to get a couple of first-class men from a first-class London accountant's office to come down here on Monday and go over all the books of the estate—all the books, mind you; the farm books in particular. I suppose that although you haven't been near the farm for the past eighteen months yourself, you know all about the expenditure, and will be able to say if it was I who paid for the feed of those greyhounds of Verrall's and what has been done with the milk of that splendid herd of cows that I saw at the farm. The game books and the timber books will be gone through carefully by the accountants with me sitting at one side and you at the other, Mr. Dunning. Now I have acquainted you with my intentions as you told me I should, and I've no doubt that we'll get on all right together in the future."

"What do you mean, sir?" cried the agent. "Do you mean to suggest that I—that I—I have fallen under your suspicion? Do you suspect that I—I—"

"Good Lord! Is it me—suspect—suspect—you? Mr. Dunning, you have risen too early—you can't be quite awake yet."

"I think that your remarks can bear but one construction, Mr. Wingfield. They suggest that you have unworthy suspicions in regard to my integrity."

"You never were further mistaken in your life, Mr. Dunning. All I suspect is your capacity. One of the most important of the farms has been vacant for over three years because you refused to allow a man who understood his business a year's grace to carry out a scheme which a little consideration by a competent person would have shown to be a first-rate one. That meant some thousands of pounds out of my pocket, and you have shown your incapacity to judge character by allowing Verrall to have a free hand with the home farm, though he wasn't a tenant but a paid manager. Wherever I go I see evidence of carelessness and incapacity."

"I did not come here to be insulted, Mr. Wingfield."

"No, you came here to do the insulting, Mr. Dunning. You came here thinking to browbeat me—assuming that I was a juggins—a juggins, Mr. Dunning—in other words, a mug. I saw what you thought of me the day you pretended to set before me the principles of the management of the property. But all the same I took a note of those matters which you waved your hands over, telling me that they were not in my line—that I should not understand them. I daresay I led you on to think poorly of me, Mr. Dunning, and to put your tongue in your cheek when I had gone out of your office and you were alone with your clerk; but though I may have been a juggins at heart I wasn't one at head, you must know. Now will you stay and have some breakfast?"

"No, thank you, Mr. Wingfield. I must consider my position, after what you have said to me; I feel that it is necessary in justice to myself to consider my position. I should be very unwilling to resign the position of trust in which I was placed on the death of your grandfather."

"I don't doubt it, Mr. Dunning. Pray don't let anything that I have said lead you to believe that I fail to appreciate how highly you value your position. I have expressed myself badly if I have said anything that suggested that to you. I think that Bacon and Tiddy are good enough accountants for my purpose; but I know that Farside, Kelly and Ransome have a big name for estate work. What do you think?"

"I shall have to consider my position, Mr. Wingfield. I shall have to do so very seriously."

"I will give you till to-morrow morning to consider it. If I don't hear from you by the morning I will conclude that you have sent me in your resignation, and act accordingly. Six months' notice, I suppose? But of course you will go into the books with the accountants."

"I shall have to consider that point seriously also. I wish a couple of strangers luck if they try to make anything out of the books without me."

"Oh, you will not desert me—I think I know better of you than to fancy that, Mr. Dunning. You must know what impression would be produced if you were to clear off at such a time."

"Sir, my position in the county—your grandfather—he was high sheriff that year—he headed the subscription list for the presentation to my father."

"That was before I was born. Somebody told me that your father's name was in the county family list. I daresay the Dunnings were a power in the land when the Wingfields were making money in the West Indies. You are still a power in the land, Mr. Dunning, and you'll let me know by the first post to-morrow without fail." Mr. Dunning went forth into the sunshine without a word. He had an impression of awaking from a singular dream. He scarcely knew how he came to be outside the house which he had entered so jauntily half an hour before. He now felt not jaunty, but dazed—queer. He could not understand how he had left the house without saying what he had meant to say. He had meant to be very plain with that young Wingfield and to give him to understand once and for all what were their relative positions, but he had had no notion that it would be necessary for him to take the extreme step of threatening to resign. He had really no wish to resign. His position as agent of the Wingfield estates was worth something over a thousand a year to him, but what was he not worth to the property? Of course, juggins though that young Wingfield was, he had still sense enough to recognize the value of such an agent, and to know that without such an agent, he and his property would be in the cart.

No, he never thought that he should have to play that trump card of his—the threat of resigning; all that he meant to do was to bring the young man to his senses and to let him know that when all was said and done he was only the owner, and as such, he had no right to make such a decisive move as the removal of Verrall behind his agent's back.

And yet now he was walking away from the Manor House feeling that he and Farmer Verrall were practically in the same boat—that they had both got a shove off from the solid shore by the rude boot of a youth who was really little better than an interloper, and that they were now adrift on a choppy sea.

But how it had all come about he could not for the life of him understand. He had not been in the house for more than ten minutes; and surely he had brought the young man within measurable distance of an apology to him for his high-handed conduct, and yet—what had he said?—accountants from London—books of the estate—the farm—the milk—the pheasants—the timber—the underwood—and with all this he, Mr. Dunning, J.P., the agent of the estates, the man whose father had received a presentation of plate—whose name was in the only authentic list of County Families—was to make up his mind by the next morning whether he would remain and give the accountants from London his help in going through the books or clear off with Verrall!

The whole business was extraordinary and not to be fully realized in the course of a morning stroll. He had reached the end of the paddock before he was able to summarize his feelings up to that moment. His summary assumed the form of an exclamatory sentence:

"Who the devil would have thought that the chap had it in him?"

As for young Wingfield, he was nearly as much puzzled by the issue of his interview with Mr. Dunning as that gentleman was himself. When Dunning had left the house Jack hurried to the breakfast-room, whistling an uncertain air. The butler blew out the spirit lamp that heated the breakfast dishes, and laid the latter on the table, with the coffee. But the moment he had left the room, Jack Wingfield put his hands in his pockets and walked away from the breakfast table to one of the windows, and, standing with his legs apart, stared out, allowing his omelette to get chilled and the coffee milk to get a surface on it. Jack Wingfield was also puzzled to account for all that had occurred. Dunning had always occupied in his mind a place of the deepest respect; and his attainments he had been accustomed to think of with something little less than awe. And yet he had been able within twenty-four hours to discover his gross incompetence and, moreover, to tell him of it, and to send him away with no more ceremony than he had thought necessary to employ in clearing out Farmer Verrall and his greyhounds!

The whole thing was too wonderful to be grasped immediately by such an intellect as his. It required a deal of thinking out; so he stood at the window staring at the garden for several minutes.

At last he too thought that he might make a brief summary of the situation and its development up to that moment. He whirled round and gazed at the breakfast things. Then he removed his hands from his pockets, and doubling up his right struck the palm of his left vigorously, saying:

"By the Lord Harry! She has made a man of me!"

CHAPTER XVII

When he told her that his mother would be greatly pleased if she would pay her a visit, her face became roseate. She hesitated before answering him. She had usually her wits about her, and rarely failed to see in a moment the end of a matter of which the beginning was suggested to her; but now everything before her was blurred. She could not utter even the merest commonplace word in response.

Three days before she had seen that sudden light come into his eyes when she had been trying—and not without success—to make him think better of himself than he had been disposed to think, and she had felt startled. She had gone home with that look impressed upon her. What did it mean? She knew very well what it meant That is to say, she knew very well that it meant that he was in love with her—for the moment, yes, for the moment; and that was by no means the same as knowing all that it meant. For instance, she could not tell if it meant that he would be in love with her the next day and the day after. She did not know if it meant that he would ask her to marry him, in the face of the opposition of his family—she assumed the opposition of his family, just as she assumed also that it was unnecessary for her to take into consideration the possibility of his being influenced by what the people of Framsby would say. He would of course snap his fingers at Framsby, but his family was a very different matter. She wondered if he would be strong enough to ask her in the face of his family. She was not quite sure of him in this respect. One sees the effect that her experience of men and their professions of love had upon her. She had been made thoughtful, guarded, determined to refrain from allowing a second man to make a fool of her—determined to do her best to repress all her own feelings in the matter before it would be too late to attempt to do so—before she had seen what his falling in love with her would lead to. That was why she had gone away so suddenly on the first day they had met on the tennis ground, and that was why she had taken the trouble to keep beside her friends on the other days: she wished to give herself every chance—to keep herself perfectly free in regard to him, so that, should nothing come of the little flame which she saw flicker up behind the look that he had given her, she would not have a lasting disappointment.

At first she patted herself on the back, so to speak, for her circumspection. She was behaving with wisdom and discretion, and with a due sense of self-respect. But on the second day, when she had had no more than half-a-dozen words with him, she returned to her home with her heart full of him, and feeling the meanness of her circumspection—hating her caution and abhorring her discretion. When she was combing out her hair that night, she caught sight of herself, as she had done before upon one occasion that has been noticed, in the tall glass, but this time she seemed to have a glimpse of a strange girl in whom she was greatly interested. She looked at herself curiously through that fine network of hair that flowed around her, covering the white draping of her white shoulders with a miraculous lacework of silk. And then, in the impulse of a thought that suggested an instinct, she unfastened the button of her drapery and allowed it to fall down about her feet so that she stood there a warm white figure of a bather ready for the plunge into the water, the foam of which was coiled about her ankles.

She looked at her reflection shyly as though she had surprised a strange girl. But the strange shyness gave way to a strange interest in that figure before her. She seemed to have acquired an interest in her body from her head to her feet such as she had never known before, and she found herself actually posing before the glass. Only for a minute, however; with a little laugh that had something of maidenly merriment in it and the rest of maidenly passion, she flung her hair away from her figure and rushed to her bed.

She did not go to sleep for a long time. The window of her room was open and she could hear faintly the notes of the nightingale that was singing in a plantation beyond the orchard.

And somehow the song of the nightingale also seemed quite new to her. She could not understand how it was that she had ever thought of it as sad.

She turned rosy when he asked her if she would pay his mother a visit, and she did not answer him at once.

"Did you tell your mother who I am—what I am?" she enquired, without looking at him.

"She knows all about you," he replied.

"And are you sure that she wishes to see me?"

He did not answer at once. At last he said,

"I don't think that she wants particularly to see you. She doesn't care a great deal for seeing strangers. But I wish her to see you, and I wish you to see her."

"In the ordinary course of life I should not pay your mother a visit," she said. "I know my place."

He laughed at the humour of her demureness, and she laughed because he was laughing; but only for a second.

"There's nothing to laugh at," she said. "I made a plain statement. In the ordinary course of life social visits are not exchanged between the ladies of the Manor and the girls of the farm; but in this case, and if you will save me the trouble of explaining how it is that I go... and yet I don't know that you can explain it or that I can explain it... oh, you had better not try to explain anything."

"Is there anything to explain?" he asked.

"There is a great deal to explain, but nothing that can be explained," she replied. "I will be pleased to pay Mrs. Wingfield a visit. That's all that need be said on the matter. I am sure that she will be very nice to me, and I know that I will be as nice to her as I can be to any one. Haven't I always been nice to you?"

"Nice—nice?" he repeated. "That's hardly the word. You have been nicer to me than any one I ever met What have you been to me? There's a word that just describes it, if I could only find it. Guardian—no—no—some other word?"

"Pupil-teacher?" she suggested with some more demure humour.

He paid no attention to her. He was not in the humour for humour at all.

"I know the word, if I could only find it," he said, musingly. "By George! I have it—good angel—that's the word. You have been my good angel. You have indeed."

"That was a word worth waiting for," she said gravely. "I don't think that there is any word that I should like better to hear any man apply to me than that word—good angel. It simply means, of course, good influence; and that is woman's mission in the world of men; it is not so much to do things herself as to influence men in the doing of things. And when you come to think of it, woman has played a rather important part in the history of the world by adopting this line. She hasn't actually done much herself, but she has been a tremendous power for good or evil in her influence upon man. That is the sort of woman I should like to be—an influence for good."

"A good angel—you have been my good angel," he said in a low voice. "You have plucked me by the hair of my head out of—out of—of—well, out of myself; and—if you knew what I think of you—if you knew what I hope—what my heart is set on—what——"

"What your heart is set on just now is that I should visit your mother," she said quickly. She had no notion of leading him to fancy that she had spoken to him of what was in her heart in order to induce him to speak to her of what he fancied was in his heart. If he had confessed to her there and then that his heart was set on marrying her she would have refused to listen to him further, and all might be over between them. But she had no idea of allowing this to come about. She cared far too much for him for this. She had read the instructive Bible story—the finest story that was ever written in the world—of a man being handed over by God for Satan to try to make what he pleased of him. She thought that God might be very much better employed in handing over a man to a woman to try what she could make of him. She wondered which of the witty Frenchmen would have replied that God, being merciful, would only make the transfer to Satan. Anyhow, leaving theology aside for the moment, the longing in her heart was that she might be given an opportunity of standing by this man while he worked out his own salvation, and she knew that the salvation of a man is the recognition by himself of his own manhood.

That was why she stopped him so quickly when he was going to say something that would have spoilt his chance—and hers.

"Your heart is set on my visit to your mother—at least I hope so, for mine is," she cried quickly, with a nod to him. "Now tell me how and when I am to come." For a moment he felt angry that she had checked his all too rapid flow of words; he was not quite sure that the trend of their conversation, and that accidental introduction of a word or two that gives a man his opportunity, if only he is on the look out for it, would ever be so favourable to him again. But he quickly perceived that he had been too impetuous, and that if he had been allowed to go on he would have ruined every chance that he had.

"May I say Saturday?" he asked. "This business"—they were close to the tennis courts, and had just arisen from lunch—"will be over by Saturday."

"And you'll have carried home the cup—don't forget that," she said. "Yes, Saturday would suit me very well, and I hope it will suit your mother."

"You may be sure that it will," he said. "I have a very good chance of the cup, haven't I? There are only two lives between me and it. If Donovan is killed by a thunderbolt to-night and if a brigand stabs Jeffares with a poisoned stiletto in the course of the evening, to-morrow I'll carry off the cup. It will be plain sailing after that."

"No, you must win it," she said.

"Wish me good luck, and—I suppose you don't happen to have about you that ring which you habitually wear—the one with the monogram of Lucrezia Borgia done on it in fine rubies, and the secret spring that releases the hollow needle-point with the deadly fluid? No? Ah, just my luck! you could put it on and then offer your hand to Donovan."

"I have left it at the chemists to be renewed," she said, turning halfway round in speaking, for they were in the act of separating. "Yes, I have used up a lot of the fluid of late; I really must be more economical. If I'm not I'll not have enough money left to get it recharged for Miss Metcalfe, who lost you the M.D.s." And so they parted with smiles and fun.

And it so happened that he carried off the silver cup, for he beat Mr. Donovan the next day, and Mr. Jeffares, the holder, found that he had strained a tendon on the Saturday morning, and so declined to contest it and also Mr. Wingfield's offer to play for it when the tendon should be in working order. (There were some people who said that it was very sporting of Mr. Wingfield to make such an offer, and others that it was very sporting of Mr. Jeffares to decline entertaining it. But in the inner circle there were whispers that Mr. Jeffares' tendon was a most accommodating one, for it had been known to strain itself upon two previous occasions when he had to meet an opponent who was likely to give him some trouble.)

She did not allow him to drive her up to the Manor House on Saturday—indeed, he did not make the suggestion that she should do so. She walked up to that fine old Georgian porch at the right visiting hour, and she had already been talking to Mrs. Wingfield for some time before Jack put in an appearance.

Again she was dressed in white, but her garments were not those of the tennis meeting. They were simpler and consequently more expensive, for there is nothing more expensive than simplicity in a woman's toilette if it is to be the best; and second-class simplicity is in worse taste than abject display. Mrs. Wingfield knew all that was to be known about lace of all lands and of all periods, and she saw in a moment that the Mechlin which made a sort of pelerine for her dress was a specimen. But she felt that it was not a bit to be worn by a farmer's daughter at any time—that was her first impression. A little later, when she found how graceful and natural and well-mannered was this particular daughter of the farm, she came to the conclusion (reluctantly, it must be confessed) that that piece of Mechlin not merely suited her extremely well, but that it was exactly the right thing for her to wear.

She was greatly impressed by Priscilla's beauty; but more by her way of speaking, and most of all by her manners. Manners with Mrs. Wingfield meant an absence of mannerisms, just as distinction meant nothing that could be seen distinctly, and good taste something that was only known when a breach of it took place. Mrs. Wingfield did not find her deviating from the straight paths of good taste when she referred to her position in relation to the best set of Framsby. She did not boast of not being "received" by these ladies; nor did she sneer at their want of appreciation of her merits. She did not refer to Lady Gainsforth as "the dear Countess" or to Lady Cynthia by her Christian name, to impress upon Mrs. Wingfield the intimacy existing between her and Lady Gainsforth's daughter. Indeed it was Mrs. Wingfield who introduced these noble names, and Priscilla knew that Mrs. Wingfield's son must have mentioned them in connection with her own; so she merely said that the skating at Ullerfield Court, the Ullerfields' place in Norfolk, had been very good indeed when she had stayed there with Lady Cynthia and Katie Ullerfield.

And then—also in response to Mrs. Wingfield's enquiry—she went on to speak of her dairy experience. She thought that on the whole there could be no more interesting work than dairy work. They were in the middle of the dairy when Jack put in an appearance.

When they had had tea he took her round the greenhouses. She could talk freely with him on this tour; she had no sense of being restrained by the looming of a grave question ahead. She knew that although two days ago he had been at the point of blurting out something that it would have been impossible for her to reply to satisfactorily then, he would never regard such an incident as the flowering of a yucca in a hothouse as a legitimate excuse for asking her the question which she had restrained.

She had no fault to find with him upon this occasion. He talked about the patience of his mother alternately with the bother of orchids and the merits of the Phoenix Barbonica for indoors; and brought her safely back to the drawing-room, where she put a crown upon the good impression she had already produced upon Mrs. Wingfield by showing more than a mere working knowledge of Wedgwood. It so happened that Priscilla had worked up Wedgwood every year to beguile the tedium of her visits to her aunt Emily. The town where her aunt lived contained a museum of the products of the English Etruria, and she had a visiting acquaintance with every piece in the collection. Thus was the good impression which she produced upon Mrs. Wingfield sealed with a Wedgwood medallion. A girl who could wear without reproach a Mechlin lace collar of the best period and who could detect Hackwood's handiwork on a tiny vase which was attributed to somebody else, could not be far wrong.

When she had gone away and his mother had come out from the drawing-room and was about to take a turn round the garden, he lit a cigar and gave her his arm. He was talking rapidly, not of Miss Wadhurst, but of his approaching struggle with Mr. Dunning. His mother knew, from the persistency with which he rushed away from every chance she offered him of touching upon Miss Wadhurst, that he was anxious to an extraordinary degree to get her own opinion of their visitor.

It was not until he had led her to her favourite seat in the curve of an Italian balustrade overlooking the stonework of a pond with a fountain in the centre that she said, "I don't wonder that you are in love with her, Jack."

"Great Gloriana! I—in love—with—whom?" he cried. "She is, I think, the nicest girl I ever met," continued his mother. "She has elegance, and that is the rarest quality among the girls of nowadays—the elegance of a picture by Sir Joshua; and her dress—there was not a single jarring note. I thought at first that that piece of Mechlin round her neck was rather overdone—it is worth sixty or seventy pounds—ah, now you perceive how outrageous is my taste—appraising the value of a visitor's dress. Dreadful!"

"Monstrous! But you think——"

"I think that she is the only girl who could carry off such a thing without self-consciousness. She is a girl of the greatest taste."

He shook his head.

"That's bad news," he said.

"Bad news?"

"Bad. If she has any taste what chance should I have?" His mother smiled. She knew girls a good deal better than did her son. She had come to think of her son as the one who chooses and the girl as the one who is chosen. She never thought of the girl as having any choice in the matter. It was her *metier* to be chosen, and all the others stood by envying her.

It was no wonder that she smiled at his suggestion.

"I only wish—but it is too late now. After all, it is only people who have not seen her—who do not know her—that will sneer at her being only a farmer's daughter," she said.

"Only fools," he cried. "Only—such fools—Framsby fools! Gloriana! What better can any one be than a farmer? I'm a farmer. Not that that settles the question once and for all," he added, with a laugh. "Lord, how rotten is all this rot that one hears about family and trade and that! It's a dreadful thing for a chap to have a shop, and, of course, society, as it's called, shuns him; but if he multiplies his offence by a hundred he's all right, and no matter what a bounder he may be, society opens its arms to him, and the bounder becomes a baronet. If a chap like me sets up a dairy and sells the milk, people say that it's sporting; but if a real farmer—the right sort of man—runs a dairy of the highest order, he is called a dairyman, and is put on a level with gardeners and grooms. So far as family is concerned, the Wadhursts are as far above us and any of the rotters that control society at Framsby as our family is above the Gibman lot who are hand in glove with Royalty. The Wadhursts were in this neighbourhood at the time of the Heptarchy."

"I think she is the nicest girl I ever met," said his mother, when the smoke had time to clear away. "Poor girl! How could she have made such a fool of herself?"

"What do you mean? Who made a fool of herself?"

"You recalled the story—it was in all the papers. But I called her Miss Wadhurst."

"There's a difference between a girl making a fool of herself and being made a victim of, isn't there?"

"But the notoriety—it is not her fault, I know, but still——"

"Still what?"

"I don't know what. I don't know anything. I only feel." He looked at her for some time—at first with a frown creeping over his face, but it did not develop into a frown; on the contrary, it vanished in a smile. He took her hand and put his arm about her.

"Thank God that you can feel, mother, for it's more than most women can do nowadays," said he. "And what you should feel is that if that girl was a fool once she may be a fool again and marry me; and that if I have been a fool always I may be wise once and marry her, if I can. I tell you that she—she—by God! she has made a man of me, and that's a big enough achievement for any girl. Thank God, my dear mother, that I've set my heart on a girl that can do this off her own bat."

"I will, my son," said she, quietly; and they walked back to the house without a word.

CHAPTER XVIII

She never once looked back in any sense, when she had passed out of the gates of the Manor. She had known that it was laid upon her to go through this ordeal of standing before the mother whom he loved, to be approved by her. She had faced the ordeal without shrinking, because she loved him. She was as sure of him and his love for her as she had been certain of the deceit of the wretch with whom she had gone through the empty ceremony of marriage in order that her mother might die happy—though the result was that she died of her misery.

She knew that if Mrs. Wingfield were pleased with her, Jack would be delighted and ask her to marry him the next time they met, if he did not force a meeting with her for the purpose; but if his mother did not approve of her, and called her heartless because her dress was white instead of black, and flippant because she had appeared several days at a sporting meeting within a couple of months of her husband's death, he would be greatly downcast, but he would ask her to marry him all the same.

But she had set forth to face the ordeal by visit as firmly as she would have gone to meet the ordeal by fire or the ordeal by water, had she lived in the days of such tests of faith. She knew that, whatever should happen her faith in him would not be shaken and his faith in her would remain unmoved. But she had made up her mind to find favour in the sight of his mother, and she now felt that she had succeeded in doing so. If she had failed, she would have been miserable, but she would have promised to marry him all the same.

The sense of exultation which was hers was due to her knowledge of the fact that she had found favour in the eyes of the mother of the man whom she loved, not to her feeling that she would, as the wife of Jack Wingfield, occupy a splendid position in the county—such a position as her poor mother had never dreamt of her filling. Beyond a doubt, she found it quite delightful to think of owning that beautiful park through which she had been allowed as a great privilege to stray while the house was empty. Every part of the grounds was a delight to her—the deep glen with its well-wooded sides sloping down to the little stream that twinkled among its ferns and mosses and primroses—the irregular meadow where stood the tawny haystacks like islands in the midst of a sea of brilliant green—the spacious avenues of elm and oak that made her feel when walking in their shadow, that she was going through the nave of a cathedral—she loved everything about the place, and it would be the greatest joy to her to live all her life there—with love; without love she would as soon spend the rest of her life in one of the cottages on her father's farm.

She felt exultant only in the thought that he was to be her companion when she went to that place. She had all her life been looking forward to a life of love; and it had been puzzling to her when she found that year after year went by without bringing her any closer to love. She was not conscious of being fastidious in her association with men; but the fact remained the same: she never had the smallest feeling of love for any of the men who had told her that they loved her—and she never had a lack of such men about her.

For the months of her engagement to that man, Marcus Blaydon, her thought was that this was the punishment that was laid upon her for the hardness of her heart—this prospect of living with a man who could never be anything to her but an object of dislike. He never awoke in her a slumbering passion—not even the passion of hate. She merely disliked him as she disliked a foggy day; and yet she was condemned to spend the remainder of her life with him with love shut out. Was that to be her punishment for having rejected the many offers of love which had been laid at her feet by men whom she liked well but could not love?

And then with the suddenness with which a great blessing or a great calamity is sent by Heaven (according to the Teachers) there had been sent to her the two best things in the world—Freedom and Love. She knew that if this man had been one of her father's shepherds and had asked her to love him she would have given herself to him. Her sense of being on the way to fill a splendid position socially was overwhelmed by the feeling that she was beloved by a man whom she loved as she never thought it would be given to her to love any man. That was her dominant thought—nay, her only thought—while she walked through the lanes to her home.

And it never occurred to her that she was reckoning among her possessions a great gift which had not yet been offered to her. It never occurred to her that she might be mistaken in taking his love for granted. Even if weeks and months were to pass without his coming to her, she would still not entertain so unworthy a thought as that he was not coming to her. But she was not subjected to the ordeal of his absence. He came to her on Monday morning, the first thing. It was surely ridiculous for him to set out on this mission before the workers in the fields had left their beds; but so he did. He went forth and wandered for miles across the Downs. He went within sight of the sea, by a curious impulse, and he sat on the turf in the early sunlight, listening to the great bass of the breaking waves beneath him and to the exquisite fluttering flutings, of a lark in the sky above him. Then he turned and found the road that led down to the snuggest of villages—he owned every house, though he did not know it—and up again to a region of ploughed fields—enormous spaces of purple-brown surrounded by great irregular hedges of yellow gorse.

It might have been fancied that, with his heart so full of the great intention, he would be walking like one in a dream, taking no thought of the things about him; but so far from his being like this, he looked upon everything that he came across with an affection such as he had never known before. He felt that these things of Nature were closer to him than they had ever been—in fact, for some of them he felt as would an explorer in a strange land who suddenly comes upon a number of people and recognizes in each a relation of his own. He had never been in such close touch with Nature before, and every step that he took was one of rejoicing.

He dallied so much in strange ways that it was actually as far on in the day as seven o'clock before he found himself in that narrow steep lane close to a narrower and steeper one, which led up to Athalsdean Farm—this was where his motor had broken down, and she had come upon him searching (by the aid of his chauffeur's eyes) for the cause of the mischief. He had not yet reached the exact spot, when he saw her turning from the farm lane to the one through which he was walking; but she was not coming toward him; her turn took her in the opposite direction.

He shouted to her, and she glanced round, and then stood still. She was at that instant under an ash that was not yet fully clothed with leaves; the sunlight shone upon her bare head. Bare? Well, scarcely bare with that splendour of wreathed tresses crowning her; but she wore no hat, and carried no sunshade. Her dress was a print, made very short, so that her serviceable shoes and her ankles were fully exposed. Such leaves as were upon the boughs cast dark shadows upon her dress, but her head was altogether in the sunshine.

She waited for him, rosy and eager—she could not control her eagerness—she could not trust herself to speak a word of greeting in reply to his.

"I have been in search of you," he said.

"For long?"

"For long? All my life, Priscilla. I want you, Priscilla—I never wanted anything so much. I need you. I cannot do without you."

He had not released the hand that she gave him, but he did not hold it so tightly but that she could have taken it from him if she had been so minded; but it so happened that she was not so minded. She allowed him to keep it, and he drew her to him. He put his other hand on her waist, and then slipped it up to the back of her head. That was how he kissed her, with his hand at the back of her head; and that was how she allowed him to kiss her at 7.5 a.m. on that fresh June morning, when the hedgerows were giving in scent to the sun the dews that had lain upon them, keeping them fresh through the night.

"You do not say a word," he complained, when he had kissed her and kissed her—on the cheeks, the chin, the eyes, and the mouth—when he had held her so close to him that she felt deliciously dishevelled, and for some seconds found it difficult to breathe. "Not a word!"

She gasped, and kept him away with one hand. He was holding the other so tightly by now that she had no chance of recovering it.

She laughed.

"A word? What word?" she gasped.

"Any word—the word that is in your heart." There was no use talking loud. His arm was about her again.

"There is no word in my heart—you have squeezed it out," she managed to say.

"You would not let me lay a finger on you if you did not love me—I know that," said he.

"You know that, and yet you ask me to say something to you. Talking is a sinful waste of time."

"So it is, my darling girl. You have said it: out of the fulness of the heart the mouth——"

"Kisses—that is what it does; it doesn't speak—it cannot."

"Since when has that knowledge come to you, Priscilla."

"I confess that it is newly acquired. You make an excellent coach for a backward girl, my master."

"You are not backward; it is only that your education has been neglected."

"And you look on yourself as a successful crammer? Haven't you seen the advertisements, 'particular attention paid to neglected children'? You are paying me particular attention. Don't you think that my education is pretty nearly complete, Jack?"

"Oh, you have a lot to learn yet; but you are coming on. You have learned that my name is Jack—that's a distinct advance. Oh, my dear girl, the delight of teaching you all—all—all!"

"I had no idea that you were so ardent an educationist. Ah, I knew you would come to me! But what I have been asking myself for several days is, Were there no girls in your own station in life——"

She could not finish her question for laughter; the phrase which her father was very fond of using sounded very funny coming from her lips, which were—as she had found out—exactly on a level with his own.

"Station of life? Station of life? Your lips are the waiting room—a first-class waiting room in the station of life," said he.

That was how he received her suggestion that he was ready to make what his relations would undoubtedly call a *mesalliance* in asking her to be his wife; though, as a matter of fact, he had not yet asked her to be his wife. Perhaps she should have regarded his movements during the previous five minutes merely in the light of a friendly attention to enable him to see if she was amicably disposed toward him.

"Let that be the last word of frivolity between us," she said. "I want to be serious. Be sure, my dear Jack, that this is the most serious moment that has come into our lives."

"I know it—I know it, my beloved," said he. "I know that meeting you was the most important thing in my life. And I know that marrying you will be the wisest. You are the first person in the world who gave me credit for having any backbone. You are the first person in the world to give me a sort of respect for myself. My mother is the dearest soul on earth; but she has never thought it necessary to help me on to anything. She was quite content that I should live and inherit the property, and follow her to the grave and then go there myself, doing as little as possible in the interim. It's wonderful how little a country gentleman can do if he only puts his heart into the business of idling. I think it quite likely that I might have made a record in this way. But you came into my life, and—and you have become my life. That's why I want you to stay with me—to stand by me, and you've promised to do it?"

"Have I?" she said. "Yes, I suppose I have; at any rate, whether I have or not you may be sure that I'll do it. And don't you doubt, Jack, that we'll do something in the world before we are parted. A man without a woman beside him represents an imperfect scheme of life. Life—that does not mean a man, nor does it mean a woman; it means the man and the woman. So it was in the beginning, so it is to-day. Life—the man and the woman, each living for the other. That's life, isn't it?"

"It is; and we'll do some living, you and I, Priscilla, if others have failed."

"The failures are those who forget—the woman who forgets that she is a woman and seeks to do the man's work—the man who forgets that he is a man and treats the woman as if she were the same as himself. Oh, here we are talking of the philosophy of life when we should be living. But that's the way of philosophy: it keeps a man learning the best way to live, and by the time he has learnt it it is time for him to die."

"Hang up philosophy and give us life, say I. Dear girl, you have made me happy and—hungry. I left my bed at four this morning, and now it's past seven."

"You will come with me and have breakfast. I wonder if any man up to this day ever asked a girl to marry him before breakfast."

"I wonder. But a chap feels so much fresher in the early morning, I think it should be tried more frequently."

"It was a bold experiment, Jack. But it might only succeed when carried out in connection with the dairy industry."

"That is how you come to be up so early. Shall I have a chance of seeing your dad if I go with you? I suppose a dad has always to be reckoned with."

"No one has to be reckoned with except myself in this matter. I am myself, and I know myself, and will obey myself and none other this time—this time."

She spoke with some vehemence, and her last sentence was uttered with a touch of bitterness. He knew what she meant. Providence had come to her rescue once, but a second interposition on her behalf was too much to expect. He could appreciate her feeling.

"You will not have to meet my father until you please," she said. "Just now he is miles away—at Galsworthy. We shall be alone."

"I'll not shudder at the prospect," said he. "We can't have everything in this world, can we?"

They went together up the lane to the farm with as much decorum as was consistent with the possibility of being discovered by some watcher in the fields, and they had breakfast face to face at an old Tudor table in one of the panelled rooms of the farmhouse, and beneath the old oak beams—a lovely room that had undergone no change in even the most trifling detail for three hundred years. The bowls of wallflowers on the table and on the lattice shelf were of blue delft, and the plate-rack on the wall held some dishes of the same colour.

"You suppose all this is old?" he said, looking around.

"Oh, no; but it wasn't bought in my lifetime," she replied. "I can show you in an account book exactly what was paid for everything. The date of the last entry in the book is the 'Eve of the Feast of the Purification, 1604.'"

"Three hundred years ago. But that's nothing in the history of your family. Have you a ledger that goes back to the Heptarchy?"

"I'm afraid that that one is mislaid. But the eggs are fresh; if we don't boil them now they will be three hours old at nine."

"You might have some relic of the Heptarchy, Priscilla."

"Alas! nothing remains from that date except our name."

"And yet you are content to submerge it in the mushroom-growth Wingfield? Have you no reverence for the past?"

"Just now I confess that I am thinking more of the future. Oh, the future, Jack, my boy—the future!"

She laid a hand upon his shoulder and stood in front of him in the attitude of a true comrade.

"My pal!" he cried, taking the note from her. "My pal, was there ever a time when we didn't know each other?"

CHAPTER XIX

ONLY one stipulation will I make, my dearest, and that is that we shall not be married in a church."

He was taken somewhat aback when she said this—they were sitting together among the apple blossoms of the orchard. She fancied that she felt his hand loosen slightly on hers at the moment; but it might only have been fancy.

"I thought that women always went it blind for the church and 'The Voice that breathed o'er Eden,' with the Wedding March to follow," said he.

"They do. I believe that there are dozens of girls who get married solely for the sake of the ceremony," she replied.

"And I can swear that there are thousands of men who will have nothing to do with it simply on account of the ceremony," said he. "If there was none of that nonsense of carriages and clergymen and top hats and a new frock coat, the marriage-rate would soon go up instead of down. What has the parson to do with the thing any way?"

"He can be done without, and so can the whole service, which is really only a melancholy mockery. Oh, never, never again will I repeat those phrases formally at the bidding of a clergyman or any one else. The 'love, honour, and obey' will be between you and me, Jack, and two of the three will be contingencies."

"Oh, I say!"

"I sympathize with you and all that, of course; but I can only promise to love you; the honour and obedience———"

"Oh, throw them in to make up weight!"

"They are both conditional. But we can hope for the best.... Jack, I would not go through another marriage ceremony in a church even if there was no other way of getting married. The horrible mockery! Think what would have happened if that man whom I had promised before God's altar to honour, love, and obey had come straight to me on getting out of gaol! Could he not have claimed me as his wife?"

"Not he. There is no law that could compel you to go with him."

"Then there was no sacred obligation implied in the vows, as they call them; and every sensible person is aware of this, and yet the mockery of repeating the words is carried on day by day. Jack, I am willing to believe that God instituted marriage, but not the marriage service according to the Church of England."

"I agree with you, my dearest; but for the sake of peace and quiet, and all that, don't you say that to my mother."

"Nothing will induce me. I am not given to forcing my views on this or any other subject on people who may have feelings or prejudices in favour of the conventional. If I were to suggest to my father a marriage before a registrar or in a British Consulate he would look on me as an outcast."

"He goes back to the Heptarchy. Yes, what you say is quite right. This little affair of ours concerns our two selves only."

She gave him her hand and he put it to his lips, but she could not help noticing that his eyes were fixed musingly upon a promising gooseberry bush. She wondered if he was considering how he was to break the news to his mother; or was he wondering how she was to break the news to her father? Either the one problem or the other would, she knew, entail a fair amount of musing.

And that was why she sent him away—it was actually approaching noon, so quickly does a day pass when lovers who have recognized each other as such for the first time come together. They had not stirred from the apple orchard. When they had left the house immediately after breakfast there had been some talk between them about the great dairy; he avowed himself to be dying to see the dairy and she had promised to make him acquainted with all the details of it's working. But they had not stirred from the orchard. She sat among the apple blossoms; all the world before their eyes was filled with apple blossoms; apple blossoms were trembling in the air between their eyes and the blue sky, and with every gracious breath that came among the overhanging boughs a snow of apple blossoms fluttered to their feet.

And then the high walls of the orchard gave them such a sense of security.

They never went near the dairy. Neither of them had a thought for it; even though its management was on the borders of the sublime. The first move that they made meant separating (for the time being), and they were long in making it. Of course it was she who sent him away. She thought that she would do well to meet her father alone and break the news to him.

When her lover had gone from her, she ran into the house and up the stairs that led to a small gable room with a window commanding a view of the steep lane through which he would have to pass crossing the country to the Manor. She waited breathless until he swam into her ken. He remained in her sight for the better part of three minutes, and then his occultation took place by the denseness of the foliage of the hedgerow. But that three minutes!...

Slowly she went to her own room and threw herself into an easy chair—the very one in which she had sat scarcely more than a month ago when reading the batch of American newspapers. That was the thought which came to her now, and with it came a sense of the enormous space of time that lay between the events of that day and the event of the hour in which she was living. It was impossible to believe that it was to be measured by weeks and not by years. Had she no premonition on that afternoon, when the earth was smiling in all its newly washed greenery, that the man whom she had seen for the first time that day would become so much a part of her life—a part?—nay, all—all her life? She could not remember having had such a thought suggested to her at that time; but that only made her feel that her memory was treacherous. She felt sure that she must have had such a premonition. Even though she had had a great deal to think about on that afternoon she must have had space to ask herself if she did not hope to meet him again.

She remembered how extraordinary had been her sense of relief when she had sat at this window in this same chair trying to realize the truth—trying to realize that she was once more free—that the course of life which she had planned out for herself and to which she was becoming reconciled, as men who have been sentenced to imprisonment for life become reconciled to their servitude, was to be changed—that she was free to live and to love as she pleased.

It had taken her a long time to realize the exact extent of what the news meant to her; and among the details of the vista of realization that opened itself out before her then, the figure of Jack Wingfield sitting by her side among the apple blossoms had no place. She had never so much as dreamt that within a month she should be within a step of possessing that park through which she had been walking and that house with the spacious rooms she had always admired, but, of course, in a distant and impersonal way.

Now she thoroughly realized how extraordinary was the happiness which was within her reach; but, as is usual in the case of imaginative people in similar circumstances, there came to her a cold suggestion of the possibility of disaster—a feeling that it was impossible for such happiness as hers to continue—a dread lest the cup which was being filled for her lips should be shattered before it reached them. She had experienced these pranks of Fate before now, and she had found that it was wise not to count upon anything on which she had set her heart, taking place in all the perfection in which it existed in her imagination.

That was why she now made herself miserable for some time, saying in her heart:

"It is too bright—the prospect is too full of sunshine. He will be killed in a motor accident—the house will catch fire and he will be burnt in his room—something will happen—I know it! It is not given to any girl to realize such happiness as I see before me."

In another minute, however, she was rejoicing in her thought: "Never mind! Whatever may be in store for us of evil, we shall have had our day—neither Fate nor any other power of malice can make us unlive to-day. His kisses, the clasp of his arms, the sense of possessing me which he had, delighting me to feel that I had surrendered myself to him—these cannot be erased from the things that have been. The joy that is past cannot be taken away from us."

This stimulating reflection was enough for her. She went over all the delightful incidents of the morning from the moment of her hearing his voice until that last kiss of his had left its mark upon her cheek—she could feel the brand of his ardour upon her face; it was still burning her white flesh, and she had seen its glow when she had passed the looking-glass. It was very sweet to her to recall all such incidents, even though a quarter of an hour had scarcely passed since the last had taken place; and gradually she groped her way free from the gloomy forebodings which she had forced upon herself so as to cheat Fate out of some of the malignant surprise which that power might be devising for her undoing. The roseate tint of that kiss which lay upon her face had tinted all the atmosphere of the past and the future as a drop of blood tints a basin of water, and she saw everything through this medium. When a girl believes that all her future life will be as exquisite as that of a pink flower—as exquisite as that carnation bloom which she wore on her cheek—she can have no serious misgivings—even when she hears the heavy boot of her father. A father's boot may awaken one from a pleasing dream, but it need not portend disaster.

He was hungry and hot when she joined him in the dining-room. He had had a tiring day, and he had been compelled to wear a hat. He was a quarter of an hour too soon for the early dinner which was the rule at the farm; but still he thought that it should have been ready for him, because he was ready for it.

She managed to clip five minutes off his waiting, but he did not think it necessary to applaud her achievement. It was an excellent meal and he did ample justice to it, scarcely speaking a word—certainly no word that had not a direct bearing upon the joint before him. It was not until the cheese was being brought into the room that she noticed the marks of a smile on his face. (She wondered if he saw the marks of something else on hers.)

"A funny thing has happened," said he. "You remember that we were talking some time ago about Mr. Dunning and his pigheadedness in letting Glyn give up his farm rather than allow him a year's rent in starting a market garden? Well, it seems that young Wingfield has been out at the farm and has come to the conclusion that Dunning did wrong, and down he came upon Dunning like a sack of potatoes the other morning, accusing him of cheating him out of two years' rent and so forth; and then nothing would do him but he looks up Verrall at the Manor Farm, and makes it pretty lively for everyone there, winding up by turning out Verrall neck and crop. I saw Verrall just now at Gollingford looking for a job. He gave me his version of the story; and I asked him if he hadn't left out the part about his being drunk—I took it for granted that he had been drunk; he wasn't many hours off being drunk at eleven this morning. He was, I fancy, mid-channel between. Wingfield is less of a fool than we fancied. Why are you laughing in that queer way, Priscilla, eh?"

"I am laughing because I was about to mention Mr. Wingfield's name to you, in a way that may possibly make you believe that there's a great deal more in him than you could believe, for he has been with me all the morning, and long before eight he had asked me to marry him, and I—I—gave him my word—at least, I gave him to understand that I would marry him."

While she was speaking he had cut up his cheese. He paused with a piece on the point of his knife in the act of conveying it to his mouth. It never reached its destination. When she had spoken he did not give a start, nor did he make an exclamation; he simply lowered the point of his knife slowly until the cheese dropped off it, and then he laid the knife across his plate, staring at her all the time.

He stared at her, but he could not utter a word. She saw him make the attempt, and smiled.

"Of course I have given you a great surprise," she said; "but I am sure that it must be a pleasant surprise, father. You did not know that I was acquainted with Jack Wingfield."

But her speaking thus easily had not, it appeared, done much to help him. After the lapse of a minute or two, however, she saw a gleam come into his eyes. He groped for his tankard of beer on the table-cloth, for he had not taken his eyes away from her face. Nor did he do so even when he was swallowing his beer; his eyes looking over the rim of the tankard gave him a very comical look.

Her smile became a laugh, and then the blank look on his face became a very definite frown.

"I don't see the fun in such jokes, girl," he said moodily, and he picked up the piece of cheese in his fingers and jerked it into his mouth. "I can't for the life of me see how you—you, with the experience you have had, can make a jest of anything that has to do with marriage."

He pushed his chair back from the table and got upon his feet, brushing to the floor some crumbs that had clung to his knees.

"I have told you the truth, father," she said. "I have been acquainted with Jack Wingfield for some time. I liked him very much from the first, and I could see that he came suddenly to like me. I paid a visit to his mother—such a charming woman! I expected him to come to me some of these days. He came to-day—quite early in the morning, and—I gave him breakfast; but that was, of course, afterwards. That's the whole story."

"Marriage—does he mean marriage—marriage? You are sure that he doesn't mean to make a fool of you, girl?" he said in a low voice that had a good deal of meaning in it. "I have heard that he is a scamp—an empty-headed man who was expelled from college for bad conduct. Would his grandfather have tied up the estate, think you, if it hadn't been that he knew the young fellow would make ducks and drakes of it? Does he mean marriage?"

"What else does a man mean when he asks a girl to marry him?"

"There's such a thing as a left-handed marriage. I know these idle gentry. Game rights—some of them believe that the maidens on their estates are fair game. The rascals! Is that what's in this youngster's mind, do you think?"

"He brought me to see his mother."

She spoke in a low voice, and rose from the table.

"Why didn't he come to me in the first place?" said her father. "What business had he making advances to you before he had got my consent—tell me that?"

"I told him my story," she replied. "Perhaps he gathered from it that, having once obeyed the commands of my parents, I should take care ever after to act on my own judgment. He talked to-day about seeing you; I told him that there was no need."

"Why should there be no need if he means to run straight? I would see that he meant right before I gave my consent. I don't want you to be fooled by him or any other man even if he was a lord. You're not in his station in life, and you know it. If he was making up to some one in his own station he would have to see her father first. What is there to laugh at?"

She had become rosy, and had given a laugh when he made use of the old phrase; but she could scarcely explain to him that her laugh was due to her recalling the sequel to her introduction of the same phrase a few hours earlier.

"I can't tell you how funny—I mean how—how—no; all that I can tell you is that I have accepted Jack Wingfield and that I mean to marry him and be a good wife to him."

"You can say that—you can talk about marrying another man before two months have passed! I'm ashamed of you."

At first she did not know what he meant by his reference to two months—two months' since what? Then all at once it flashed upon her that he had in his mind the incident that should have been appropriately commemorated (according to his idea) by widow's weeds.

"I think that we had better not return to that particular matter," she said. "We can never look at it from the same standpoint. I married once to please you and my mother; I will marry now to please myself."

"Decency is decency, all the same, whatever your notions may be," said he. "No daughter of mine with my consent will become engaged to a man so as to outrage every sense of decency. A year is the very shortest space of time that must elapse—even a year is too short for good taste."

"A year and more has passed since you gave me to that man—the man you choose for me—a year since I outraged a sense that is very much higher than your sense of decency by promising to honour a wretch who was trying to accomplish my dishonour."

"What do you mean, Priscilla? Didn't he marry you honestly in the church? Give the man his due. I doubt if this young Wingfield's intentions are so honourable."

She rose from the table saying: "I will talk no more to you on this subject, father. I thought that after my year of suffering—oh, my God! what I suffered! And you could look on and know nothing of it! Was ever a girl plunged as I was into such a seven-times-heated furnace of shame? Was it nothing to me, do you think, to walk in the street and see women nudge one another as I came up—to see myself pointed out to strangers and to hear them mutter 'Poor thing!' or 'What a pity she made such a fool of herself!'—to have it set down to me that I was a girl so anxious to find a husband that I jumped at the first man that offered, without making the least enquiry as to his character? I told you that when that man wrote to you for your consent—he was so scrupulous, you know, he would do nothing without your consent—I told you that I disliked him—that I distrusted him—that I could never be happy with him, and yet you put me aside as if I were not worthy of a moment's consideration—you put my opinion aside and urged on my poor mother to make her appeal to me, the consequences of which killed her. With all that fresh in your mind—with some knowledge at least of what my sufferings for that horrible year must have been—feeling my life ruined—linked for ever to that man's handcuffs—in spite of all this you can still question my right to choose for myself—you can still insult both me and the man whom I have promised to marry! That being so we would do well not to talk any further on this topic."

She walked out of the room, leaving him still in his chair, his head set square upon his shoulders and his lips tight shut. He allowed her to go without a word from him. The truth was that she had given him a surprise and a shock. Never once had she accused him during the year of having failed to do his duty as a father in protecting her from the possibility of such a calamity as had befallen her. Never once had she referred to his persistence in urging her to marry Marcus Blaydon; so that he had come to fancy, first, that she had forgotten this circumstance, and, later on, that he had been all too ready to condemn himself for the part he had taken in insisting on her marrying that man. Whatever slight qualms he may have felt during the days of the man's trial, when the infernally sympathetic newspapers were referring to his daughter as a victim, and pointing their usual moral in the direction of the necessity there was for fathers to take a stricter view of their duties as the protectors of their daughters from the schemes of adventurers—whatever qualms he may have felt about this time at the thought that, but for his persistence and his daughter's sense of duty, Priscilla might never have been subjected to such an ordeal, had long ago waned, and he had come to think of himself once again as a model father. The thought that his daughter was about to make what worldly people would call a brilliant match, quite without his assistance, was displeasing to him. Still, he might have got over his chagrin and given his consent; but that long speech of hers had taken his breath away. It had left him staring at the tablecloth and absolutely dumfounded.

She had clearly been having a little savings bank of grievances during the year, and now she had flung the result of her thrift in his face.

It was no wonder that he remained dumb.

CHAPTER XX

WAS there any reason why they should wait for a year?

That was the question which came up for discussion between them every time they met, which was usually once a day. It was, as a rule, at the hour of parting that the question came up for dispassionate consideration. And they discussed it quite dispassionately, he with his arms clasping her shoulders, and she enjoying an extremely close inspection of the sapphire in his tie, at intervals of pulling his moustache into fantastic twists, merging through this medium his identity into that of many distinguished personages, Imperial as well as Presidential, and even poetical.

"A year! Great Gloriana! What rot! A whole year? But why—why?"

"Why, indeed? But your mother—she takes the year for granted."

"And I suppose your father would turn you out of his house if you were to marry me inside that time?"

"That would be almost certain. It is generally assumed that a year——"

And here there would be an interval—a breathless interlude in the academic consideration of that nice question in the etiquette of wedlock.

And then they got tired of discussing it, and it was relegated to the lovers' limbo of the unnecessary.

But if there were grave reasons (in the eyes of such people as accepted the conventional as the inevitable) why they should not be married for a year, there did not seem to be any reason why the intentions of the pair should be concealed for the same period. Mr. Wingfield appeared several times in the High Street of Framsby with Miss Wadhurst beside him in his motor; and after the third time of observing so remarkable an incident, some of the onlookers made an honest attempt to account for it. The best set discussed it, and agreed that, being people of the world, they would not shake their heads in condemnation of the antics of a young reprobate. When a young reprobate has a rent roll of something approaching fifteen thousand a year his peccadilloes must be looked on with the eye of leniency.

The fiat having gone forth to this effect, the members of the best set looked indulgently into the shop windows when they noticed the approach of the motor with the silly young man and the foolish young woman side by side. This was very advanced, the best set thought—it put them on a level of tact with the best set in Trouville or Monte Carlo, where they understood such incidents were quite usual. But of course when the mothers came upon Mr. Wingfield when he was alone, they did not fail to recognize him or to do their best to induce him to accompany them home to tea. Equally as a matter of course when they met Priscilla they either looked across the street or at the telegraph wires between the roofs in front of them. The elderly ones sniffed, and the younger ones sneered.

But when one day Miss Wadhurst appeared by the side of Mrs. Wingfield in her victoria the impression produced in Framsby was indescribable. It was paralysing. A four-line whip was passed round the members of the best set calling them to their places in the front row of the pavilion seats at the Tennis and Croquet Club to discuss the situation.

"The poor old lady! She could have no idea of what has been going on!"

"It would be an act of duty—certainly of charity—to give her a hint."

"Or write her a letter—not necessarily signed—charity is sometimes all the more effective when bestowed anonymously."

"That girl is artful enough for anything."

"And pushing enough for anything. Did you notice how she was always throwing herself in the way of the Countess at the Open Meeting?"

"Surely Mr. Possnett will think it his duty to warn Mrs. Wingfield."

(The Reverend Osney Possnett was the Vicar of Athalsdean.)

So the discussion of the grave and disturbing social question went on among the members of the front row; and the caterer, observing askance the amount of tea and tea cake incidentally consumed, made up his mind that if another question came forward demanding the same amount of sustenance as that—whatever it was—which was now being dealt with, he would be compelled to increase his *per capita* charge from sixpence to ninepence.

And then, just when they were warming on the question, stimulated by copious cups, the effect of which all the cucumber sandwiches failed to neutralize, Rosa Caffyn entered the pavilion with Mrs. Bowlby-Sutherst, and asked for tea for two.

Mrs. Gifford, the wife of the Colonial Civil Servant, who was the leader of the best set, was quick to perceive her opportunity. She knew that Rosa Caffyn was, in the face of all opposition, the friend of Priscilla Wadhurst, and so might be made the means of conveying to that young woman some idea of the grave scandal that her conduct was exciting. She rose from her place and hurried to Rosa's table.

"We have just been discussing a very disagreeable incident," she remarked, after greeting the girl and Mrs. Bowlby-Sutherst.

"Oh, then we have arrived quite opportunely to give you a chance of discussing a very delightful one," cried Mrs. Bowlby-Sutherst.

"We have not heard any delightful one," said Mrs. Gifford.

"What, do you mean to say that you have not heard that that pretty Miss Wadhurst, the girl with that wonderful hair, you know, is engaged to Jack Wingfield? Why, where have you been living? Don't you take in the *Morning Post*? No? Oh, well, I suppose it would not contain much to interest you."

Mrs. Bowlby-Sutherst was very much of the county; she was indifferent to Framsby's "sets." She watched with malicious interest the collapse of the leader of the best and resumed her revelation.

"Oh, yes; it was in the *Post* this morning, 'A marriage is arranged,' and the rest of it. I knew that you would all be glad to hear of it, but I thought that you would be the first to get the pleasant news. Rosa and I are driving to the Manor to offer our felicitations. Miss Wadhurst is staying there with Mrs. Wingfield. It's so nice when a handsome and clever girl like that is making a good match; and the poor girl deserves something good as a set-off against that unlucky affair of hers."

"She is a clever young woman," said Mrs. Gifford spitefully. "Oh, yes, a very clever young woman! I hear that she milks her father's cows."

"Oh, my dear Mrs. Gifford, you are very far behind the times," laughed Rosa. "Nobody milks cows nowadays. You might as well talk of Priscilla using one of the old barrel churns. It's all done by machinery."

"And will you have some of the machine-made in your tea, Rosa?" asked Mrs. Bowlby-Sutherst, poising the jug over the cups which had just been brought to the table.

"Thank you—that's enough," said Rosa. "And let me offer you some of the machine-made butter on the machine-made bread."

"I think I'll try a hand at a hand-made sandwich," said Mrs. Bowlby-Sutherst. "There's a joke in that somewhere, I feel—can you catch it?"

"Hand-made sandwiches made by the handmaid of the caterer—is that it?" asked Rosa after a thoughtful frown—the frown of the habitual prize acrostic-solver and anagram-maker of the English vicarage.

Mrs. Gifford felt rather neglected when the two others laughed together quite merrily. She rather thought that she would take a stroll round the grounds.

"One of the cats," whispered Rosa.

"The leader of the tabbies," assented Mrs. Bowlby-Sutherst. "But don't you make any mistake, my dear: although she's wild to hear that your friend is doing so well for herself——"

"And for Mr. Wingfield."

"And for Mr. Wingfield—in spite of that, you may rest perfectly certain that she will leave cards with pencilled congratulations upon the Manor people as early as possible to-morrow. Another sandwich?"

And that prognosis turned out to be correct. Several members of the best set called at the Manor the next day and left congratulatory cards. They had in view the possibility of future *fêtes* at the Manor; they would do any reasonable amount of calling or crawling to get invited to a garden-party given by a county person; and Miss Wadhurst was to be promoted over the heads of a large number of aspirants to a position in the county.

Although there were a certain number of persons who affirmed that she was showing very doubtful taste indeed in becoming engaged to any one, even a man with a rent roll of something like fifteen thousand a year, within a few months after receiving the news of the death of the other man, still Miss Wadhurst got quite a large number of cards of the same nature from ladies who had done their best to keep her in her place in the past, and who were clearly hoping that their failure to do so would prejudice her in their favour in the days to come.

But when a month had passed and the people of Framsby had almost ceased discussing the question of the advancement of Miss Wadhurst, there came a faint rumour to the effect that the *rapprochement* between the young couple was not quite so complete as it had been. They were no longer seen together either on foot or in the motor, and while heads were being shaken and significant winks exchanged, the definite announcement was made (by Mrs. Gifford) that a final rupture had taken place. The engagement was broken off, and the principals to that pencilled contract had separated.

A small and discreet commission of enquiry made their report on the subject, the tenor of which removed any doubt that might possibly remain on any mind. Investigations proved that the young man had elected to run away; and the fact that his mother had affirmed that he had gone on business, even specifying this business and alleging that he was endeavouring to find a substitute for Mr. Dunning, the agent, whose health had unfortunately broken down, necessitating his taking a long voyage, suggested that she had had a hand in the breaking off of the engagement. As for the young woman, it was thought very natural that she should desire to avoid the humiliation of meeting, under altered conditions, her Framsby friends, whose cards of congratulation she had never so much as acknowledged.

Rosa Caffyn knew all about her, and when interrogated, said that Priscilla had gone to pay a visit to a girl friend of hers in Dorsetshire, who was at the point of leaving England with her father, a major-general in the army, about to take up an appointment in the Bengal Presidency. This was Rosa's story, and every one acknowledged that Rosa was a staunch friend to Priscilla, unfortunate though the latter had been; for she was ready to deny the breaking off of the engagement—to be exact, she had not quite gone so far as to deny it in so many words: being the daughter of a parson, however, she was sufficiently adroit in choosing words which by themselves expressed what was the truth, and could not be regarded as compromising, should it be found out, later on, that they had been the means of promulgating a falsehood. "Every one knows how guarded clergymen can be in this way," said Mrs. Gifford and her friends.

Rosa's exact words, when questioned, were these:—"She said nothing to me about the engagement being broken off."

Oh, yes; Rosa was a staunch friend, but it could do her no good to suggest in this way that the engagement was still unbroken; the whole truth was bound to come out eventually.

Of course, Mrs. Wingfield could not be asked directly if there was any truth in the report. Being a semi-invalid she was rarely at home to any of the Framsby people. But as ten days had passed and her son had not yet returned to the Manor, it might surely be assumed that the lady's story about her son's expedition in search of a new agent was partaking of the character of Rosa Caffyn's statement. Estate agents were not so rare as black swans, they said; a man on the look-out for one could certainly manage to obtain a specimen in less than ten days.

Then there was Farmer Wadhurst; he was a straightforward man and a man of business, and though officially connected with the church, yet without that adroitness at misleading through the medium of verbally accurate phrases, which—according to Framsby's best set—is characteristic of parsons and the members of their families—Mr. Wadhurst might be approached on the subject of his daughters engagement. But Mr. Wadhurst was not easy of approach on social matters, though always ready to talk of "cake." He had his theories regarding this form of confectionery for milch kine, and was always ready to say which breed should take the cake, and in what quantities. But he quickly repelled the approach of such persons as came to congratulate him on the engagement of his daughter—a fact that caused them to wink at their friends and say that that was the right position for a yeoman to take up in respect of his daughter's engagement to the young squire. He was not going to stand congratulations on such a thing. He was an English yeoman and he paid his way, and he wasn't the man to regard an alliance with the Manor as a tremendous thing for him or his daughter either. He knew all about the Wadhursts, and he knew all about the Wingfields, and he wasn't going to truckle down to any Wingfields, or, for that matter, to the Duke himself; no, not he.

This was Farmer Wadhurst. But someone, stimulated by a desire to find out the exact truth, managed to approach him—a tradesman who enjoyed the Gifford custom.

"We haven't seen your young lady about of late, sir," he remarked when the business excuse had been completed. "We hope that she's well, and nothing wrong, sir."

"You could hardly have seen her here, for she's been in Dorset for the past fortnight, and so far as I know she's in good health," said Farmer Wadhurst. But in the act of leaving the shop a thought seemed to occur to him. He turned round, and looked at the tradesman suspiciously.

"What did you mean by that?" he asked.

"Mean by what?"

"By 'nothing wrong'? What do you suspect is wrong?"

The man held up horny hands of protest.

"Bless your heart! Mr. Wadhurst, you musn't take me up like that," he cried. "I meant nought more'n or'nary remark. I'd be the last man in Framsby to hint at ought being wrong; I would indeed, sir, as I hope you know. I've all'ays said that in this case it is the man that's the really lucky one, and I don't care who knows it, Mr. Wadhurst."

Mr. Wadhurst gave a searching glance at the man, and then left the shop. He was not quite satisfied with the explanation which the man had given him of his use of that very ordinary phrase. "Nothing wrong—nothing wrong—we hope there's nothing wrong"—the words buzzed about him all the time he was walking down the High Street. "Nothing wrong!" Why, what could there be wrong? What could there be wrong? What sort of gossip was going about? Who had been saying that anything was wrong?

He went down the street to where his dogcart was waiting for him, and mounting to his seat, drove off in the direction of the farm; but before he had gone more than half a mile along the road he turned his horse about, and drove quickly back to Framsby. He pulled up at the post office, and, descending, entered the place and, after a considerable amount of thought, composed and wrote out a telegram.

Then he mounted his dogcart and drove off to his farm.

CHAPTER XXI

It was barely ten o'clock the next morning when Mrs. Wingfield, telling her maid that she felt that this was going to be one of her good days, got her seat moved out of the shady part of the terrace into the region of the fitful sunlight that had followed a liquid dawn. The day was a grey one, with lazy pacing clouds very high up in the air; and the occasional glimpses of tempered brilliance which the land was allowed between the folds of the billowy vapour, were very grateful to the lady. She had letters and a book and a writing-case.

She had scarcely settled herself down among her cushions before she heard the sound of wheels on the carriage drive—she could not have heard it if her chair had remained on the shady part of the terrace. Then came the sound of a man's voice—imperative—insistent—set off by the murmured replies of the butler. The insistence became more insistent, and the replies louder—more staccato. Then the butler appeared on the terrace.

"Mr. Wadhurst is here, ma'am—says his business is important. I told him that you were not at home to anyone in the morning unless by appointment; but he said it was very important—in fact that he must see you, ma'am. I did my best to put him off——I did indeed, ma'am; it was no use. He's not easy put off. So I said I would see if you would. If not, ma'am, I'll——"

"Certainly I'll see Mr. Wadhurst," said Mrs. Wingfield when the butler had murmured his explanations to her. "Ask him to be good enough to come on the terrace. Draw that cane chair closer."

"Very good, ma'am," said the butler, retiring with dignity and leaving the lady to wonder what Farmer Wadhurst could possibly want with her at that hour of the morning. She had never seen Farmer Wadhurst.

She saw him now. A large man with big bones, a slight stoop and a suggestion of Saxon sandiness about his hair and beard.

She rose to greet him, and the butler once more retired.

"I am very pleased to meet you, Mr. Wadhurst," she said. "I think it is very likely that, if you had not come here to me, I should have ventured to pay you a visit."

"What, have you heard something?" he asked eagerly.

"Heard something? Well, nothing more than your daughter told me, Mr. Wadhurst," she replied. "But, surely, if my son and your daughter have made up their minds, you and I should not turn cold shoulders to them. Priscilla, I know, feels deeply your——"

"Where's your son to-day, ma'am?" cried Farmer Wadhurst, interrupting the gracious words of the lady. "Where is he to-day, and where has he been for the past fortnight?"

"He has been in several places," she replied. "He went to look after an agent—Mr. Dunning has left us—it was very awkward—first to Buckinghamshire, then to Lincoln. I got a letter from him yesterday from Sandy-cliffe; he is having some yachting—a week of yachting. I fancy he saw his chance now that Priscilla is visiting her friend. I don't think he would have been so ready if she——"

"Read that," cried the man, interrupting her once again, laying a telegram—almost flinging it—on the table before her.

"What is this?" she enquired, looking about for her *pince-nez*. "It is a telegram from Jack. What—what—oh, don't tell me that something has happened—that he is hurt—something dreadful—that you were sent to break it to me."

"Read it," he said. "Something dreadful! Maybe not so dreadful to you; not so strange either. You are his mother; you may have heard something like it about him before."

She had found her glasses, and picked up the telegram with shaking fingers.

"*Priscilla no longer here left week yesterday?*"

"What does this mean?" she asked. "She was staying with Miss Branksome at Lullton Priory. Is this from General Branksome?"

"I got wind of something being wrong," said he, "and I telegraphed last evening to the Branksomes asking if she was with them. That's the answer I got. You know what it means. But I warned her. God knows I did my duty by her in warning her against him. She would not listen to me."

"I don't know what you are thinking of. Can you not tell me what it is that is in your mind? You surely do not suppose that Priscilla—that my son——"

"What's in my mind is that your son is a scoundrel, ma'am—that's what's in my mind—a rank, foul scoundrel! He has induced her to run away with him, and for the past week they have been living together as man and wife, wherever he is."

"You lie, sir; I tell you, you lie. My son may have his faults, but he was never a seducer of women."

"Then he has begun now; every wickedness must have a start. He has started with my daughter. I knew that he meant no good. I warned her—God knows that I warned her, not once, but twice—every time that I'd a chance of words with her. It wasn't often of late; she had a way of stalking out of the room every time that I opened my lips to warn her against him."

"Mr. Wadhurst, you are mistaken. I feel certain that you are mistaken," she cried. "What object could he have in carrying out so shocking a scheme? There was no obstacle in the way of their marriage. I had received Priscilla as a daughter."

He smiled. "Mothers know nothing of the ways of their sons," he said. "I've known some that looked on their sons as saints, when all the time——"

"I don't care what you knew," she said. "I know my son, and let me add that I also know your daughter—apparently I know her a good deal better than you ever knew her. Don't behave like a fool Mr. Wadhurst. Don't waste your time in this foolish way—every moment may be precious. Priscilla may have gone to pay another visit; but on the other hand, something may have happened to her. She may be in danger. One reads of such things in the papers, never fancying that they may one day happen to our own friends—in our own families. No time should be lost in making enquiries. I will telegraph to my son, and you may be sure that he will do his best—he will know what should be done. He would be distracted at the thought that she is in danger."

Mr. Wadhurst smiled more bitterly than before. "In danger! She has been in danger from the first moment she set eyes upon him. An evil hour it was—an evil hour. What have I done that these evils should fall upon me?" He had turned away from the lady, and was standing with his hand clenched over the crumpled telegram as if he was addressing the carved satyrs' heads on the stone vases that stood on the piers of the balustrade. "What have I done that these things should happen to me?" He seemed to have an idea that Providence kept books on a proper system of double entry, and every now and again, by the aid of a competent staff of recording angels, posted up the ledgers and struck balances. Farmer Wadhurst could not understand how, if this was done systematically, he should be so badly treated. He believed that he had still a large balance to his credit.

"Don't waste any more time; it may be precious," suggested the lady again; and he turned upon her with an expression of fierceness.

"I'll take your advice," he cried. "I'll not waste any more time. I'll find her—and him—and him. I know where to look for her; wherever he be, she'll be there too. I'll go to her—and him."

"And I'll go with you," she said, rising. "I'll go with you to Sandycliffe, and he will, I know, confide in me. He is certain to know where she is to be found; but if he does not, he will know what should be done. He would be distracted if anything were to happen to her."

He seemed to be startled by the suggestion. He looked at her for several seconds; then his eyes fell.

"You think that I mean to kill him?" he said in a low voice.

"No," she replied. "You would not try to kill him unless you-found them together, and I am confident that they are not together."

"You need not be afraid for him—it is not him that I mean to kill."

"I am afraid neither for him nor for her, Mr. Wadhurst."

"Come, then, if you're not afraid. It's only a two-hour journey to the coast. There's a train in forty minutes from now—no, half an hour from now. I've been here ten minutes. I looked it up. You will catch that train if you mean to come. I'll make sure of it myself."

He spoke almost roughly, and when he had spoken he turned round and strode away. She called to him, begging him to come back, but he paid no attention to her. He seemed anxious to make it plain to her that he refused to recognize the fact that they were acting in concert in this business—to make it plain that he was going for one purpose, and she for quite another. She felt that he was a nasty man—a detestable man. She liked Priscilla not merely because Jack loved her, but also because Priscilla embodied all that she considered admirable in a girl; but now she wished with all her heart that she had never come across her son's track.

She perceived that there was no time to lose if she meant to catch the 10.47 train from Framsby to Gallington Junction, where one changed for Sandycliffe.

She also perceived that it would never do to allow that man to go alone to the place. She was positive that Jack and Priscilla were not together, but she distrusted Mr. Wadhurst. She had no confidence in his powers of deduction or in his self-restraint. She saw as in a picture the meeting between that man and her son—she could hear the irritating words that the former would speak—-the sharp and contemptuous replies of the other— exasperation on both sides, and then perhaps blows—blows or worse.

It would not do to miss that train.

She had set the household moving within a minute or two, and the motor was ordered to be at the door in ten minutes. Her maid was overwhelmed at the very idea of a start like this at a moment's notice. She began to remonstrate, but her mistress was peremptory; and amazed her by the vehemence with which she commanded her to hold her tongue and get out a travelling dress. It was only by much straightforward speaking that the flight was accomplished in good time, and the railway station reached with four minutes to spare. The maid found such a period all too short for the full expression of her grievances in being compelled to start on a journey in her house-dress with a most inappropriate wrap to conceal its true character as far as possible—it was too short a space of time for her purpose, but she certainly did her best.

At first Mrs. Wingfield thought that Mr. Wadhurst had not arrived at the station. He was nowhere to be seen. It was not until the train had come in, and Mrs. Wingfield and her maid had taken their seats, that the man appeared—he had hidden himself in the goods office, utilizing his time by an enquiry regarding some crates of machinery which he expected. He went past the first-class carriages without looking into any compartment. When the change was being made at the junction she failed to see him. But when Sandyclifle was reached she found that he had travelled in a second-class compartment, that was next to her first-class carriage. He took no notice of her, but walked with those long strides of his out of the station in front of her.

He was in a position to take notice of her when she met him face to face coming out of the hotel door when she was at the point of entering.

"Go in and make your enquiries, ma'am," he said grimly. "You will find out whether your opinion or mine of your son is the true one."

"What, is it possible that—that—he—they——"

"They are here. Make your enquiries."

He went away, and she entered the hotel and hastened to the office.

Oh, yes; Mr. Wingfield was staying there, the young lady said.

"Alone?" asked the mother.

"Only Mrs. Wingfield. They will be in for lunch at one. They have been sailing since morning," was the reply.

Mrs. Wingfield could scarcely walk so far as the coffee-room. When she managed to do so, she found that her maid had justified the character she had always borne for thoughtfulness: a slice of cold chicken and a small bottle of dry Ayala were on the table in front of her.

"You must eat and drink now," she said. "This promised to be one of your good days; but that rush to the train and that long journey will go far to make it one of your worst if we are not careful."

Of course the maid knew, as did every one at the Manor, of the ridiculous visit of Farmer Wadhurst, and she was one of the few who guessed rightly what was its purport. She was fully aware of all that was meant by this breathless flight to the coast, and, as she had had something like forty years' experience of the world and the wickedness of men and the credulity of women and the ambiguity of the word Love, she had never for a moment doubted what would be the issue of this journey. It was not at all necessary for Mrs. Wingfield to say to her, as she did while the champagne was creaming in the glass:

"Walters, Mr. Wingfield is here, and I have just learned that Miss Wadhurst is here also—you saw Mr. Wadhurst and you will know, I am sure, that it would never do for them to meet."

"It must be prevented at any cost, ma'am," acquiesced Walters. "Where's Mr. Wingfield and Miss Wadhurst just now?"

"They are out sailing; they will be here for lunch at one. It is necessary that I should meet them."

"Quite so, ma'am. It's a pity; but you'll do it. This is one of your good days. To-morrow will most likely be one of your worst. But it can't be helped."

"It cannot be helped. If I were to fail to meet them before—before anyone else can meet them—there would be no more good days for me in the world, Walters."

"Drink the champagne, ma'am, and rest quite still for half an hour and you'll be able to do it without risk."

Mrs. Wingfield obeyed her. She took some mouthfuls of the chicken and then drank two glasses of the champagne. Her maid had spied a comfortable chair overlooking the tennis lawns close at hand and the sea in the distance. To this she led Mrs. Wingfield, and there she left her with a wrap about her knees, to wait for her anxious half-hour.

The day was less grey at Sandyclifife than it had been at the Manor, and certainly the air was cooler. A breeze was blowing shorewards, bearing in every breath the sweet salt smell of the Channel. It came very gratefully to that poor weary lady sitting there waiting for what the next hour should bring to her.

But what could it bring to her except disaster? The man had told her that he had no intention of making an attempt to punish her son; but what did it matter about the man or his intentions? It was not the consequences of the act that troubled her, it was the sin of the act.

The thought that a son of hers—her only son—should be guilty of anything so base, so cruel, so mean, so selfish, made her feel sadder than she would have felt had the news been brought to her that he was dead.

She felt that so long as she lived there would cling to her the consciousness that she had brought into the world a son who had been guilty of an act of vice which she could never condone. That was what her whole future would be—clouded with that consciousness, when she had been hoping so much that was good for the days to come.

And then, like every other good woman who is a mother of sons whose feet have strayed from the straight road, she began to think if she had any reason to reproach herself for his lapse. Had anything that she had said or done led up to his commission of the baseness? Was she to be reproached because of the ease with which she had withdrawn whatever distaste she had at first felt for the idea of his wishing to marry a girl who was not socially in his own rank of life? Surely not. If she had opposed his wishes as so many other mothers would have done, she might find reason for some self-reproach; but she had been kind and sympathetic and had taken the girl to her heart; and yet this was how he had shown his appreciation of her kindness—of her ridding herself of every prejudice that she might reasonably have had in regard to his loving of a girl situated as Priscilla was. This was how he was rewarding her!

The impression of which she was conscious at that moment was only one of disappointment—supreme disappointment—such disappointment as one may feel at the end of one's life on finding out that the object for which one has lived and laboured from the beginning to the end is absolutely worthless. She felt sad, not angry. She felt that if her son were to appear before her she could weep, but she could not denounce him.

While she sat there thinking over the whole matter, her tears began to fall before she became aware of it; and it was while she was holding her handkerchief to her eyes that they came up, her son and Priscilla, walking across the springy turf of the lawn so that she heard no sound of their approach.

When she removed all the tears that a handkerchief can remove—it only touches the outward ones—they were standing before her.

She did not cry out; she did not start. She only looked at them and turned away her head.

"Speak to her," said he in a low voice, and he too turned away his face from the accusation of his mother's tears.

Priscilla took a step forward and knelt before her, leaning across her knees with caressing arms about her waist.

"You will forgive us, dearest mother," she said. "You will forgive me because I did it out of love for him, and you will forgive him because he did it out of love for me. Whichever of us is most to blame you will forgive the most because that one is the one that loved the most."

The mother looked down at the lovely thing that pressed against her knees. She laid a hand upon her shoulder, and at the touch the girl's eyes became full of tears. The other felt them warm on the hand that she was pressing to her lips.

There was a long silence.

"Mother," he said at last, for he noticed that some of the guests of the hotel were strolling about the further edge of the lawn, and they might choose to enter the dining-room by the French window that opened behind his mother's chair. "Mother, you will not blame either of us. We had both the same feeling that we should make sure of such happiness as we saw awaiting us lest it should be snatched from us by that malignant Fate which delights to spoil a man's prospects when they seem brightest. That was why I forced Priscilla to marry me on the sly."

"I knew that you would detest the very name of a registrar, and I could never bring myself to face the ceremony in the church," said Priscilla. "But indeed I will be as good a daughter to you as if the Church had had a voice in the ceremony. Bless me, even me also, O my mother, and our marriage will be blessed."

Then the mother fell on her neck, kissing her, and saying:

"It is I who have to ask your forgiveness, dear. I cannot tell you what—I thought—base—base! Oh, my darling, you have made me so happy; you did what was right. I will never accuse you again."

She was looking up smiling through her tears as she held out a hand to her son.

"I knew that you would not be like other women," he said. "You are the best woman in the world—the best mother that a man with a mind for wickedness could have. You don't know all that you have kept me out of. But why did you come to us to-day, mother? Did you suspect—great Gloriana! Here's your father, Priscilla. A regular family party—what!" Mrs. Wingfield the elder laughed quite spitefully—quite triumphantly as Mr.

Wadhurst hurried across the lawn. He had spent half an hour on the beach waiting for the approach of a yacht that was standing off and on in the light breeze. He could not know that the hotel people had made a mistake and that Mr. and Mrs. Wingfield had not left the shore.

He was hurrying across the lawn, and on his face there was a look which his daughter was able to interpret. That was why she spoke before he had time to utter a word.

"Father," she said, "I don't think that you ever met my husband, though I daresay you know him by sight as well as he knows you. Jack, this is my father."

He looked at her and then at him. His mouth was very tightly closed. He stood quite a yard away from them and ignored Jack's very cordial salutation.

"You must forgive these light-headed young people, Mr. Wadhurst," said Mrs. Wingfield the elder. "But it was really very naughty of them to take the law into their own hands and get married by a registrar instead of going properly to the church."

"Married!" said the churchwarden. "Married within three months of the death of her husband! You did well to do it in that hole-and-corner way; for you knew me too well to hope that I would give my consent."

"That's quite true," said she. "But I told you long ago that I had made up my mind that a woman's marriage is her own affair, not her father's. I had one experience of the union that receives the blessing of the father and the blessing of the Church."

He looked at her. His mouth was tightly shut once again.

"Look here, Mr. Wadhurst," cried Jack. "We're just going in to lunch. If you didn't give your consent to our marriage, you have still time to give us your blessing. Hurry up. The lobsters in the dining-room will be becoming anxious."

He still kept his eyes fixed upon his daughter. He did not seem to hear Jack speaking. But the moment that Jack had said his last word, Mr. Wadhurst glanced at him, and then, turning round, walked straight across the lawn.

They watched him in silence until he became occulted by the pavilion.

"The lobsters will be getting impatient," said Jack, helping his mother to her feet.

CHAPTER XXII

Another delightful week elapsed, with yacht cruises and adventures by flood and field, and then Priscilla, never giving herself up with such complete abandonment to the intoxication of the first month of marriage as to be incapable of observing the changes of time and temper and temperature—the variations in the pulse of that little spiritual animal known by the pet name of Love, began to perceive that Jack was thinking about home; and that meant that she had been wholly successful in her treatment of that happiness of his which demanded the wisest nursing, with a mental chart of its variations from day to day. Women who are wise adopt the modern system of therapeutics, and devote all their thought to the nursing of that happiness which has been entrusted to their care when it is still in its cradle, and do not trouble about the Pharmacopoeia. It had been her aim to lead him to think about his home—their home—as that was where she meant him to spend most of his time; and the wife who can keep her husband's attention most closely directed to home is the wisest as well as the happiest. The accountants who were going over the books of the estate, kept in a culpably slovenly way by Mr. Dunning, were, he was informed, approaching the end of their labours; and the new agent, who had been found with really only a reasonable amount of difficulty, was by the side of the accountants and the stewards and the bailiffs, mastering the details of the old system, which had been far from systematic, and, as Jack and Priscilla could see by his letters, instituting a new *regime* on a proper basis.

This was satisfactory; but Priscilla could see that the establishment of routine did not greatly interest her husband. He was imaginative, though no one but herself had suspected it, and she meant that he should have something to appeal to his imagination. Even before they had been married she had seen some splendid possibilities in connection with the trout stream that flowed through the glen, though at that time she had not so much as hinted at them; but now she felt that she could do so with good effect if the opportunity should arise; and when an imaginative young woman is on the look-out for an opportunity, the opportunity invariably presents itself. A letter from Mrs. Wingfield mentioned the services of a new footman who had succeeded in putting out a fire—the result of a lamp accident in the still-room and a housemaid's carelessness. Owing to the exertions of the man and the training which he had received at his last place, the fire had done very little injury; but if it had not been dealt with in time the Manor House would certainly have been done for, said the letter.

"Confound those lamps! That's the third fire within two years, and all through those antiquated abominations," cried Jack.

"Sell them for scrap metal, and trust to electric light," said Priscilla in a second.

"Who is to pay for a cable from Gallingham—nine miles?" he enquired.

"No one, my dear. There is no need to go so far or to spend so much money, when you have that lovely cascade going to waste in Primrose Dell."

"What has the cascade to do with it, my girl? I wasn't talking about a fire engine; though with these lamps——"

"With some elementary engineering and a simple dynamo you can make an electric installation for the house, and stables, and yard, and farm, and gardens, that will cost you little more than the wages of one man—say, twenty-five shillings a week."

"Make it thirty."

"Well, thirty. Mind you, you will be able to put stoves in all the bedrooms, and you will be able to run machinery for pumping water, for cleaning harness, for churning, for brushing your hair, if you wish for it."

"I don't wish for it for brushing my hair, but I do for everything else. Is this a dream of yours, my girl, or have you been reading a pictorial advertisement?"

"I went into the question two years ago, hoping that we might be able to introduce electric power on the farm; but unhappily we have no stream of water to work the dynamo and it would not pay to use coal; we might as well use the coal energy direct. I went so far into the matter as to visit a place where a private installation had been made, and my eyes were opened."

He gazed at her admiringly in silence for some time. Then he cried:

"Great Gloriana! You are a bit of a wonder, Priscilla! You carry me off my feet; and the worst of it is that I feel I must do everything that you suggest. If I try to look the other way I see something that sends me back to you. I'm like the master mariner whose adventures worried us at school—in trying to avoid what's its name, he fell on the other—you know."

"Scylla and Charybdis?"

"That's it—Scylla—in my case, Priscilla and Charybdis. Priscilla and Charybdis—that's how I am. But by the living shrimp, you're a wonder!

Where can I get any books that will go into the business? I suppose the dynamo people are those to apply to in the first place. But I know nothing worth talking about of electricity."

"What is there to know about such a simple adaptation of it as is necessary for our purpose? I assure you that the sparking of your motor is a thousand times more complicated, and you know all about that. Long ago people thought that to be an electrical engineer enough to light up a house required years of training, and people's sons were to become electrical engineers instead of being doctors or lawyers; but now they are only something between plumbers and gasfitters. Isn't that so?"

"By the living shrimp! we'll have the whole place in a blaze before the winter," She lay back and laughed at his enthusiasm and the unfortunate way in which it led him to prophesy.

"I hope it will not be quite so bad as that," she said. For the next three or four days he could talk of little else than the electrification of the Manor. She explained to him the way in which the course of the stream could be diverted at a trifling cost and at the sacrifice of none of the picturesqueness of the place of primroses.

"I would not have a primrose interfered with," she cried. "The Primrose Dell is a sacred place."

"I will take steps to have it incorporated on our coat of arms," he said. "And I will see that it has a special motto to itself. Yes 'Priscilla and Charybdis.' Oh! we mustn't spoil the primroses. If it hadn't been for them where should I be to-day? What should I be to-day?" And then some of the books arrived, and with his usual aptitude for picking up new ideas, he mastered all the essentials to the schemes which Priscilla had initiated.

But before he had quite made up his mind as to the most suitable part of the stream to touch, something occurred which interfered materially with the development of his plans; for one morning he got a telegram signed "Franklin Forrester," enquiring if he could be seen at 2.30 that day. "Very important."

"What the mischief!" he exclaimed. "How does he know that I'm here? What can Franky Forrester want with me that's very important?"

"Who is Franky Forrester?" asked Priscilla.

"Oh! Franky Forrester was one of the chaps who just escaped being sent down at Oxford when I enjoyed that distinction," he replied. "Franky was a little too sharp for the powers. He had a genius for organizing; and that's how he got through. He could organize a row with any man, but it was invariably part of his organization that he should be outside the row when it was going on. He has made his way in the world by the exercise of his genius. I saw him in London a few months ago. He is still organizing things—politics, I believe he said, What can he want with me?"

"Money," suggested Priscilla. "I have heard that funds are the soul of politics, if principles are the body."

"He'll get no money out of me," said Jack. "But somehow I don't think that it's money he wants. I suppose I had better see him. He is a nice chap and well connected. He never loses sight of a man that's well off or that's likely to be well off."

"That's the art of organization in a nutshell," said she. "I suppose it is," he said. "Anyhow, the phrase is a good one. There are a lot of good phrases knocking about; it's a pity that so many of them are in nutshells—some of them are hard to crack. Franky was great at phrases. You always needed to carry a pair of nutcrackers in your pocket when he was in the offing. I wonder how he heard that I was here."

"I suppose you will see him, Jack. He says 'very important.'"

"Yes; but he doesn't say whether it's important to me or to himself. Oh, yes, I suppose I must see him." Although Priscilla did not think that he had reached that period of honeymoon delight when a man is ready to welcome the arrival of a friend, or even an enemy, she was still pleased that a new element was entering into their communion. She had a strange longing to be presented to some of his friends, and to hear him say:

"I want to introduce you to my wife, old chap. She's dying to know you."

And she was gratified shortly after lunch that day; for those were the very words he employed when making her known to Mr. Franklin Forrester.

She saw by the expression of the visitor's face when he looked at her that he was both surprised and pleased.

"He is appraising my value as a possible asset to a political party," she said to herself; and that was precisely what Mr. Forrester was doing.

He was a well-made and rather good-looking man, with a Vandyck beard, inclined to fairness. He had a moderate supply of hair on the front of his head and he made praiseworthy, and on the whole successful, attempts to conceal the fact that it was becoming rather thin on the top. His eyes would possibly have been accounted good had he ever given anyone a chance to see them long enough to form an opinion upon them. As it was, most people saw them only long enough to see that they were restless. Still, Jack's wife had managed to interpret the general expression of his face pretty accurately.

"And now maybe you'll tell me how you got my address here," said Jack, when they had said a few words about Sandycliffe and how it was being developed. Mr. Forrester knew who was most interested in its development, and how the hotel shares had been worked off.

"I sent a wire to Elliot—you know Compton Elliot—at Framsby to find out if you were at home. I believe that it was from Mrs. Wingfield, your mother, that he got your present location. Useful man, Compton Elliot," said Mr. Forrester.

"Yes, infernally useful," assented Jack.

"My dear Wingfield, you may be sure that I would not have thrust myself upon you at this—this—this interesting time if I could have avoided it," cried the visitor. "At the same time, I must honestly confess that I'm rather glad to find you so circumstanced———"

"Gloriana! What a word—'circumstanced'!" murmured Jack.

"Well, I mean that I'm pleased to be able to make an appeal to you in the presence of some one who will, I am sure, advise you to listen to me, and not condemn me without thinking the whole matter over."

"Isn't he artful?" said Jack. "He has just killed a political opponent and he is about to appeal to my better nature not to give him away. He knows that women are invariably on the side of the criminal. Go on, F. F."

"Mrs. Wingfield, I ask you if this isn't ungenerous on the part of your husband. Here I have come down from the intoxicating pleasure of the London season solely to ask this man to become a member of Parliament, and this is how he receives my proposition."

Mr. Franklin Forrester had very rarely to be so straightforward as he was in this speech. As a matter of fact, his resources in this particular direction were so limited that he found it absolutely necessary to economise them; and the general opinion that prevailed among his political opponents was that he was very successful in his exercise of this form of thrift. But his excuse to himself for having resorted to an unaccustomed figure of speech was that this was an exceptional case that demanded exceptional treatment.

He had been straightforward almost to a point of abruptness, and he perceived that the end had justified the means: Jack Wingfield was voiceless and gasping, and Mrs. Wingfield was silent and flushing.

He saw what manner of woman she was—yes, up to a certain point. He saw that she was far more appreciative of a compliment paid to her husband than her husband was; and he also saw that she was more anxious for her husband's advancement than her husband was.

He had rendered them speechless; and he knew that that was the prehistoric method of woman-capture; and that up to the present a more effective method has not been devised by the wit of man. Stun them, and there you are.

He felt that he had captured Mrs. Wingfield. She had flushed with surprise and delight. He had heard all about her from his useful friend, Compton Elliot, of Framsby. She was a farmer's daughter, and having played her cards well, she had married a man with a fine property and not too rigid a backbone. She was sure to be ambitious to achieve a further step—one that should carry her away from the associations of the farm into the centre of London society—for the greater part of the year.

That was what Mr. Franklin Forrester's analysis of the situation amounted to. It was not quite accurate; but there was something in it.

He had not expected the farmer's daughter of Compton Elliot's confidential report to have so pleasing a personality. He had rather visions of a stoutish young woman with an opulent bust and dark eyes, combined with a knowledge of how to use them. But the difference between his ideal and the real lady did not cause him to change the plan of attack which he had arranged for her capture.

"Now the murder's out," he said, looking not at Jack, but at Jack's wife. "We want a good man who will make a good fight for Nuttingford, and we believe that we can hold the seat."

"Then why the mischief didn't you go to a good man?" enquired Jack.

Mr. Forrester smiled. He did not tell him that he had already approached two very good men; and that, being shrewd as well as good—politically good, which represents a condition that is possibly not quite the same as ethically good—they had shaken their heads and told him to go on to the next street.

No. Mr. Franklin Forrester regarded those communications as strictly confidential; he did not think it necessary to allude to them.

"I have come to the right man, if I know anything of the Nuttingford division," was what he did say; "and I think I know something of the Nuttingford division," he added.

"I don't doubt it; but you don't know quite so much about the man you've come to, or you wouldn't have come," suggested Jack. Then he glanced at his wife, and Mr. Forrester noted that glance with great interest.

"It's because I know you, my friend, better than you know yourself—I won't say better than Mrs. Wingfield knows you—that I have come to you," said the politician. "You are the sort of man that we want—that the country wants."

"Oh, I say, why drag in the poor old country by the hair of the head? It's almost indecent," remonstrated Jack, and once again he glanced at his wife. She smiled back at him, but spoke not a word. She was a wise woman. A wise woman is one who has a great deal to say and remains silent.

"You are the man that's wanted at this time," resumed Forrester. "By the way, what are your politics?"

"What politics do you want?" asked Jack. "I fancy that if I were to stand I could accommodate you; but I shan't."

"You're the man for us. Most of us inherit our politics with the family Bible and our grandfather's clock, and we rarely change them, unless, like our young Zimri—the unsuccessful Zimri—we are at the tail end of a Parliament, and are certain that there will be a change of government in the next—a change of government has usually meant a change of politics with the family of our aspiring Zimri. His father was the successful Zimri, but he didn't have peace; and the founder of the family elevated Zimriism to a fine art—he didn't have peace either—on the contrary, he had a wife. All things are possible with such men; but I don't care what your politics are; we'll put you in for Nuttingford, if you'll agree to stand."

"This is rot, Forrester, and you know it. What good shall I be in your House of Commons? What good shall I be to your blessed Party anyway?"

Mr. Forrester could quite easily have answered this question, had it been prudent to do so. He could have told him that he was wanted by the Party because there was a difficulty with two men, each of whom believed that he had a right to the reversion of the seat, and would certainly contest it in view of the other coming forward. In such a case the seat would undoubtedly be seized by the solitary representative of the Other Party. But Mr. Forrester perceived that such an explanation would occupy a good deal of valuable time; and he wished to spare his friend and his friend's charming wife an acquaintance with details which possibly a man, and certainly a woman, looking into the arena of politics from a private box, might regard as sordid. So he merely laid his hand on his friend's knee, and said:

"Leave that to us, my dear Wingfield. You may be sure that we would not take you up unless we saw that you could do something for us that would pay us for our trouble. Now, don't you decide against us in a hurry.

Talk the matter over with Mrs. Wingfield. I wouldn't give much for a man who didn't take his wife into his confidence on such important things."

"And how much would you give for a man who did, and then decided by her advice against you?" asked Jack.

"The constituency is a peculiar one," said Forrester, ignoring the question. "They hate politics. If we were to send them a well-known politician he would have no chance with them. What they want is a man like yourself—a simple ordinary, everyday, good-wearing English gentleman—plain commonsense—that's what they want; nothing very definite in the way of a programme; they don't want a windbag or a gasometer; they're not going in for air ships at Nuttingford. You know what Cotton is?"

"Cotton? Who the mischief is Cotton that I should know of him?"

"That's the best proof of the accuracy of what I've been telling you. Cotton is the man who has sat for the constituency for the past fifteen years, and yet nobody has heard of him."

"And why shouldn't he continue in the obscurity of the House of Commons for another fifteen years? Nobody wants him outside, I suppose."

"He has been ordered off by his doctor, and he is applying for the Chiltern Hundreds at once. He will mention your name in his valedictory address, and we'll do the rest—that is, of course—you know what I mean?"

"Blest if I do, quite!"

"Oh, I mean that having provided them with the right man for them—the man they want—we'll see that they are loyal to you."

"'Wingfield and the Old Cause'—that'll be the war cry, I suppose. You'll have to coach me on the old cause—only there'll be no need, for I haven't the remotest idea of standing. I'm going in for a big electric scheme, Forrester, and I'll have no time for politics."

"I refuse to take your answer now. I should be doing you a grave injustice. I didn't except you to jump at my offer before it was well out of my lips. Heavens, man! a seat in the House of Commons——"

"Mother of Parliaments, and the rest."

"You needn't sneer. I tell you it's a position that carries weight with it. I don't wonder that it's so coveted. Men spend thousands of pounds trying to reach it—thousands of pounds and years of their life."

"I'm not one of them, Forrester. Don't look angrily at me because other men make such fools of themselves."

"I won't, Wingfield, because I know that you won't make a fool of yourself by refusing this offer. But I have said my last word of encouragement. After all, you know best what will suit you. It would be an impertinence on my part to suggest that you are not competent to decide for yourself. Don't be in a hurry. Now, what about this electrical scheme?"

CHAPTER XXIII

Not one word had Priscilla uttered while that artful Mr. Forrester was talking to her husband, and, incidentally, giving her many opportunities for expressing her views either in accordance with or in divergence from those he expounded so fluently. Her silence surprised their visitor. He thought his friend Jack Wingfield an extremely lucky chap to have married a wife who knew when to be silent and was very generous in her time limit on this point.

He was all the more amazed when he found that she was quite capable of expressing herself on such subjects as the future of electricity and the novels of Anatole France, with originality and distinction. A farmer's daughter, was she? Well, all that he could say was that agriculture, which was laid on mankind as part of a Bible Curse scheme, and which has been the subject of a pretty fair amount of reprobation within recent years, deserved a good word if this young woman had come into the world under its auspices.

But he took a leaf out of her book—one of the blank pages—one that had no word upon it—and went away, without another reference to the subject of his mission to the developing seaside resort.

When he had gone, Jack suggested a stroll along the beach, and she picked up her hat in a moment Among her most artful perfections was her readiness to move at a moment's notice. She was at all times prepared for everything. She never kept her husband waiting while she went to her room for a hat or coat.

Of course he began to talk immediately of the possibility of Sandycliffe's becoming developed out of all recognition of its charm. It was jolly rum, he thought, how places like that come and go. One year a place was the solitary right one to go to, and the next it was among the places that should never be so much as visited by anyone who wished to be thought anything; and such people were becoming more numerous every day.

She agreed with him. She wondered if there were any people in the right set who decreed which watering-places on the coast should be visited, and which left alone, just as the best set in Framsby decreed in regard to persons.

This was very interesting, of course, but she knew that he had not asked her to walk with him solely to discuss the vicissitudes of coasts towns. Still, they had gone on for quite half a mile before they had exhausted the topic, and seated themselves on one of the new chairs on the end of the concrete path. Even then he did not speak about Mr. Forrester and his mission for some time. At last he said casually:

"What brought that chap down to me to-day, do you fancy?"

"He came to you because he knows that you are the sort of member that the Nuttingford people want," she replied with the utmost promptitude.

"Bless my heart and soul! Why should they be such fools? You mustn't believe all that old F. F. tells you, my girl."

"All? I don't think that he could induce me to believe a quarter of what he says," she replied. "But I'm positive that he believes you would have a better chance of being elected than anyone who is likely to come forward. What I felt from the first moment that he broached the subject was that he and his Party are somehow in a tight place in regard to the Nuttingford division. It occurred to me that someone whom they expected to come forward had thrown them over, and for some reason or other he thought that he might fall back on you. I wouldn't go as far as to say that he expects you to win, but he expects you to make a good show for the Party on the day of the election; and so you will, Jack, only you'll be at the head of the poll." He jumped up from the seat as if he had been stung by a wasp.

"What do you mean?" he cried after a long pause, which he utilized in collecting himself. "Do you mean to think for a moment that I would make such a fool of myself as to go among strange people for the sake of getting a licking at a cost of a thousand pounds or so?"

"My dearest boy, I want you to go in for this business if only for the sake of showing that clever, far-seeing man that you're not quite such a fool as he fancies."

"The best way I could do that would be by laughing at him as I did."

"There's a better way still: take him at his word—a little better than his word—and amaze him by getting returned. He doesn't believe that you could get returned for the division, but he thinks, as I said, that you will make a good fight for it. Now you must pull yourself together and fight every ounce there's in you. Jack, you *must* do it, out of compliment to me."

"Look here, my girl, you are making a man of me—I know that. Didn't I call you my guardian—my good angel—once upon a time? Well, so you are—so you showed yourself to be; but are you not going ahead with me a little too fast?"

She rose from the seat and put her arm within one of his arms.

"Let us stroll on a little farther," she said.

"I don't like it," he said. "Just beyond that iron railing there is the cliff and some horrid rocks below. If we walk on through that railing we shall come a cropper among the rocks. See?"

"I see your very apt allegory. Jack, if you don't want me to urge you to go in heart and soul for this business, you made a grave error in that last remark of yours. Jack, the man who could turn the topographical condition of a place into a forcible argument and a picturesque one into the bargain, is the man to convince a constituency that they badly want him to represent them in Parliament."

"You're hustling me, Priscilla. I repeat that you're hustling me, and I'm beginning to be mortally afraid of you."

"You needn't be afraid of me. I'm not so stupid as to want to hustle you. I'm not such an idiot as to start life with you by trying on a system of nagging. In my eyes you'll always be the man with the *bâton*, and I'll always be ready to play any tune that you beat time to. If I urge you all that I can to do something, and you refuse to do it, don't fancy for a moment that I'll dissolve in tears or get a hump or say, 'You wouldn't take my advice,' when you come to grief through having your own way. I promise you that I'll do none of these things. You're the man and I'm your helpmeet. Heaven forbid that I should ever try to make my opinions take the place of yours; but heaven forbid also, that, having opinions, I should keep them to myself."

"Amen to that, say I."

"All that I can do is to lay them at your feet, Jack, and—no, that's too humble altogether: I won't lay them at your feet, I'll try to make them look their best in front of you, and if you like them you can adopt them as your own. That's all that I can do. You'll find that I know my place, dear."

"I see that you do; you know it a deal better than you know mine, if you fancy that my place is on a leather bench in the House of Commons."

"Maybe you're right, Jack; but what an experience to one is an election campaign! I've been longing all my life to be so placed that I should be able to go through an election fight—not a hollow thing, mind you, but a splendid tingling close fight. That's the thing that develops whatever character one may have—whatever strength one may have within one. The only way by which a man can be made a man of is by a fight."

He looked at her and laughed.

"And you're determined to make a man of me, are you?" he said; "by a fight—an election fight? Well, that's all very fine; but supposing I should win, where would we be then?"

"In the House of Commons, ready to carry the fight into the enemy's country; and that's where you'll be as sure as you take off your coat—and you *will* take off your coat, Jack."

"And my waistcoat, if necessary. And what am I to fight for? I've no definite opinions about anything in politics."

"You begin by defining your opinions, and you'll very soon find out how definite they are. But don't you bother about opinions; the fight's the thing that matters. Any excuse for a fight is valid."

"You have a drop of Irish blood in you somewhere, my girl. Upon my word you have almost persuaded me to say 'Agreed' to Forrester's proposal. But mind you, if I get in I'll blame you. Let there be no mistake about that."

She took a hasty glance around. She saw the strategical conditions of their surroundings. She thought that when they should get a step or two beyond the little peninsula of sea wall, she could do it.... And she did. She had an arm about his neck in a moment, and he felt delightfully near strangulation. He could not cry out for help, because there were two middle-aged ladies with books and a clergyman with *The Guardian* on the seat in the hollow of the cliff.

"You are a perfect darling!" she cried. "You are doing this thing just to please me, because you know I have set my heart on it—and I *have* set my heart on it, Jack, dear. I admit that I am ambitious, Jack, but only for you, dear—only because I know what there is in you, and I want it brought out. I want people to accept you at your true worth. My ambition is bounded by you."

He did not say anything in response to this confession. But he pressed her arm very close to him, and so they walked on in silence, until he said:

"My girl, my girl, shall I tell you what I feel just now? I feel that I should like to do something to justify your belief in me. Until you began to talk to me I used to be inclined to grin at those old chaps who used to bump about in armour—Lord! the noise they made must have been like a tinker's horse running away with a cartload of tin kettles—looking out for doughty deeds to do so that they might appear big Indians in the eyes of their ladies fair. They spelt—such of them as could spell, and there weren't a lot—'lady' with an e at the end. I say I used to laugh at them and think them howling bounders; but by the Lord Henrietta! since I came to know you I've had just the same feeling. I tell you that I should dearly like to do something big, so that you might be able to say, 'He did it, and he's my husband, and it was I taught him how.'"

"And you will do it—I have no fear for you, Jack. You will show people what you can do, and I shall feel—I may boast of it, too—that I have had an influence for good upon you, not for evil."

"If anybody wants to hear further of what that influence has been to me, send them along, and I'll tell them. My dear girl, you've now set me a job of work to do, and if you stand by me I'll do it."

"I'll stand by you, Jack; I've no interest in life except to stand by you. If I wasn't quite sure that you'll be a success in the fight to get into Parliament, and a still bigger success when you get in, I shouldn't say a word to urge you on to this job. But I know enough of you to be sure that there's no one in the House of Commons who has a greater capacity than you for grasping the practical side of things, and seeing the rights and the wrongs in every question. Of course you may say that I don't know all the members of the House of Commons and that I don't know so much about you, if it comes to that."

"Well, I admit that something like that did occur to me."

"I daresay it did. But don't you think that I'm going to retract anything that I said on that account. I'm not. I've read the newspapers like a student for the past four years, and I've read you like—like a lover for the past two months. These respective times are quite long enough to enable me to pronounce the definite judgment that I did in making my comparison. Oh, Jack, I can see quite well that people won't have oratory at any price, in these days. What they want is men like you, who will say in common language—colloquial language—what they think. After all, the great thing is the thinking and the doing; the talking is quite a secondary consideration. Goodness! Here have I been making a long speech to prove to you that there's no use for speech-makers nowadays."

"You have spoken good sense and to the point, my girl, and that's more than can be said of the majority of orators. Well, I've taken on a big contract, and you've promised to see me through with it. All that we've got to do now is to search for principles to take the place of politics. Have you any outline in your mind at present?"

"Not even the most shadowy."

"That's satisfactory. We don't start on this campaign with any foolish prejudices in favour of one thing or another. We can be all things to all men in the Nuttingford division of Nethershire."

"And to all women—don't forget the women. I look to them to make a strong muster on our side."

"Whatever our side may be."

CHAPTER XXIV

It was in this happy spirit that they approached Mr. Franklin Forrester the next day, Jack having had a chat with him through the telephone.

Mr. Forrester was delighted—at his own sagacity in playing his hand so as to win Mrs. Wingfield to his side. He took care to make his principals aware of his sagacity in this particular, and they also were delighted. They smiled, of course, at the suggestion that the seat might be taken by his friend Wingfield, but he would come forward and contest it in their interest, and that was something. People, especially those of the opposition, must not get it into their heads that The Party could not put a man into the field to oppose Lawford, who would, of course, win the seat, but not so easily as he expected—not so easily as to reflect seriously upon the resources of The Party who were running Wingfield.

That was the way the leaders of the organization to which Forrester belonged looked at the candidature of Wingfield. And the way Forrester himself looked at it was that the fact of his being able to bring Wingfield up to the scratch—that was his metaphor in referring to his success—would raise him to the extent of another rung in the political ladder which he had set himself to climb some years before, and up which he had already made a creditable ascent.

One thing he saw clearly, and that was that his candidate's having married the daughter of a farmer—not a gentleman farmer nor an amateur farmer, but a farmer, and a farmer, too, who was well known to make his business pay—was a distinct point in his favour. It would assuredly be accounted to him for righteousness by a constituency like Nuttingford, which was so largely agricultural.

He mentioned this to Jack, who, he found, was fully alive to the importance of making every legitimate use of this claim upon the electorate. So far as he could make out, it was the solitary claim which he had to their attention, and this made him value it all the more highly. He delighted Mr. Forrester by the ease with which he showed himself ready to adapt himself to circumstances and circumstances to his candidature. Most high class men, Mr. Forrester's experience had shown him, had been at first inclined to take a very high tone on approaching a constituency, striking the attitude of a patriot or a philanthropist and assuring him that if they could not be returned solely on their own merits without such adventitious aids as family interests or business interests or the interest which attaches to an interesting wife, they would much prefer not to be returned at all. Such high-toned men very soon got such nonsense knocked out of them. One of them, who was the father of two little girls with lovely eyes, had the mortification of seeing his antagonist romp in ahead of him solely because he had appeared every morning on the balcony of the hotel carrying on his shoulder a flaxen-curled little boy in a Little Lord Fauntleroy suit, though he had only borrowed the child for the election.

"What did the crowds outside the hotel care whether the boy was his or not?" cried Mr. Forrester. "They gave him their votes; and there was the other man thrown out, though he might have played off his two lovely little girls against the borrowed brat with every chance of success. Oh, children are simply thrown away upon superior men like that!"

But Wingfield showed himself superior to such ridiculous affectations of superiority and high-tonedness. He knew enough about practical politics to be aware of the affinity of the cult to the pastry industry of the roadside. To attain success in the making of mud pies one must not be over-careful of one's hands. There is no making mud pies without mud, and there is no dabbling in politics if you mean to devote your best energies to the culture of lilies—not the speckled variety nor even the golden, but the pure saint of flowerland, the snow-white sort.

Of this fact Jack Wingfield was well aware, so he did not resent—certainly not openly—Mr. Forrester's advice: "You must run your wife's connection with farming for all that it's worth."

"And it's worth a good deal," assented the candidate. "Yes, we'll rub it in, never fear."

And Priscilla also showed herself to be quite alive to the value of this connection.

"I'll give a practical lesson daily on 'How to make farming pay,'" she cried. "I'll take care that he has not a monopoly of the farm in his speeches."

"Oh! those speeches are what I dread," groaned Jack. "Psha! you've no idea how simple this part of it is," said Mr. Forrester. "All you've got to do is to get well grounded on about half a dozen topics and speak all you know of all of them at every meeting. Don't on any account commit anything to memory, for so long as you don't make use of the same words no one will recognize any sameness or repetition in what you say. I'll take care that you have a proper number of repartees made out for you upon every occasion. These will be typewritten on slips of paper, and placed in order on the table in front of you, so that when the conscientious objectors, for whom we will arrange, ask you their questions from the body of the hall or the gallery, you will have nothing to do but glance at the repartee before you and repeat it with whatever inflection you may think necessary. Only you mustn't forget to turn down each repartee when you have delivered it, or you'll find yourself at sea."

"I can easily believe that," said the candidate.

"And then we shall have to arrange for an effective interruption now and again. But your appeal for the man to be allowed to remain and your joke on the matter will also be typewritten in front of you. Some men prefer to commit the joke to memory, but it's never safe to do this. Oh, you'll have no trouble when once you get into the stride of the thing."

"I'll do my best to accommodate my faltering steps to its majestic swing," said Jack. "This is a nice business I'm learning, Priscilla," he added, turning to his wife.

"It's the most interesting game ever invented—so much is clear to me," said she. "It's the game of musical chairs on a heroic scale. You face the music, and the moment it stops you make a struggle for a seat, and if you don't mind a little rough-and-tumble business you'll get your seat, Jack—I see that clearly."

This coaching took place during the first day or two after Jack's announcement of his decision. And then he went off with Priscilla to the town of Nuttingford to make the acquaintance of the local organization of The Party, and to be grounded on all local questions, so that the soundness of his views on these points might never be open to suspicion. Then at the right moment the member for the division, Sir Christopher Cotton, applied for the appointment of Steward and Bailiff of the Three Hundreds of Chiltern, and this being an office of emolument, his seat automatically became vacant, but he did not offer himself for re-election.

His valedictory address appeared in all the papers, and it contained a very handsome recognition of the abilities of the gentleman who had, he said, come forward at considerable personal sacrifice to solicit the suffrages of his friends in his place. He could not doubt, he added, that the electorate would view with a friendly eye the candidature of Mr. John Wingfield, who, though not personally connected with the division, had many interests in common with the electors and was sound on all matters of Imperial bearing.

Beneath this graceful tribute to the worth of a gentleman of whom he knew absolutely nothing, appeared the address of that gentleman himself. It was of the simple, straightforward, manly type—and its burden was the shameful way in which the agricultural industry—the most important industry in the country—had been neglected not by one Government only, but by all. He frankly admitted that the one aim of his life was the placing of agriculture on a sound basis, and whether he was returned to Parliament or not, his opinion would remain unaltered, that prosperity to the country meant prosperity to the agricultural interests of the country. At that point in the address the candidate's frankness became even more apparent.

"I am prepared to hear it alleged," his address went on, "that my views on this matter are not wholly disinterested, that in fact my own interests are largely bound up with the agricultural industry. Gentlemen, I own that it would be futile for me to make an attempt to deny this accusation. My own interests are identical with those of agriculture. It is for you to say if this fact disqualifies me from being regarded as a fitting representative of such a constituency as yours."

Now, considering that Jack Wingfield and Priscilla his wife had composed this address without the least aid from Franklin Forrester, the encomiums which it received from that critic were accepted by them with pride—of a certain sort. But when it is known that Jack, after reading over the address in the newspaper out loud, appealed to Priscilla to say if it contained a single false statement, and that she replied that it really did not contain a paragraph that was absolutely untrue, it may be gathered that their pride in its composition was tempered by some misgivings. When two people find it necessary to assure each other from time to time of the purity of their motives, one may perhaps go so far as to assume that neither of them is absolutely convinced on this point. It is understood that during an election certain ethical indulgence is allowed to the candidates and their immediate supporters, just as, at certain times of fasting, the representatives of the most rigid form of Church government grant exemption to some persons from obedience to the strict letter of the law, and just as ingenious Jews have in all ages contrived to effect a compromise with their conscience in the acceptance of the Mosaic injunctions in regard to the observance of the Sabbath (though the Jew has always paid in something on account, so to speak). But whether or not such an explanation of the ethics of the easy-going may be considered satisfactory by the Judge Flynns—the "high-toneder" people of the world, Jack Wingfield and Priscilla his wife soon found themselves too busy to subject themselves to any tests of the searching character of those that Farmer Wadhurst's daughter had instituted in his dairy. The use of a spiritual lactometer would be extremely inconvenient during a contested election, and the contest at Nuttingford promised to be an unusually brisk one.

They both plunged into it. They had got the start of the other candidate—a solicitor by profession, who had made a former appeal to the same constituency—and they meant to keep ahead of him.

From the first it was seen that the sagacity of Mr. Forrester had not misled him when he had suggested that Mrs. Wingfield's presence would tell largely in favour of the candidate of The Party. Priscilla stood by her husband at all times; but she refused to say to anyone:

"I want you to give your vote to my husband."

"It's entirely a matter between yourselves and him," she would say with a smile and a wave of her hand. "If you think him the man for you, as I know him to be the man for me, you can't do better than send him into Parliament as your representative; but if you don't, well, there's no harm done—I'll have the more of him to myself."

Moreover, she never made a suggestion to him as to what the character of any of his speeches should be. It was only when he talked over some question with her and asked her advice that she put forward an opinion.

She saw as clearly as did Mr. Forrester that Jack's form of oratory was the sort that must tell at an election meeting. It was not classical; it was far better: it was colloquial. He told stories by the score, and everyone of them bearing upon his own experience in many countries—just the sort of stories that people like—about lions and tigers and killing things—about niggers (with a sly word or two about the scantiness of their attire)—about a cricket match in the South Seas which had lasted three weeks with a hundred and twenty on each side, and a free fight at the close—about a football match in Africa, where the football was a cocoanut in its original husk, and how they kicked it to pieces with, their bare feet, and how the referee was treated almost as badly as he is upon occasions in the Midlands. "But the great pull that those chaps have over us is of course that a black eye is never noticed." This commentary was received with laughter and cheers; and under the cover of this demonstration Priscilla scribbled a few words on a piece of paper, and pushed it before him. When the yells had passed away, he resumed:

"I suppose you think that that about the black eyes has nothing to do with us at this election. Well, you're wrong. I was about to say when you interrupted me—there really was nothing to laugh at. Do you think a black eye is something to laugh at? (Great laughter.) Well, you're wrong again! (More laughter.) I should know, for I've had many a one myself. (Renewed laughter.) In fact, at one time of my life I had so many black eyes that my friends used to call me not blackeyed Susan, but black-eyed Jack. (Great laughter.) My mother said, 'This can't be my own beautiful boy, for my son had lovely dreamy blue eyes, and this boy's are—' (The remainder of the sentence was inaudible owing to the laughter and cheers.) But to come to the point. I was about to say that my opponent's disclaimer with regard to the labourers' cottages resembled that nigger's black eyes. He declares that the opinions which I said were his were not his opinions at all. Ladies and gentlemen, if you had asked that nigger if he had a pair of black eyes he would have denied it. My opponent holds those opinions without knowing it, and we accept his disclaimer, feeling sure that he made it in good faith—as good faith as the nigger's who denied his lovely black eyes, and so we part good friends." (Loud cheers.)

That was his style of oratory, and it did very well. But of course, he was not always so successful as he was upon this occasion in dragging in a connection between one of his stories and an election topic. Priscilla was not always at hand to give him a hint of the possibility of turning a story to good account. But his audience cared no more for the appropriateness of a story to an election issue than children care for the moral of a fable. They wanted to be entertained and he entertained them, and they found him a jolly good fellow, and affirmed their belief in varying keys the moment he got upon his legs and the moment he sat down.

Mr. Forrester began to feel that there was more than a likelihood that the Wingfields would win. He took care to arrange with the local organization to have a sufficient number of sound dull speakers to precede Jack's efforts and to follow them up. The difficulty of providing such speakers is never insuperable in an agricultural constituency, or for that matter, in any other constituency.

But the *coup de theatre* of Jack's campaign was due to the happy accident of a conscientious objector—not one of those who had been provided by the management—being present in the gallery one night, when Mr. Wingfield had been affirming (for the fiftieth time) that he was heart and soul an agriculturist.

"Look here, mister," this person sang out. "Look here, we've heard a deal about you and the lady (cheers and cries of 'Turn him out!') No, nobody will turn me out."

"You're right there, my lad," cried Jack. "We don't want anybody turned out. We want somebody turned in—into Parliament, and I've the authority of that person for saying that he doesn't want to be turned in by turning other people out. Go on, my friend. It's a free country."

"So I was hoping, sir. Well, what I want to know is this. Did ever you or your lady do a real day's work yourselves? That's what I want to know."

There was some laughter and some confusion at the back of the hall, for it seemed that there were conscientious ejectors present as well as the conscientious objector. While order was being restored, Priscilla said something in Jack's ear, and at once he held up his hand for silence.

"Our friend has thrown us down a challenge, and we're only too glad to take it up," he cried. "Has either of us ever done a real day's work? he asks. Well, here's my wife's answer. Here we are in this hall to-night. Now, to-morrow morning at 10 o'clock my wife will show all who honour her with a visit in this place whether anyone in this neighbourhood can tell her something she doesn't know in dairy work. She'll do a day's butter making with her own hands, and you'll be able to judge for yourselves whether or not I have been over or under the mark in my claim that we understand what we're talking about. If my speeches here haven't contained much butter it's not because we don't know what the real thing is or that one of us at least can't make it with it the best in the land. There's no duchess in this country or any other that can beat Mrs. Wingfield at butter making (laughter), but it's not for me to talk to you of it; you come here, any of you that know what butter is, and you can judge for yourselves to-morrow and maybe the day after. One friend up there talked of a single day's real work. Well, we accept his challenge and double the task—two days—three—four—if he insists. Now, mind you, this is no joke. You'll find that it's no joke if any of you hope to beat the butter that will be made here to-morrow and as much longer as you please."

He sat down "amid a scene of indescribable enthusiasm," as the local newspapers had it, only they said that "he resumed his seat." The man who had asked that question from the gallery was the driver of a traction engine, and he had long been suspected of harbouring unworthy socialistic theories. He thought it prudent to leave the hall before the close of the meeting.

"How will you get out of it?" asked Mr. Forrester of Priscilla. "That husband of yours has either made himself or marred himself by his attempt to get the better of that man in the gallery. How does he mean you to get out of the business?"

"He doesn't," replied Priscilla. "It was I who told him to take up the challenge. Oh, Mr. Forrester, we're all sick to death of this vulgar talk, talk, talk day after day and night after night. Thank goodness that I have now a chance of turning from that unwholesome stuff to a good clean worthy job of butter making. I'll win this election for my husband in the legitimate way of work as opposed to words."

And she did win it for him.

By eleven o'clock the next morning she had turned the hall into a dairy, and in the daintiest dairymaid's costume that had ever been seen, with her white arms bare to the elbow, she churned her milk and turned out pat after pat of the finest butter that had ever been seen in that neighbourhood. By the evening she had produced sufficient to stock a shop for a day, and she had leisure to make all the farmers' daughters acquainted with the scientific tests by whose aid alone could the best results be obtained.

The only trouble that there was in carrying out her scheme was in regard to the regulation of the crowds of people who flocked from every quarter to see Mrs. Wingfield respond to the challenge that her husband had accepted on her behalf. The local police were quite unequal to the duty of marshalling the crowd. Volunteer stewards had to assist them to prevent the hall being rushed. But in spite of all their exertions the doors had to be closed several times during the afternoon. At the dinner hour of the working population the whole street was packed with interested young women and still more interested young men, and the sound of their cheering was as continuous as the firing of a battery of machine guns.

"What chance have I against that kind of thing, Forrester?" enquired Jack's opponent of the manager of Mr. Wingfield's party. "I suppose this is another of your clever tricks" he added, "I should be proud to be able to father it, but I am not," said Mr. Forrester.

"You mean to say that you did not arrange for that challenge?"

"I do indeed. It was sprung on us—the whole thing was sprung on us. I give you my word for it. The fellow sang out some rot from the gallery, and while they were calling to put him out, Mrs. Wingfield saw her chance. She put Wingfield up to it, and he only did what she told him. I didn't know where I was standing when I heard him accept the challenge; but in a minute or two I saw what could be made of it."

"Butter! I don't know what we are coming to in England when the grave issues of an election contest are decided in this way—I really don't."

"I'm not sure that that young woman hasn't inaugurated, a new state of things. Speech-making is played out as an election force."

"And butter-making is to take its place! Why not have a milking match between the candidates to decide which of them should be returned? Mrs. Wingfield is a clever young woman, and her husband's a lucky man. We all thought him a bit of a juggins."

"So he was; but she has made a man of him."

"She has made a member of Parliament of him," said Jack's opponent; and whatever enthusiasm he may have felt at the thought, he managed to prevent it from being noticed in his voice.

He spoke the truth. Mrs. Wingfield's husband was returned as the Parliamentary representative of the Nuttingford division of Nethershire by a majority of eleven hundred and sixty-one votes.

When the enthusiastic electors and non-electors—the latter are invariably the more enthusiastic—blocked the street in front of the hotel and shouted for Mrs. Wingfield, that lady appeared on the balcony, but after a long interval.

Everyone saw that she was smiling, but only those people who were close to her saw that her smile was that of a woman who has wept and is still weeping.

CHAPTER XXV

The Wingfields as a topic were becoming too much for Framsby. No sooner had the curiosities of Mr. Wingfield's engagement to the daughter of Farmer Wadhurst been discussed than the news came of that hole-and-corner marriage of the pair. Agriculture was looking up, some people said, while others asserted that it was manorialism that was coming down. There was a feeling of indignation at being cheated out of the marriage; the offence was in their eyes on a level with the promise of a presentation of a stained-glass window to the church and then sending one done on "Glacier" transparent paper. The act, if not absolutely fraudulent, was certainly in very bad taste, a good many people said; but there were others who announced that they were not surprised at that young woman's desire to avoid publicity being obtained for such an act as her marriage to a second husband before her first had been dead more than two months. These were the people who had invariably referred to Priscilla as Mrs. Blaydon, and pretended not to understand who was meant when anyone spoke of Miss Wadhurst.

The right set agreed that the whole affair, from the engagement to the marriage, was disgraceful, and hastened to leave a second relay of cards upon Mrs. Wingfield the elder, and to enquire with a most interesting expression on their faces, if they were fortunate enough to get a word with that lady, when the young couple would be at the Manor, so that they might leave cards upon them as well.

It might reasonably have been expected, Framsby thought, that the Wingfields had absorbed enough of the conversation of the community up to this point; but it seemed as if the Wingfields had set themselves up as a perpetual topic; for while the buzz about the marriage was still in the air, there came the news, announced in ridiculously large type under the heading of "The Nuttingford Vacancy," that the Wingfields were in this business as well. "The Candidature of Mr. Wingfield" soon became the most conspicuous line in every newspaper; and the way even the most respectable London organs lent themselves to this new scheme for pandering to that young woman's insatiable desire for publicity showed, in the estimation of Mrs. Gifford and her friends, with deplorable emphasis, how depraved was the taste of the readers for whom the newspapers catered.

The same censors were, however, just enough to affirm that the woman was at the bottom of it all. They rehearsed the various items in her progress of publicity; and the result was certainly a formidable total. The first was, of course, the sensation of the arrest of Marcus Blaydon at the church door; and then came his trial, and the pathetic appeal made by the prisoner's counsel to the judge and jury on behalf of the young wife, every line of which appeared in the papers. But this was apparently not enough for that young woman, and her name must be dragged into the published account of the death of her husband. Two months later she had married Mr. Wingfield in a way that was eminently open for discussion, and now here she was urging her poor husband—the poor rich man whom she had inveigled into marrying her, to make a fool of himself by coming forward as a candidate for the representation of an important division of an important county.

They marked off the items on their fingers after the convenient method of Lord Lovat in Hogarth's picture, and then enquired where it was all going to end. When were those newspapers who gave four or five snapshots every morning of Mrs. Wingfield engaged in canvassing for her husband, and now and again a cabinet portrait of herself, coming to reason? When were they going to cease lending themselves to the ambitious schemes of the farmer's daughter? Everybody knew, and several newspapers asserted, that Mr. Wingfield had no chance whatsoever of being returned to Parliament for Nutting-ford, so what on earth was the sense of pushing that young woman before the eyes of the public? That was what the censors were anxious to know.

But when the butter-making scenes came, and the papers were strewn with snapshots of this transaction—when the great London organs gave column reports of it, with occasional leading articles, and when finally the news came that Mr. Wingfield was returned by an enormous majority—the members of the best set hurried out to the Manor with a fresh relay of cards. Surely the new member and his wife, out of gratitude for the distinction conferred upon them by the electors of Nuttingford, would provide the people of Framsby with a series of *fêtes* on a scale unparalleled by any remembered in the neighbourhood.

Now there was in Framsby a population of some 9,000 who belonged to none of the recognized sets, and who had never so much as heard of the existence of these sets; these are the people who matter in every community, not the retired civil servants, not the retired undistinguished officers of Sappers or the A.S.C.; and these were the people who felt that something should be done to show how proud Framsby was of having given Nuttingford a member and of having given that member a wife who had her portrait looking the whole world in the face out of the pages of the illustrated papers. These are not the people who hire halls and elect a chairman and pass resolutions to the accompaniment of long, commonplace speeches. But they get there all the same, and they got there when they felt that they should do something to show their admiration for Mr. Wingfield and his wife.

What they perceived they could do in this way was to meet the train by which the pair whom they desired to honour would arrive at Framsby, and, removing the horses from their carriage (they had found that the motor was not to be used), harness themselves to the vehicle and drag it through the streets and along the road to the Manor. From the steps of the porch the new member of Parliament would address them, and possibly his wife would follow him; they would all cheer and sing that about the jolly good fellow, and then the final and most important act of appreciation would take place: the health of the young couple would be drunk by the crowd at the young couple's expense. Moreover, a little reflection was sufficient to convince the good people that the occasion represented what was known as a double event: the celebration was not only of the home-coming of Mr. and Mrs. Wingfield, after their honeymoon; it was also the celebration of the splendid and successful election contest in which they had both been so actively engaged.

The good people pulled themselves together. They felt that it could be done. They felt themselves quite equal to doing the honours of the double event, and no one who knew them would have ventured to suggest that the confidence which they had in their own powers was misplaced.

There was very little organization in the matter—very little was required. Half-a-dozen house painters prepared as many lengths of canvas containing the simple manly English words "Welcome Home," and half-a-dozen young gentlemen in the drapery line got together some slices of bunting which they shaped and glued on to rollers, so that they became bannerets in a moment. For the necessary bouquets they knew that they could depend upon the Manor gardeners; so the arrangements for the demonstration did not occupy much time or thought. The musical accompaniments were suggested by the Town Band, and then it was that Mr. Mozart Tutt, Mr. Morley Quorn, and the other members of the Framsby Glee and Madrigal Meistersingers had a chance of putting into practical form their recognition of what Mrs. Wingfield had done for them upon one occasion, for they prepared some choice serenade music with which to greet the lady and her husband in the course of the night.

Someone suggested that they should practise a chorus beginning "See, the Conquering Hero Comes" for the railway station; but Mr. Tutt was too wise to enter into any contract that would involve competition with the band and the cheers of the public.

And on this scale the home-coming of Mr. and Mrs. Wingfield was arranged for; and as neither of them had been informed of the intention of Framsby, they were rather surprised when, late in the evening, their train steamed into the station, and slowed down into an atmosphere of yells. Beyond the barrier there was a sea of faces whose waves were caps with an occasional straw hat, and here and there a bowler—all were in the air undulating fitfully, and lapping the base of a headland bearing the inscription "Welcome Home."

"Gloriana!" cried Jack. "Is this for us? And I fancied we had been done with all that sort of thing until the next general election."

"Of course it's for us," said Priscilla. "I had no idea that Framsby would rise equal to the occasion."

"Framsby is rather more than equal to the occasion," growled Jack. "What I want to know is, what has Framsby got to do with the election?"

"This isn't an election demonstration. Can't you see that it's only a welcome home?"

"Dammitall!" murmured Jack.

It is part of the penalty which people have to pay for being popular that when they are trying to get into the church where a clergyman is waiting to marry them, their admirers prevent them from entering; when they are leaving a public meeting where they have made a stirring speech, they have to fight their way to their carriage, and when they are met at the railway station they are all but deafened first and suffocated afterwards. Jack and his wife tried to stem that sea of faces that roared in front of them, but they found it impossible. The platform exit was narrow, and now it was choked with human life. But this circumstance did not affect the enthusiasm of the people beyond. They cheered and waved and quite prematurely broke into the "Jolly Good Fellow" chorus which, properly speaking, should only find its vent when Mr. Wingfield should announce from the porch of his house that he hoped his good friends would honour him by drinking to the health of his bride.

It was not until the railway authorities had admitted a force of police that Mr. and Mrs. Wingfield were able, following in the hollow of the wedge which they inserted between the masses at the barriers, to reach the outer atmosphere, which was resonant and throbbing with the fifes and drums of "See, the Conquering Hero Comes," though the moment they put in an appearance, the strains were overwhelmed by cheers as completely as the flame of a candle is overwhelmed when the extinguisher is dropped over it. The whole space in front of the station and the streets to the right and left were crammed with warm human life, cheering in battalions.

It was all very flattering and overpowering, and unless a man had gone through a fortnight's electioneering he would not know what to do to restore the *status quo ante*. Happily Mr. Wingfield was such a man. He sprang upon a trunk—a weight-carrier of the Saratoga type—and taking off his cap, raised his hand. At once the cheers began to wane and then they ceased altogether in the region of the station, though further away they died hard.

"My friends," said Jack, in strident tones. "My friends—" and so on. Everyone knows what he said—everyone present knew what he was going to say, and he said it. It lasted just three minutes, and before the crowds had recovered from the effects of that spell of silence, he was in the carriage with Priscilla by his side. The coachman had taken good care to send the horses that had been taken out of the traces, back to their stables, so as to prevent the possibility of a mistake being made by the crowd. He had heard of enthusiasts taking the horses out of a carriage upon a similar occasion and failing to return them.

It was a triumphal progress of Mr. and Mrs. Wingfield from the railway station to the Manor. Never could such a home-coming have been looked for by either Jack or Priscilla when, in accordance with the terms of an agreement which they had entered into at the office of the registrar of marriages, they had left that station a couple of months earlier, she having returned to Framsby for one day only from her visit to her Dorsetshire friends, and he from his interesting interview with his promising agent.

The sun had just set when the carriage was dragged along the road to the Manor House, the crowds trotting on each side. It was a warm evening, and they were getting into fine form for the beer which they knew was awaiting them. On through the gates and up the avenue the carriage was dragged. The band had been left some distance behind, so they were spared any more suggestions of the "Conquering Hero," but the full choir of the Framsby Glee and Madrigal Meistersingers now ranged around the Georgian porch, and in response to the beat of Mr. Tutt, struck into "Hail to the Chief that in Triumph Advances," and the effect was certainly admirable, especially as the blackbirds and the thrushes supplied an effective obbligato from the shrubberies. There are several stanzas to that stirring chorus, and the young couple had ample time to greet Mrs. Wingfield, who had come to the head of the steps of the porch to welcome them, before the strains had come to a legitimate close. Jack had also time to ask the butler if he had made any arrangements about those casks of beer, and to receive a satisfactory reply.

When the last notes of the melody had died away and the cheers began once more, he stood with Priscilla by his side (she was carrying the beautiful bouquet with which she had been presented: every flower had come from the garden before her) at the top of the steps.

"My dear friends," he began, and then he said the rest of what everyone expected him to say—even his final words, referring exclusively to the drinking of his health and the health of Mrs. Wingfield, were not unexpected—at any rate, they were quite as well received as any part of his speech; and then came the true and legitimate rendering of the anthem which marks the apotheosis of the orator, "For He's a Jolly Good Fellow," followed by the "Hip, hip, hip, hooray!" thrice repeated, with one cheer more in case that the enthusiasm had not found an adequate vent by the triplex scheme, though the latter certainly did not seem to be ungenerous in its application.

The butler responded to the sentiment of the cheer.

Priscilla went upstairs to her room to change her travelling-dress, but Jack, with his arm about his mother, went into the dining-room, where some cold eatables had been laid out, with a refreshing "cup" in an old cut-glass jug. No candles had yet been lighted; there was no need for them; the glow of the sunset came through the windows and imparted the show of life to the portraits, each in its own panel along the wall on both sides of the fireplace.

The man glanced round the room with a look of satisfaction on his face.

"Ha, my old friends," he cried; "how have you all been since I saw you last? Somehow you don't seem quite so surly as you used to be when I first came among you. You're not altogether so sneery as you were, my bold ancestors—what? Do you know, mother, I always had a hang-dog feeling from the first day I found myself among these impressive Johnnies—I had a feeling that they were jeering at me; and I was afraid to argue it out with them on the spot. But now I can face them without feeling that I'm like the dirt beneath their feet. I've done something—I've married the right wife for a chap like me—she has done it all, mother. I never should have had the cheek to try it off my own bat. She made me go in for it, and then she pulled it off for me. And all so quietly and tactfully; no one would fancy that she was doing it When Franklin Forrester was stating the case to me, she sat by and never uttered a single word, and so it was to the very end. I tell you she almost succeeded in inducing me to delude myself into the belief that I was doing the whole thing. Oh, she's the wife for me!"

"Indeed I feel that she is," said his mother, still keeping her hand upon his arm. "I am so glad that I have lived to see your happiness, Jack. I am so glad that I loved her from the first."

"I knew that you would, dearest. That made you doubly my mother. I felt that I was giving you a daughter after your own heart."

She pressed his arm, and held up her face to him. He kissed her silently on each cheek, and then on the forehead.

"Good-night, my boy," she said. "I must leave you now. You will be together."

"Don't think of going yet," he cried.

"I have not been quite so well to-day," she said. "I just got up so as to be able to welcome you both, but it has been too much for me. You will say good-night to her for me."

"You do look very pale and frail, my dearest," he said. "You should not have left your bed. We could easily have put off our return for another day."

"Oh, I'm not so ill as all that," she said, with a laugh. "But you know how I need to be careful. If I have a good night I may be able to breakfast with you in the morning. Good night, my own boy. God bless you."

"God has blessed me," he said. "I have the best mother in the world—the best wife in the world."

He put her in the hands of her maid, who was waiting for her in the corridor at the head of the staircase. Then he walked to the further end of the same corridor and stood at the window, looking out at the dissolving crowds below, hearing the "chaff" of the boys and the girls, and the cackling laughter of incipient but certainly not insipid love-making. The advances of the young men were no more deficient in warmth than was the retreat of the young women. The giggle and the shriek were, of course, the natural accompaniments of this playfulness.

And the Meistersingers were giving their serenade in a self-respecting style. Mr. Tutt knew all about how that sort of thing should be done. He had spent close upon three months at Leipzig, studying music on its highest plane and becoming thoroughly familiar with the varying aspects of German sentimentality.

Jack was waiting for the sound of Priscilla's door and of her steps on the corridor. Half-an-hour had passed since she had gone upstairs, and she was not the girl to be making an elaborate toilet at this time. She should have been ready long ago.

He returned half-way down the corridor, and entered his own dressing-room to change his coat and brush his hair. The bedroom was in silence.

"Hallo!" he said, without opening the connecting door. "Hallo, Priscilla, what are you about that you haven't come down yet?"

He heard her voice say, "Jack, come to me—come," but he scarcely knew the voice to be hers; it was the voice of a stranger.

He opened the door and passed through.

She was standing in the centre of the room, still in her travelling-dress—she had only taken off her hat.

"I say, what's the matter?" he began at the moment of entering. But then he stood still, as she turned her face to him. "Good God! Priscilla—dearest, what is the matter? You are as pale as death."

He thought that she was about to fall—she was swaying as a tall lily sways in a breath of air. He hurried to her and put his arm about her.

"My God! You are ill. You have been doing too much. You have been overdoing it at that beastly election, and this is the reaction. Pull yourself together, darling."

She seemed trying to speak, but no word would come. She gasped. Her attempt to speak was choking her. At last she managed to make herself audible. Clutching at his shoulders rather wildly and with her face rigid, pushed forward close to his—with wild eyes and cheeks as pale as moonlight, she cried in gasps:

"Jack—Jack—my own Jack—my husband—swear to me that you will stand by me—that you will never leave me whatever may happen."

"My darling! Calm yourself! Tell me what has happened."

"What? What? Only one thing—one thing! I saw his face in the crowd—close to the carriage. He was not drowned—he's alive—he has returned."

"What do you mean?—he?—who? God above—not—not that man?"

"Marcus Blaydon—I tell you I saw his face. He smiled—such a smile! There is no chance of a mistake. He is alive, and he has returned."

The Framsby Glee and Madrigal Meistersingers were giving a spirited rendering of "Auld Lang Syne."

Should auld acquaintance be forgot,

And never brought to min',

Should auld acquaintance be forgot

And days o' lang syne?

CHAPTER XXVI

The moment that she had spoken he flung a protective arm about her—his left arm; his right arm was free, and he had turned his face away from her with a jerk and had alert eyes fixed upon the door. His man's instinct had forced him into the protective attitude of the primeval man when threatened by a sudden danger of another man or another animal. He had not in that second realized the details of the danger that her words had disclosed; his action was automatic—the inherited instinct of the cave-dweller ancestor.

As such its force was felt in every nerve by the woman who was clinging to him.

The silence was broken by the dwindling laughter of the dissolving crowds outside the house, where primeval man was carrying on his courting of primeval woman after the manner of their tribe, among the shrubberies.

"I knew that you would hold me from him," said Priscilla. "I knew that I need not fear anything with you near me, my man, my man!"

At her words the man, for the first time, was startled. He turned his face toward her, drawing a long breath, and looked into her eyes.

In another moment he gave a laugh.

"Yes," she said, smiling and nodding her head, interpreting his laugh by the instinct of the forest. "Yes, let anyone try it."

There was a long interval before his hand fell away from her waist. He felt with that hand for the back of the chair out of which she had risen on his entering the room—his eyes were still upon her face; they were still upon it when his groping had found the chair, and he sat down slowly and cautiously.

"My God, my God!" he whispered, and once again there was silence. He could hear that she was shivering as if with cold. There was more than a hint of chattering teeth.

"Sit down," he said, after a long pause. "Sit down and tell me what—what has happened."

She fell shivering into his arms, a dead weight. He thought that she had fainted, but she had strength enough left to reassure him. She was clinging to him and her head was upon his shoulder.

"You will keep me, Jack, you will keep me from him," she said in a gasping whisper. "I saw him there, I could not be mistaken—and the way he smiled.... But I knew that something like this was in store for us. It would be impossible for such happiness as ours to last. It is always when one has built up one's happiness bit by bit, brick by brick, a palace—a palace was ours, Jack—a hand is put out and down it topples. That was why I married you in such haste, my darling. I told you, when you asked me, that I was afraid of losing you. But I haven't lost you, dear; I have you still. I have you still!"

"You have, Priscilla. Whatever else may be doubtful, you may be certain that you have me still. I will not fail you. Oh, what a fool I should be if I let anything—or anyone—come between us! Where should I be without you? What should I be apart from you, darling? I know—I know what I should be because I know what I was before you came into my life. Do you fancy that I would shrink from killing a man who tried to part us? Let him try it!"

Then he started up with such suddenness that he almost seemed to fling her away from him. He stood in the middle of the room with clenched hands, and cursed the wretch who had done his best to wreck her life—who had not been content with what he had done in this way more than a year before, but who had been guilty of this contemptible fraud—pretending that he was dead so that he might return and complete the work that he had begun—the work in which he had been interrupted. He cursed him wildly—madly—his teeth set and his eyes like the eyes of a hungry wolf—worse—infinitely worse. And she sat by, listening to his ravening and glorying in it as the woman of the cave gloried in the anger of her man when he heard the wolves howl in the distance. She knew that her man would fight them and get the better of them. She knew that the man is fiercer than the wolf and forces the wolf to retreat before his anger. Every curse that Jack uttered—and he uttered a good many—added to her love for him. That was what she had come to by the stress of circumstances.

But she knew that when the passion of the wolf in the man had spent itself, the god in the man would take the upper hand. If there had not been a bit of a god in man he would have remained a wolf.

She noted the dwindling of the impromptu Commination

Service which he conducted without the aid of an acolyte. He paced the room for a while and then stopped in front of one of the windows looking out into the sapphire glow of the summer twilight. Before he turned to her the room had become perceptibly darker. She could not see the expression on his face, for his back was to the light, but she knew what it was by the sound of his voice, when he said, "Forgive me, Priscilla; I forgot myself."

"You did, dear, you forgot yourself; you remembered only me," she said. "Sit down, Jack, and let us talk it all over. I have recovered from the effects of that first sense of terror that I had. I suppose it was natural that I should be terror-stricken."

"Terror-stricken! I cannot understand how you managed to restrain yourself for so long. You saw him shortly after we left the station, you said?"

"Yes, I think I must have cried out, but, of course, you could not hear me on account of the cheers."

"Ah, those cheers! A triumph—a triumphal progress! A joyful welcome home—that ruffian's smile.... You could not have made a mistake. I don't suggest so obvious a way out of this trouble. You saw him."

"I saw him."

"And yet you were strong enough to bear yourself as if nothing had happened! No woman alive except yourself could have done that, Priscilla. And then—then you were strong enough to tell me all there was to be told. Another woman—any other woman—would have tried to keep it secret, would have paid the fellow his blackmail until his demands became too monstrous, and then—what might happen? Heaven only knows. But you were straight. You did the right thing. You told me—you trusted me."

"Whom should I trust if not you, my husband?"

He took the hand that she stretched out to him. He kissed it over and over again. But this was not enough for him; he took her into his arms and put his face down to hers.

"You knew that I was not a fool," he said. "What should I be without you?... And what is to come out of it, Priscilla? Can you see what is to come out of it all?"

"Everything that we think—the worst—the very worst is to come of it," she said. "I see quite clearly all that is before us—well, perhaps not all, but enough—oh, quite enough for one man and one woman to bear. Oh, Jack, if you were only a little less true, all might be easy. But you would not let me leave you even if I wished."

"Take that for granted," said he. "But what is to come of it all? There would be no use buying him off, though I've no doubt that that's what he looks for. The infernal scoundrel! There's nothing to be bought off. If he were to clear off to-morrow matters would only be the more complicated."

"Not a step to one side or the other off the straight road must we take," she cried. "We must begin as we mean to end. No compromise—there must be no thought of compromise. You are married to me and I am married to you, and to you only—I never was married to that man—that is the truth, and nothing shall induce me to deviate from it, Jack."

"That's the way to put it—I don't care a tinker's curse what anybody says; and take my word for it, a good deal will be said. Oh, I know the cant. I know the high-hand inconsistency of the Church. But we'll have the sympathy of every man and woman who can think for themselves without the need of a Church handbook on thinking. Yes, I'm pretty sure that we shall have all the minds on our side if we have the ranters and the canters against us. At any rate, whether we have them with us or not, you'll have me with you and I'll have you with me. That's all that matters to us."

"That's all that matters to us. Only—oh, Jack, your mother—your poor mother!"

He was silent for a long time.

"Look here, Priscilla," he said at last; "when a man marries a wife he throws in his lot with her and he should let no consideration of family or friendship come between him and his wife—that's my creed. But we can still hope that my mother will see with our eyes."

She shook her head.

"I have no hope in that way," she said. "She will go away from us when we tell her what we have resolved upon. But she is so good—so full of tenderness and love for us both. Oh, Jack, I would do anything—anything in the world rather than wound her."

He saw at once that her feeling for his mother would make her relinquish her purpose. He would need to be firm.

"Look here, my girl," he said; "there is only one course for us to pursue. We have no alternative. You spoke the truth just now when you said that it would not do for us to deviate in the least from the straight track in this business. The moment we do so we're lost. That's all I have to say. Change your dress and follow me downstairs. I'm hungry and thirsty. You must be the same. It will not do for us to let ourselves run down just when we most need to keep ourselves up. We'll have the devil and all his angels to fight with before we're done with this affair."

"I don't mind the devil," she said, "it's the angels that I dread—the angels with the haloes of their own embroidering and the self-made wings. Oh, Jack, I wish we could have the angels on our side."

"That's a woman's weak point; she would go any distance to get the patronage of an angel."

"Do you remember the day when you called me your good angel, Jack? Alas, alas! Jack!"

"I called you that once, my girl, and I'll call you so again—now. I never felt greater need of you than I do now. I am just starting life, dear, and that is when a chap most needs a good angel to stand by him."

"And for him to stand by. Oh, Jack, if I hadn't you to stand by me now I would give up the fight. If I had not married you, where should I be when that wretch came and said, 'I have come for my wife'? You have saved me from that horror, Jack."

"I wish I knew how to keep you from the horror that you have to face, my Priscilla."

"You will learn, Jack, every day you will learn how to do it."

He gazed at her from the door for some moments, and then went slowly downstairs and into the diningroom. A footman and the butler were in waiting. He sent them away, telling the latter that Mrs. Wingfield was a little knocked up by the attention of the townspeople, and would probably not come downstairs for some time; there was no need for the servants to stay up.

She came down after an interval, and he persuaded her to eat something and to drink a glass of the "cup" which had been prepared in accordance with an old still-room recipe in the Wingfield family.

Afterwards they went out together upon the terrace, and he lit a cigar. They did not talk much, and when they did, it was without even the most distant allusion to the shadow that was hanging over their life. When there had been a long interval of silence between them, they seated themselves on the Madeira chairs, and he told her how on that evening long ago—so very long ago—more than two months ago—he had sat there longing for her to be beside him; how he had put his face down to the cushion thinking what a joy it would be to find her face close to his.

"And now here it has all come to pass," he said. "This is the very chair and the cushion, and the face I longed for."

He sat on the edge of her chair and laid a caressing hand upon her hair; but he did not put his face down to hers—he could not have done so, for her face was turned to the cushion; but even then her sobs were not quite smothered. He could feel every throb as his hand lay upon her forehead. He made no attempt to restrain her. He had an intuition—it was a night of instincts—that her tears would do much more to soothe her than it would be in his power to do.

For an hour they remained there, silent in the majestic silence of the summer night. It was without the uttering of a word that she rose and stood in front of him at last. He kissed her quietly on the forehead and she passed into the house through the open glass door, and he was left alone.

He threw himself down on his chair once more, but only remained there for a minute. He sprang to his feet in the impulse of a sudden thought.

He went down by the terrace steps to the shrubberies, walking quickly but stealthily, and moving along among the solid black masses of the clipped boxes and laurels and bay trees. So he had stalked a tiger that he wanted to kill on his last night at Kashmir. He moved stealthily from brake to brake as though he expected to come upon an enemy skulking there. And then he crossed by the fountains and the stone-work of crescent seats and mutilated goddesses and leering satyrs, into the park and on to the avenue that bent away from the country road. He moved toward the entrance gates and the lodge with the same stealth of the animal who is hunting another animal, pausing every now and again among the trees to listen for the sound of footfalls.

He heard the scurrying of a rabbit—the swishing rush of a rat through the long grass, the flap and swoop of a bat hawking for moths—all the familiar sounds of the woodland and the creatures that roam by night, but no other sound did he hear.

"The infernal skunk!" he muttered. "The infernal skunk! He has not even the manliness to claim her—he does not even take enough interest in her to see where she lives—to look up at the light in her window. He lets her go from him, and he will come to-morrow to try on his game of blackmail. I wish I had found him skulking here. That's what I want—to feel my fingers on his throat—to throttle the soul out of him and send him down to..." and so forth. He completed his sentence and added to it several other phrases, none of which could be said actually to border on the sentimental. He stood there, a naked man among his woods, thirsting for a tussle with the one who was trying to take his woman from him.

It was not until he had returned to the chair of civilization and had begun to think in the strain of fifty thousand years later, that he felt equal to contrasting this wretch's bearing with that of the sailor man about whom his mother had read to him when he was a boy and she had thought it possible to impart to him a liking for the books that she liked—a sailor named Enoch Arden who had been cast away on a desert island—he had had great hopes of any story, even though written in poetry, which touched upon a man on a desert island. Enoch Arden returned to England to find his wife married to another man and quite happy, and he had been man enough to let her remain so. But Jack had not forgotten how that strong heroic soul had looked through the window of her new house the first thing on reaching the village. Ah, very different from this wretch—this infernal skunk who had preferred boozing in a bar at Framsby and then staggering upstairs at the "White Hart" to his bed. He had a huge contempt for the fellow who wouldn't come to Overdean Manor Park to be throttled.

But soon his train of thought took another trend. He knew that Priscilla was womanly, though not at all like other women, to whom the conventions of society are the breath of life, and the pronouncement of a Church the voice of God. She had proved to him in many ways—notably in regard to her marrying of him—that she was prepared to act in accordance with her own feeling of right and wrong without pausing to consult with anyone as to whether or not her feeling agreed with accepted conventions or accepted canons. She had refused to be guilty of the hypocrisy of wearing mourning for the man whom she hated; and she had ignored the convention which would have compelled her to allow at least a year to pass before marrying the man whom she loved.

He reflected upon these proofs of her possession of a certain strong-mindedness and strength of character, and both before and after she had come to him as his wife he had many tokens of her superiority to other women in yielding only to the guidance of her own feeling. This being so, it was rather strange that he should now find that his thoughts had a trend in the direction of the question as to whether it might not be possible that, through her desire to please his mother—to prevent people from shaking their heads—she might be led to be untrue to herself—nay, might she not feel that she could only be true to herself by making such a move as would prevent people from saying, as in other circumstances they would be sure to do, that he was to blame in keeping her with him?

That was the direction in which his thoughts went after he had been sitting on his chair under her window for an hour. But another half-hour had passed before there came upon him in a flash a dreadful suggestion, sending him to his feet in a second as though it were a flash of lightning that hurled him out of his chair. He stood there breathing hard, his eyes turned in the direction of her window above him. He remembered how he had looked up to that window on that night in June when his longing had been: "Oh, that I could hear her voice at that window telling me that she is there!"

She was there—up there in that room now, but... He flung away the cigar which he held unlighted between his fingers, and went indoors and up the staircase.

He remained breathing hard with his hand on the handle of her door.

Would he find that that door was locked—locked against him?

He turned the handle.

She had not locked the door.

She was his wife.

CHAPTER XXVII

The interview which he most dreaded in the morning was averted, or at any rate postponed. His mother had had a very bad night and was unable to get up—she might not be able to leave her bed for a week. Her malady, though not actually dangerous, was disquieting because it was so weakening, a bad attack frequently keeping her in bed for ten days or a fortnight; and complete quiet was necessary for her recovery and long afterwards.

Jack breathed again. He had been thinking of the revelation which he had to make to his mother before many hours had passed, and the more he thought of it the greater repugnance did he feel for the discharge of this duty. He breathed more freely. She might not be in a position to hear the story for several days, and what might happen in the meantime?

He could not of course make a suggestion as to what might happen; only one happening might be looked for with certainty, and this was the visit of Marcus Blaydon.

"He will not delay in striking his first blow," said Priscilla. "You will let me see him alone? I shall know what to say to him, Jack."

But Jack felt that, clever and all though his wife was, he knew better than she did how to deal with such men as Blaydon.

"Don't think of such a thing," said he. "You and I are one. We shall face him together. I know that you have your fears for me. You need have none. I can control myself. But that ruffian—one cannot take too elaborate precautions. Such men are not to be depended on. Revolvers are cheap, so is vitriol. I know that type of rascal, and I'll make my arrangements accordingly. I have met with blackmailers before now, but I've not yet met one that adhered strictly to the artistic methods of the profession; they never move without a revolver or a knife—in the case of a woman they trust a good deal to vitriol."

"I'm quite willing to submit to your judgment, Jack," said she. "I'm not afraid of him. If you say that I should not see him I'll leave him to you, but I think that I should face him with you by my side."

"So you shall," said he.

And so she did.

They had not rehearsed an imaginary scene with the man. They had not exchanged views as to what to say to him. Each knew what was in the other's mind on the subject, so that any planning was unnecessary.

He came early—a man of good presence, he seemed to Jack to be probably from thirty-five to forty years of age. His dark hair was somewhat grizzled and so were his moustache and beard. Priscilla had thought it strange that he had not shaved his face on getting out of gaol and starting life afresh. He had always worn that short, square beard; but it now appeared to her to be shorter and to have much more grey in it. His eyes were queer, neither grey nor hazel; they were not bad eyes, and they had a certain expression of frankness and good spirit at times which was quite pleasing, until the man began to speak, and then the expression changed to one of furtiveness, for he looked at the person whom he was addressing with his head slightly averted so that the pupils of his eyes were not in the centre but awry.

The thought that came to Jack Wingfield at the moment of the man's entrance was that he could easily understand how one might be imposed on by him; but to Priscilla came the thought that she had been right in distrusting him from the first.

He had been shown into the library by the order of Jack; the room was empty; Jack kept him waiting for some minutes before he entered, saying:

"Good morning. Can I do anything for you, Mr. Blaydon?"

"You can," said the other. "I came here for my wife, and I mean to have her."

And then Priscilla entered. The man threw out both hands in an artificial, stagey way, and took a step or two toward her.

"Stay where you are," said Jack imperatively. "You can talk as well standing where you are. Don't lay so much as a finger upon her. Now, say what you have to say."

"Isn't it natural that I should cross the room to meet my own true wedded wife, sir?" said the visitor. "She can't deny it; if I know anything of her she won't deny it—we were married according to the rites of God's holy ordinance in the Church; and those that God hath joined together—but I know she will not deny it."

"You know nothing of her," said Jack. "All that you knew of her—all that you cared to know—was that her father had some money which you hoped to get your hands on to cover up the consequence of your fraud. But now you're going to learn something of her. She escaped by a hair's breadth from your clutches, and believing you to be dead—the report of your heroic death was another of your frauds, I suppose."

"I escaped by the mercy of God, sir, and my first thought was for her."

"Was it? Why was your first thought on getting out of gaol not for her? How was it that you were aboard that vessel?"

"Circumstances beyond my control—but—ah! I wanted to begin life again and not drag her down with me. I felt that I had it in me, sir; I know that I had it in me."

"You knew that the report of your death was published in the American papers and you knew that it would appear in all the papers here. That was nearly four months ago, and yet you took no steps whatever to have that report contradicted. You wished everyone to believe that you were dead."

"What better chance could I have of beginning life afresh? It seemed as if the hand of God——"

"Don't trouble about the hand of God. You didn't consider that it was due to the girl whom you had linked to your career of crime, to mention in confidence what your scheme was—to begin life again without being handicapped by your previous adventures that had landed you in gaol?"

"I wanted to wait until I had redeemed the bitter past. I wanted to be able to go to her, an honourable man, and say to her, 'Priscilla, bitter though the past may have been, yet by the mercy of God——'"

"Quite so. That was quite a laudable aspiration, and it shows that your heart is in the right place."

"All that I thought about was her happiness, sir. I said, 'If I have done her an injustice in the past, she shall find out I have atoned——'"

"You thought of nothing but her happiness? Well, now that you come here and find that she is happy, what more do you want?"

"I want her—my wife."

"Because you think that she will be happy with you? Why didn't you go to her and tell her of your plans the very moment you were released from gaol?"

"I hadn't the courage to face her after what had happened, sir."

"That was your only reason?"

"That was my only reason."

The man bent his head in an attitude of humility, and Jack Wingfield, who had spent six years of his life mingling with all sorts of men that go to make up a world, and who had acquired a good working knowledge of men of all sorts, looked at the man standing before him with bent head, and said:

"You lie, sir; you went straight off to another woman."

The man gave a start, and his humility vanished. His eyes revealed unsuspected depths of shiftiness as he looked furtively from Jack to Priscilla and back again to Jack.

"What do you know about it? Has Lyman been writing to you?"

"Never mind who has been writing to me: the fact remains the same, and I think we have you in a tight place there, Mr. Blaydon," said Jack, smiling at the result of his drawing a bow at a venture.

"Look here," cried the visitor. "I know just how I stand. I know what my rights are—restitution of conjugal rights. I've been to the right quarter to learn all that, and what's more, I won't stand any further nonsense. What right have you to cross-question me—you? It is you who have ruined the girl, not me."

"Mr. Blaydon," said Jack quietly, "you are a man of the world, and so am I. You have said enough to show me that you are no fool. Now, speaking as man to man, and without wishing to dispute the legality of your claim or to throw away good money among bad lawyers, how much will you take in hard cash to clear off from here and let things be as they are?"

"Not millions—not millions!" cried the man indignantly. "I'm no blackmailer—don't let that thought come to you. I don't ask for money. Good Heavens, sir! what have I done that you should fancy my motives were of that character? No; all I ask is for my wife to come with me."

"And supposing she went with you to-day, what could you do for her?" said Jack. "Have you a home to which you could take her? What are your prospects?"

"My prospects may be none of the brightest, Mr. Wingfield; I wasn't born so lucky as you; but I'm her husband, and it's my duty to think of her first. If she's the woman I believe her to be, she will acknowledge that her duty is to be with me."

He looked toward Priscilla, but she remained silent; she made no attempt to acknowledge his complimentary words.

Then Jack went to the mantelpiece, and drew a postcard from behind a bronze ornament—a postcard addressed to himself.

"Take that card in your hand and tell me if you recognize the handwriting," he said, handing the card to the man who took it and scrutinized the writing closely.

"I never saw that writing in all my life," he said, and Jack took the card from him smiling. The man looked at his fingers; the card had evidently been leaning against a gum-pot and got a touch of the brush on its border. He wiped his fingers in his pocket-handkerchief, while Jack replaced the postcard where it had been standing.

"If you tell me you have never seen that writing before, I am satisfied," said he. "But I have a letter or two the writing on which I fancy you would have no difficulty in recognizing. I will not produce them just yet. Now, without wasting more time, Mr. Blaydon, I wish to know from you in one word, now or never, if I offer you the sum of twenty-five thousand pounds——"

Priscilla started up.

"Don't you speak," cried Jack, sternly. "I'm prepared to be liberal. But mind, it's now or never with you, my man; for I'll swear to you that I'll never repeat my words—I say now, if I offer you the sum of twenty-five thousand pounds to clear away from here, to go to, let us say, Canada, and sign a paper never to return to England or to make any further claim upon us—well, what do you say—yes or no?"

There was an appalling pause. A great struggle seemed to be going on in the man's mind, and so there was, but he pretended that it was in his heart, but this was where he made a mistake. He overrated his gifts as an emotional actor. His shifty eyes prevented his being convincing. He turned his head away, and took out his handkerchief. Then he wheeled sharply round and spoke firmly.

"Mr. Wingfield, I've told you that I have no thought except for the happiness of my wife. I'll take the money."

"Will you indeed?" asked Jack, anxiously.

"I don't want to stand between her and happiness. I will take the money," said the visitor.

"I thought that you would decide in that way," said Jack, "and I'll pay it to you——"

"Never!" cried Priscilla, speaking for the first time.

"Thank you; that's the word I was looking for," said Jack. Then he turned to the man.

"Take yourself away from here, and look slippy about it, my good fellow," he said. "You have shown yourself to be just what I guessed you were. But I don't think that you can say so much for us: we're not just the fools that you fancied, Mr. Blaydon. You thought you were a made man when you learned that the girl you had tricked once had fallen a victim to your second deception. You'll need a bit of re-making before you can call yourself a man. How much better would our position be if you were to clear off without revealing the fact of your existence to anyone? Our marriage would be legally still no marriage. And you thought that in these circumstances we would hand you over a fortune. Now be off with you, you impudent blackmailer, and do your worst. We shall fight you, and get the better of you on all points. You may take that from me."

"I have come for my wife, and I mean to have her. You allowed just now that she was my wife," cried the man, weakly reverting to his original bluff.

"She refuses to go with you, Mr. Blaydon. How do you mean to effect your purpose?"

"I have the law on my side. I know where I stand. Conjugal rights——"

"Two conjugal wrongs don't make one conjugal right, and you'll find that out to your cost, my good fellow. We've had enough of you now, Mr. Blaydon. I've been very patient so far, but my patience has its limits. Go to the attorney or the attorney's clerk who sent you here, and ask him to advise you as to your next step." He rang the bell, and the footman had opened the door before he had done speaking.

"Show this person out," said Jack, choosing a cigar from a box on the mantelpiece, and snipping the end off with as great deliberation as is possible with a snip. Priscilla had already gone out of the room by the other door—the one which led into the dining-room.

The man looked at Jack, and then looked at the respectful but unmistakably muscular footman.

"Good morning, Mr. Wingfield," he said, picking up his hat.

"Good morning," said Mr. Wingfield. "Fine weather for the harvest, isn't it?"

"Admirable," responded the departing guest. "Admirable! Ha! ha!"

He made a very inefficient villain of melodrama in spite of his "Ha, ha!" laugh.

Yes, but he occupied a very important position as an obstacle to the happiness of Mr. and Mrs. Wingfield. He was legally the husband of the young woman who called herself Mrs. Wingfield, and who had never called herself by his name, and a legal husband is a quantity that has always to be reckoned with. His position is a pretty secure one when considered from the standpoint of English legality. In America he would do well not to step on a slide.

CHAPTER XXVIII

That's over, at any rate," said Jack, when he had come to the side of Priscilla in the dining-room. He was smiling, but his face was pale, and his fingers that held his cigar were twitching. "I didn't say just what I meant to say, but I think I said enough."

"Every word that you said was the right word," she cried. "You spoke like a man who knows that a fight has to be faced, and does not fear to face it. Dearest, you were splendid; only—what do you know about him? Who has been telling you anything?—that about the woman—who suggested to you that he had gone to a woman?"

"I have had experience of men of all sorts and conditions. I knew when I saw the fellow that I had to deal with a man on whom such a shot would tell. It was a shot, and I hope that it may turn out to have been a happy one for us. What was the name he mentioned?—someone who he said had been giving him away?"

"Lyman."

"Lyman. So it was. We must make a note of that. Lyman is the name of the man that is ready to give him away. Now, who is Lyman?"

"Lyman is the name of the captain of the barque that was wrecked on the coast of Nova Scotia. He was among the saved."

"You knew that? Well, that's so much. I'm not sure that it's a great deal, but the smallest contribution will be thankfully received."

"Another mystery—that postcard. It was from the gunmakers—about the last cartridges. What would you have learned if he had recognized the handwriting of the clerk?"

"That was a little dodge of mine to get from him a piece of undoubted evidence of his identity. You see, I wasn't quite certain that he was the man. There are so many men ready to carry out some scheme of imposture if they only get the chance. Lord! the cases that I have heard of! Now, what more likely than that someone on the look-out for a job should have read the accounts that appeared in the papers of the heroic death of Marcus Blaydon, and then got hold of the idea that it would pay to come to me with a story of how he had not been drowned, and with a demand for his wife or a pretty fair sum to keep away?"

"There can be no doubt that he is Marcus Blaydon—oh, none whatever. I wish there was even the smallest chance of a chance. But how would the postcard prove anything?"

"Well, an hour ago I found that card on the mantelpiece, and I gave it a light coating of gum. By that means I got an excellent impression of his fingers, and by good luck his thumb also. Now, if I send that card to the governor of the gaol where the man spent a year, he will tell me, in the course of a post or two, if he is Marcus Blaydon or Marcus Aurelius—see?"

She did see. She saw very clearly that the man whose education in a certain direction she had airily undertaken, possessed some elements of knowledge in another direction. He had not mis-spent his years of wandering. He had come to know something of his fellow men and their ways. She was well aware of the fact that, however resolute, however brave she might have been in meeting that man face to face at the critical moment, she would not have succeeded in getting rid of him as easily as Jack had got rid of him; and her admiration for Jack had proportionately increased. Women love a man who is successful with women, but they worship a man who is successful with men.

Priscilla gazed in admiration at the man before her.

"You got the better of him in every way," she said "He was like a child in your hands—a foolish boy."

"We'll get the better of him in the long run, too, you may be sure of that," he said.

The morning's work had immeasurably increased his admiration for her. She had only said one word during the whole of that time spent in the library. If a man esteems a low voice as a most excellent thing in a woman, he bows down before the wisdom of a woman who has a great deal to say and yet can keep silent. And surely no woman alive possessed the wisdom of his Priscilla in this respect. She had done neither coaxing nor wheedling of the electors of the Nuttingford division; she had resorted to none of those disgusting flatteries of which the wives or the sisters of other candidates whom he could name had been guilty even in bonnie Scotland, where Conscience is understood to be the only consideration to make her sturdy sons vote this way or that. No; his Priscilla had won him the election by her silence; and in the same way she had allowed him to send Marcus Blaydon out of the house.

"You don't think I was a little too high-handed with him?" said he, after a thoughtful pause.

She made an expressive motion of negation with both hands.

"The sooner it's over the sooner to sleep, dear Jack," she said. "There's nothing so dreadful as suspense. We shall never know a moment's ease until the thing is over—or, at any rate, begun. The sooner he begins the better pleased will I be."

"I don't think that I gave him any excuse for dallying," said he, grimly.

"What will his next step be, do you fancy?" she asked. "Tell me what he can do beyond making the newspapers publish the story of his escape. I know how they will do it—with the column headed in big letters, 'A Modern Enoch Arden.' They won't have the sense to see that he has nothing of Enoch Arden about him."

"We shall have to face some nasty bits of publicity but we'll face them," said he, resolutely. "He has plainly been in touch with a man of the law; he had got hold of that legal jargon about conjugal rights. He will have to appeal to a judge to make an order for you to go to him."

"But no judge will make such an order—surely not, Jack?"

"You may take it from me that he will get his order."

"Is such a thing possible?"

"Absolutely certain, I should say."

"And what then?"

"Nothing. The judge who makes the order has no way of enforcing it. Only if the man can carry you off he has the law on his side. You had much better not let him carry you off after he gets his order, Priscilla."

"Or before it. I suppose that he has the law on his side as matters stand at present."

"I suppose he has. But when he gets his order and you refuse to obey it, he will have a very good chance of getting a divorce."

"It would be hoping too much to expect that he will do us such a good turn. So then we shall be the same as before."

"That's what I have been thinking; but I've also been thinking that if you made an application to have your marriage to him annulled, the chances are greatly in favour of your having that application granted."

"Jack, you are talking like a lawyer. I did not know that you could give an opinion on these points so definitely."

"I only speak as a layman, from my recollection of certain cases that have appeared from time to time in the papers. I may be all wrong—

remember that. We may have to fall back upon something that Captain Lyman knows, and try for a divorce."

"That was why you made that shot which showed your knowledge of men such as he is."

"I confess that I hoped to get him to commit himself."

"And he did."

"Yes; but unfortunately his doing so will not count for anything in a court of law. We shall have to produce evidence as to the woman—perhaps even the woman herself. If we find that, immediately after leaving gaol he went off to her and deserted you—the court would place great stress upon his desertion of you—we might have a very good chance of getting a divorce."

"Only a good chance?"

"It would be a layman's folly—even a lawyer's folly—to talk with any measure of certainty about the result of an action at law. But I am pretty sure that in an application to have the marriage pronounced null and void, as the jargon has it, his desertion of you would play a very important part. Funny, isn't it?"

"Funny! Funny! Oh, Jack, darling Jack, will not everyone say that it was the unluckiest day of your life when you met me?"

"You may be sure that some fools will say that, Priscilla, my wife; but you may be equally sure that people who knew what I was before I met you and who have continued their acquaintance will say that, whatever may happen, my meeting you and marrying you were the best things that ever happened to me. You may be sure that that's what I say now and what I'll ever say. Now, don't you suggest anything further in that strain. Good Lord! Didn't you say that the best thing for bringing out what was best in a man was a good fight? Well, I feel that I am now facing a conflict that will develop every ounce of character I possess. That's all I've got to say just now, except that I've wired to Reggie Liscomb to meet me at his office in London this afternoon—he belongs to Liscomb and Liscomb, you know, the solicitors—and he will tell us what we should do, and I'll tell him to do it without a moment's delay. But you may leave that to Liscomb and Liscomb; their motto has always been 'Thrice is he arm'd that hath his quarrel just, and four times he that gets his fist in fust.' They'll get their fist in fust, you bet, if only to take the wind out of the sails of the other side."

Priscilla had frequently heard of the great firm of Liscomb and Liscomb, but never had she an idea that one day she would be in a position to recognize that celerity of action in the conducting of a case which had frequently resulted in the extrication of a client from a tight place.

"You are going up to London to-day?" she said in surprise. "You don't take long to make up your mind, Jack. Why, you had only the night to think over this dreadful business, and yet you were able to get that man to commit himself and show his hand, and now you know what is to be done to give us the best chance of getting rid of him for ever. Jack, I ask your forgiveness; but I didn't think you had it in you."

"Neither did I until lately, Priscilla. It was you who made me think differently. Six months ago if I had been brought face to face with a thing like this I should have run away simply to avoid the bother of it all. But now—well, now I don't think that you need fear my running away."

He went up to town by a train that arrived in good time to allow him to have a long afternoon with his friend, the junior partner in the great firm of solicitors who had "handled" some of the most interesting cases that had ever come before a court of law, and some still more interesting that they had succeeded in settling without such an appeal to the judgment of the goddess of Chance. Newspaper readers owed them more grudges than anyone had a notion of, for the persistence with which they accomplished settlements, thereby preventing the publication of columns of piquant details—piquant to a point of unsavouriness. The public, who like their game high and with plenty of seasoning—and the atmosphere of the Divorce Court is very conducive to the former condition—little knew what they lost through the exertions of Messrs. Liscomb and Liscomb; but Messrs. Liscomb and Liscomb knew, and so did many a superfluous husband and many a duplicated wife.

But here was a case that could by no possibility be regarded as one that might be settled out of court. It was bound to move forward from stage to stage until it came before a judge. Mr. Reginald Liscomb saw that clearly when Jack had given him an outline of the case which had not yet advanced to the position of being a case, but which would do so the very next day, on being "stated" by Messrs. Liscomb and Liscomb to the eminent advisory counsel whom they kept constantly employed.

"We have never had anything quite on all fours with this," said the junior partner. "What we want is a decree of nullity—that's plain enough. But shall we get it? Well, that's not quite so plain. As a matter of fact several things may seem plain, but as a matter of law there's nothing that can be so described. What's the man going to do? Is he going to do anything? Does he fancy that there's money in it? Did he suggest that when he came to you to-day? Mind you tell me everything. The man that conceals anything from his lawyer is as great a fool as the man that hides something from his doctor, only the lawyer is the more important. After all, your doctor only deals with your body and its ailments."

"Whereas you look after—no, not exactly one's soul—one's reputation—more important still," said Jack.

"You put it very well," assented Mr. Liscomb modestly—as modestly as was consistent with an inherent desire for strict accuracy.

"You compliment me," said Jack. "You may be sure that I'll keep nothing back—especially if it tells against the other man."

"Don't bother about that so much as about what tells against yourself. At present what might tell against you is the indecent haste in the marriage—within three months of the report of the husband's death by drowning. A judge may think that was not a sufficient time."

"But the man would not be more thoroughly dead at the end of a year than he would have been at the end of three months."

"No; but there was only a report of his death. The question that a judge will ask is this: Did the lady exercise a reasonable amount of precaution in satisfying herself that her husband was dead before entering into a second contract of marriage? That's a very important question, as you can understand. If the court didn't consider this point very closely, you can see how easy it would be for a man and his wife to get a decree of nullity by the one publishing a report of his or her death in a newspaper. If the proof of the publication of such a report were to be accepted as justification for a second marriage after a brief interval, the time of the court would be fully occupied in issuing decrees of nullity."

"I see—yes—there's something in that. But the circumstances of this case are not quite the same, are they? The first marriage was no marriage, so far as the—the actualities of marriage are concerned: the man was arrested within five minutes of the signing of the register; besides, the fellow had made fraudulent representations."

"Fraudulent representations are punishable by imprisonment, but they are not held to invalidate a marriage. But as you say, this particular case is not on all fours with any that has come under my notice. We were talking about the question of money, however. Did the man make any suggestion about your paying him any money?"

Jack made him aware of the points in the interview bearing upon money, and Mr. Liscomb took a note of them. No, the fellow could not be called a blackmailer: the suggestion of the twenty-five thousand pounds had not come from him; but he had clearly shown his hand. On the whole, Mr. Liscomb, speaking for himself, and subject to the correction of Sir Edward, the eminent perpetually-retained counsel learned in the law, and, more important still, in the idiosyncrasies of judges and the idiotcies of juries, was of the belief that, taking the peculiarities of the case into account, a decree of nullity might be obtained; but failing this a divorce might be tried for.

"In the meantime it is advisable that Mrs.—that the lady should go back to her father's house. You will, of course, see that this is so."

"I see nothing of the sort," said Jack. "She holds that she is my wife, and I hold that I am her husband, and so we mean to stand by one another whatever may happen. Besides, the father would hand her over to Blaydon the day she went to him; and I don't know what you think of it, but it seems to me that just now Blaydon occupies a pretty strong position. If he were to get his hands on her, and hold her as his wife, where should we be then? How could he be hindered from putting her aboard a ship and carrying her off to the South Seas?"

Mr. Liscomb shook his head.

"We should have to serve a writ of *habeas corpus* and———"

"Don't trouble yourself further on this score," said Jack. "We are together now, and we mean to remain together. Take that as final."

"Very unwise! You'll have difficulty getting the divorce. But in an exceptional case, possibly—anyhow, we'll make a move to-morrow, under the advice of Sir Edward, of course. We'll be first in the field, at any rate. So far as I can see just now, we shall enter our case at once and trust to have it heard early in the Michaelmas sittings."

"What, not before October?" cried Jack.

"Most likely November, with luck, but probably December," replied Mr. Liscomb with the complacency of a lawyer for whom time means money. "You may rely on our losing no time. By the way, has the man anything to gain by holding on to the lady—I mean, of course, something in addition to the companionship of the lady?"

"Her father is well off—a wealthy farmer," said Jack.

"Heavens! this is indeed an exceptional case—a wealthy farmer nowadays! And you have reason to believe that if she went to the custody of her father he would hand her over to the man?"

"He would do his best in that way—he would not succeed, because his daughter is stronger than he is; but he would only force her to run back to me."

"I should have thought that the old man would kick him out of his house—a blackguard who was fool enough to get caught. But I've had experience of fathers—mostly Scotch—who believe so desperately in the sacredness of the marriage bond that they would force a woman to live with the man she has married even though he has just returned from penal servitude for trying to murder her."

"So far as I can gather from my wife, her father is something like that."

"My wife!" murmured Mr. Liscomb, smiling very gently, when his client had gone away. "My wife!"

CHAPTER XXIX

Jack gave what he considered to be an adequate account to Priscilla of his interview with Mr. Liscomb. He did not, however, think it necessary to tell her what that gentleman had said respecting the wisdom of their separating until the case or cases should be heard, nor did he do more than hint at the difficulties, which Mr. Liscomb had rather more than hinted at, in the way of proving the profligacy of Marcus Blaydon. But he thought it well to prepare her for the inevitable law's delay; and he was gratified at the sensible way she received the information that three months would probably elapse before the case could come on for hearing.

"It seems a long time, Jack," she said. "But I don't think that it would be possible for us to have everything ready to go before the judge much sooner. I have been thinking over the whole matter while you have been away, and I see clearly, I think, that we shall have trouble in proving that he went away straight from the gaol to that woman of your surmise. How are we to get hold of Captain Lyman? and when we do get in touch with him, how are we to get him to tell us all that he knows?"

"Yes, all that will take time," said Jack. "The evidence on this point may help us in the nullity suit, and in the divorce suit it would, of course, be absolutely indispensable."

There was a pause before she said doubtfully:

"I wonder if Mr. Liscomb suggested that our marrying in such haste—within a few months of the news reaching me—would prejudice a judge."

"Of course he did; it was stupid of me to forget that," replied Jack; "very stupid, considering that I was thinking of it in the train on my way home. He made a remark about the haste—indecent haste, he called it."

"And he gave it its right name," said she. "That was a mistake on my part, Jack; but don't think that I'm sorry for it, or that I wouldn't do it again. Where should I be to-day if I had waited?"

"Would your father have insisted on your going to that man?"

"He would have tried to compel me—I am sure of that. In his eyes a marriage is a marriage—for worse as well as better—it makes no difference."

"I'm glad that you think so. It lets me know that I did not make a mistake in what I said to Liscomb on that point. But with reference to the indecent haste point, surely any judge that is worth his salt will see that nowadays and in certain circumstances three months are as long as a year was in the old days—the Prayer-book days! It was in the fellow's power to send you a cablegram letting you know that he was safe long before you had a chance of seeing a newspaper with the account of the wreck and his heroic conduct. 'Heroic conduct' was in the heading, I remember."

"Yes; he'll have to reply to the judge on that point. By the time Sir Edward has done with him he'll have to make a good many replies. Well, we shall wait for the next move. But three months—if the people are nasty to us it will seem a long time, Jack; you are right there."

"You'll not find that the law errs on the side of indecent haste. We shall soon see how the people behave."

He was quite right. The next day he glanced at the local paper, thinking that it was quite possible the man might have gone without the delay of an hour to make his statement public; but the paper contained no such interesting item of news. The man was plainly still in consultation with his solicitor.

In the course of the afternoon the road to the Manor was crowded with vehicles bearing card-leavers for Mrs. Jack Wingfield. The two livery stables at Framsby found the strain on their resources so severe as to necessitate their collecting the fragments of their most ancient vehicles and glueing them together in haste to respond to the demand for carriages from people who had never been otherwise than impolite, if not actually insolent, to Miss Wadhurst, but who now had a feeling that Mrs. Jack Wingfield would make her husband's money fly in *fêtes*. It would never do for them to miss invitations to whatever festivities were in the air through neglect on their part to take every reasonable precaution to secure their being invited.

But when the footman had the same answer for all—namely, that Mrs. Jack Wingfield was "not at home," the feeling was very general that it was rather too soon for Mrs. Jack Wingfield to give herself airs, though it seemed that airs were to be looked for from her as inevitably as in an opera by Balfe.

Another day brought the newspapers, but there was still no news, in even the most enterprising of them all, bearing upon the incident which had caused Mrs. Jack Wingfield to think that for some time at least she would do well to be "not at home" to any visitors.

But on the afternoon of the third day a visitor called to whom she did not deny herself. Her father was admitted and found himself awaiting her coming in the library. She did not keep him waiting for long.

"Well, father, is not this a shocking business?" she said, before he had even greeted her.

"A shocking business! A shocking business to find you still here, Priscilla," he said.

"Where should I be if not with my husband?" she said.

"Your husband! Your husband isn't here; you know that well, my girl."

"The only husband I have ever known is here. Please do not fancy that I recognize as my husband that contemptible fraud to whom you gave me."

"However badly he treated you, however grossly I was taken in by him, he is still your lawful husband. Marriage according to the rites of the Church is a sacred bond. It is not in the power of man to sever it. You swore 'for better for worse.'"

"I did not swear at all. That is one of the fictions of the Church like the 'Love, honour, and obey' paragraph. Do you tell me that I must honour a felon, love a trickster, and obey a blackguard?"

"It is God's holy ordinance; you cannot deny that, however blasphemous you may become in your words."

"Do you tell me that it is God's holy ordinance that I should worship with my body a swindler—a man who only wanted to get me into his power to prevent his swindling from sending him to the gaol that he deserved? Do you think that it would be in keeping with the holy ordinance of God for me to live with a wretch who made his scurrilous joke about the ring he had just put on my finger a few minutes before the handcuffs were put on his wrists?—a blackguard who went straight from the gaol to a woman in America—who allowed the report of his heroic death—oh, how you laid stress upon that heroic death of his, and called me indecent because I was sincere enough to thank God for having delivered me from him!—he allowed the report of his death to be published in order that he might have a chance of blackmailing my husband."

"Your husband! Your—I tell you, girl, that Marcus Blaydon is your husband, and that so long as you remain under this roof John Wingfield is your paramour. I warned you of him long ago. I did my duty as a father by you in warning you that he did not mean to wed you; and didn't my words come true?"

Her face was scarlet and her eyes were blazing. She took a couple of rapid steps toward the door; but when about to fling it open, she managed to restrain herself. She stood there, breathing in short gasps, looking at him but unable to speak for indignation.

"You are my father," she managed to say at last; "I do not wish to turn you out of this house; but if you utter such an accusation again in my hearing, out of this house you will go—straight—straight! You have made some horrible—some vile accusations against me—me, your daughter, whom you placed in the power of that wretch, though I told you that I never could love him—that I almost loathed him; but instead of showing my poor mother the cruelty of which she was guilty, you backed her up and compelled me to utter lies——lies that you knew were lies—in the church. He uttered lies too; and yet, knowing all that you know, you are still not afraid to call this duet of Ananias and Sapphira God's holy ordinance! I don't know what your ideas of blasphemy are, but I know that you have provided me with a very good example of what I should call blasphemy."

He gazed at her as he had never before gazed even when she had also amazed him by the ease with which she got the better of him. He gazed at her for some minutes, and then his head fell till his chin was on his breast.

"Oh, God, my God! how have I sinned that my girl should turn out like this?" he said in a firm voice, as if uttering a challenge to his God to lay a finger upon a single weakness in his life that demanded so drastic a punishment.

She watched him, and she had a great pity for him, knowing him to be sincere in his belief in his own integrity and in the infallibility of the ordinances of the Church.

"Father," she said, "have you not read in the Bible that those who sow the wind shall reap the whirlwind? I do not profess to know much about the ways of God toward men—there are people who, while they tell me one minute that His ways are past finding out, will, the next, interpret with absolute confidence the most incomprehensible of His acts. But I have taken note of some things that I have seen, and that is one of them—the whirlwind harvest. Here we are to-day in this horrible position—why? Because you compelled me to go to the church and make promises, and utter falsehoods by the side of that man for whom I had no feeling of love. If I had ever loved him, would the fact of his going to gaol have made any difference to me? Not the least. It would only have made me love him more dearly, knowing that my love would mitigate his suffering. If I had loved him, would I not have been by his side the moment he got his freedom? If I had loved him, would I have been capable of loving someone else and of marrying that one within three months of his death? The seed was sown, and this is the harvest. I feel for you with all my heart; but I see the justice of it all—I even see that, like every other woman, I have to pay dearly for my one hour of weakness—for my one hour of falsehood to myself."

He had not raised his head all the time that she was speaking, nor did he do so until several moments had passed. He seemed to be considering her words and to be finding that there was something in them, after all. But when he looked up there was not much sign of contrition in his face.

"Whatever you may say, there's no blinking facts, and you know as well as I do what are the facts that face you to-day," he said, shaking a vehement fist, not as if threatening her, but only to give emphasis to his words. "The facts are, first, that you are the lawful wife of Marcus Blaydon, and secondly, that you are not the lawful wife of John Wingfield, and that if you persist in living with him you are his mistress."

She opened the door this time, but not vehemently.

"Go away," she said, "go away. I might as well have kept silent. I shall work out my own salvation in the face of your opposition and the opposition of the world."

"Your salvation? Woman, it is your own damnation that you are working out in this house—this house of sin!"

He took a few steps toward the door and then wheeled round.

"One more chance I give you," he said. "Come with me now, and you will only be asked to resume your former life. I will not insist on your joining your husband—only come away from this house."

"Go away, go away," she said, without so much as glancing at him.

Only one moment longer did he stay—just long enough to say:

"May God forgive you, Priscilla."

He contrived, as so many pious people can in saying those words, to utter them as if they were a curse. They sounded in her ears exactly as a curse would have sounded.

And then he tramped away.

Jack came to her shortly afterwards.

"You have no news for me, I suppose?" he said.

"No news, indeed. The old story."

"You knew what to expect. I think that the best thing we can do is to clear off from this neighbourhood as soon as we can. Until the matter is settled one way or another we should feel more comfortable among strangers."

"I am perfectly happy here, my dear Jack," she said. "I am so confident that we are doing what is right, I do not mind what people may say. Perhaps we should do well to go when your mother is strong enough to learn what has happened. That is the only thing that I dread—telling her the story."

He shook his head sadly.

"That will be the worst moment of all," he said slowly. "Thank heaven there is no possibility of our having to tell her anything for some time. She is far from well to-day."

That same evening Jack received from Messrs. Liscomb and Liscomb a copy of the opinion of the astute Sir Edward on their case. It was not voluminous, but it was very much to the point. It was in favour of an application for a decree of nullity in respect of the marriage with Blaydon, on the grounds, first, that the man had made false representations (antenuptial); secondly, that he had deserted his wife, making no attempt to see her after his release from gaol; and, thirdly, that he had taken no step to contradict the report, so widely circulated, of his death, thereby making her believe that she was at liberty to enter into a second contract of marriage. Failing success to have the marriage nullified, there were some grounds for trying for a divorce. In this case it would of course be necessary to prove misconduct.

On the whole, Messrs. Liscomb and Liscomb were inclined to think that the court would consider favourably the application for a nullity decree on the ground that the man and the woman had never lived together—the lawyers made use of a legal phrase—and that the latter had good reason to believe, owing to the default of the former, that she was a widow when she contracted her second marriage. Of course the misrepresentations (antenuptial) of the man, though of no weight in an ordinary case of divorce or separation, might in a petition for a nullity decree be worth bringing forward. They also thought that the fact of the man's being convicted of a crime against property (always looked on seriously by a judge and jury), and of his being arrested practically in the church porch after the marriage ceremony, would influence a court favourably in respect of the petitioner.

"They have never misled a client by an over-sanguine opinion, I should say," remarked Jack when he had read to her the letter of Messrs. Liscomb and Liscomb.

"And I am sure that they have found that plan to be the wisest," said she. "But I think that they rather incline to the belief that we shall succeed."

"From all that I have heard respecting them I feel that they have in this case expressed what they would consider to be an extraordinarily roseate opinion of our prospects," said he. "I wonder what move the other side will make next, and I wonder also if his advisers will take a sanguine view of his prospects. Did you gather from anything your father said that the fellow had been with him?"

"He said nothing definite on that point; but how should my father know anything of what has happened unless he had seen Marcus Blaydon?" said Priscilla. "He is, as we knew he would be, on the side of Blaydon. Just think of it! He is on the side of the wretch who did his best to wreck my life—who shortened my mother's life and made its last months to be months of misery instead of happiness—who allowed that false report of his death to go about uncontradicted so that I should run the chance of finding myself in the midst of the trouble that has come to me now—my father takes the side of that man against us, simply because of his superstition as to the sanctity of the marriage service according to the Church of England! He does not consider for a moment that the sacredness of marriage is to be found only in the spirit in which the marriage is entered into. He does not ask himself how there can be any element of a holy ordinance in a fraud."

Jack Wingfield was a man. He had been wise enough to refrain from considering the question of marriage either from the standpoint of a sacrament—the standpoint assumed by the Church of Rome—or from the standpoint of a symbol of the mystical union of Christ and the Church—the standpoint assumed by the Church of England. He had, as a matter of fact, never thought about marriage as a mystery, or the symbol of a mystery. It had only occurred to him that these assumptions, though professed by the Church within the Church, were ignored by the Church outside the Church. The Church of Rome refused to recognize divorce; but had frequently permitted it. It called marriage between an uncle and a niece incest, but sanctified it in the case of a royal personage. The Church of England, with its reiteration about every marriage being indissoluble by man, having been made by God, smiled amiably at the Divorce Court and petted *divorces*. The Church did not attempt to assign a mystic symbolism to divorce; and though it had for years affirmed that the marriage of a man with the sister of his deceased wife was incest, yet Parliament and every sensible person had assured the Church that this view was wrong, and the Church, after a little mumbling, like giants Pope and Pagan at the mouth of their cave, had submitted to be put in the wrong.

Jack Wingfield being a student—a newspaper student—of contemporary history, was aware of the numerous standpoints from which marriage is discussed, with well-assumed seriousness, by people whom he suspected of having their tongues in their cheeks all the time; but, as has just been stated, he had never himself given a thought to the mysticism of marriage or the symbolism of a wedding. He felt that it was enough for him to know that when his time came to fall in love with a girl and to desire to make her his wife, if the girl consented, he would marry her according to the law of the land, and she would be his wife.

Well, this had all come about; he had fallen in love and he had married the girl according to the law of the land; and was there anyone to say that she was not his wife or that he was not her husband? Of course he knew that there were quite a number of people who would say so; but what was their opinion worth? If she was the wife of someone else, she should, in the opinion of these people, leave him and go to someone else—yes, go to live with that swindling scoundrel—go to be the perpetual companion of a felon and a trickster who had shown his indifference to her and to all that she had suffered as his victim. What was the value of the opinion of people who should, with eyes turned up, assert the doctrine of the sacredness of marriage, and the necessity of acting in the case of himself and Priscilla in sympathy with their doctrines? These were the people who regard the conduct of Enoch Arden with abhorrence. Was he not actually allowing his wife to "live in sin" with the man who had supplanted him?

No; Priscilla and he had married in good faith, and they should be regarded by all sensible and unprejudiced people as man and wife. There was no man living, worthy of the name of a man, who would not call him a cur if he took any other view of the matter than this.

The idea of his handing over that girl to be dealt with by a felon according to his will, simply because the rascal had succeeded in getting the better of her father and mother...

Jack Wingfield laughed.

"Let him come and take her," he said to himself.

CHAPTER XXX

That was what he was longing for—for the claimant to come in person and lay a hand upon her. He felt that he would have given half his estate for the chance of answering the fellow as he should be answered—not by any reference to the opinions of those half-pagan patriarchs known as The Fathers; not by any reference to the views promulgated in the Middle Ages by that succession of thieving voluptuaries, murderers and excommunicators, the heads of the Church of Rome; or by modern sentimentalists struggling to reach the focus of the public eye—no, but by the aid of a dog-whip.

That was what he was longing for in these days—the chance to use his dog-whip upon the body of Marcus Blaydon. But Marcus Blaydon did not seem particularly anxious to give him the chance, and this fact caused his indignation against the man to increase. He felt as indignant as the henwife when her favourite chicken had shown some reluctance to come out of its coop to be killed.

It was the Reverend Osney Possnett, the vicar of Athalsdean, who paid a visit to the Manor House. Mr. Possnett had not been able to officiate at the marriage ceremony between Priscilla and Marcus Blaydon; he had been in Italy at the time; it was his curate for the time being, the Reverend Sylvanus Purview, who had married them. Doubtless if Mr. Purview had remained in the parish he would have paid Priscilla a visit when still under her father's roof, to offer her official consolation upon the untoward incident which, happening at the church porch immediately after the ceremony, had deprived her (as it turned out) of the society of her husband; but the Reverend Sylvanus Purview had found that the air of the Downs was too bracing for him, and he had quitted the parish a few days after the vicar's return, leaving the vicar to pay for his month's board and lodging, which he himself had, by some inadvertence that was never fully explained, omitted doing, although it was afterwards discovered that he had borrowed from Churchwarden Wadhurst the money necessary for this purpose.

Mr. Possnett had, however, made up for his curate's official deficiencies, as well as his monetary, and had spoken very seriously to Priscilla, on his return from Siena, on the subject of what he termed her trial—though it was really to Marcus Blaydon's trial he was alluding.

Priscilla had listened.

And now the Reverend Osney Possnett would not accept the formal statement of the footman, that Mr. and Mrs. Wingfield were not at home, but had written a few lines on the back of his card, begging Priscilla to allow him to speak a few words to her.

"I wouldn't bother with him, if I were you," said Jack when she showed him the card. "We have no use for your Reverend Osney Possnett. But please yourself."

"I don't want to be rude," said Priscilla.

"No, but he does," said Jack.

"I don't mind his rudeness," she cried. "Perhaps—who can tell?—he may have something important to communicate to me—something material——"

"They scorn anything bordering on the material," remarked Jack, "except when they get hold of a fraudulent prospectus with a promise of eighty per cent, dividends. But see him if you have any feeling in the matter."

"I think I should see him, Jack."

"Then see him. I'm sure he won't mind if I clear off."

So Jack went out of the room by the one door and the Reverend Osney Possnett was admitted by the other. The room was the large drawing-room with the cabinets of Wedgwood; and the sofa on which Priscilla sat was of the design of that in which Madame de Pompadour was painted by Boucher. It is, however, scarcely conceivable that the Reverend Osney Possnett became aware of any sinister suggestiveness in this coincidence.

He shook hands with her, not warmly, not even socially, but strictly officially.

"Priscilla," he said—he had known her from her childhood—"Priscilla, I have seen your father. He has told me all. I felt it to be my duty to come to you—to take you away from here."

She looked up and laughed—just in the way that Mrs. Patrick Campbell laughs in "Magda" when the man makes the suggestion about the child. Priscilla's rendering of that laugh made her visitor feel angry. He was not accustomed to be laughed at—certainly not to his face. He took a step toward her in a way that suggested scarcely curbed indignation.

"Priscilla," he cried, "have you realized what you are doing? Have you realized what you are—what you must be called so long as you remain in this house?"

"Yes," she replied. "I am Mr. Wingfield's wife, and I am called Mrs. Wingfield by all in this house, and I must be called so by everyone who visits at this house!"

"You are not his wife—you know that you are not his wife," said Mr. Possnett, vehemently.

"I know that I am his wife, Mr. Possnett," she replied with irritating gentleness. "I married him in accordance with the law of the land."

"But you were already married—that you have found out; so your marriage was no marriage."

"I agree with you—my marriage with Marcus Blaydon was no marriage."

"It was a marriage, celebrated in the house of God, by a priest of God, that made it a marriage—sacred; and yet you——"

"Sacred? Sacred? Mr. Possnett, do not be so foolish, I beg of you. Don't be so—so profane. Surely the sacredness of marriage does not begin and end with the form of words spoken in the church. Surely it is on account of its spiritual impulses that a marriage, the foundation of which is love, is sacred. A marriage is made sacred by the existence of a mutual love, and by that only. Is not that the truth?"

"I have not come here to-day to discuss with you any quibble, Priscilla. You know that you can legally have but one husband and——"

"Ah! I had no idea that you would make such a sudden drop from the question of the sacredness of marriage to the question of mere legality. I understood that the Church's first and only line of defence was the spirituality of marriage—the sacred symbolism—the mystery. Now you drop at once to the mundane level of the law—you talk of the legal marriage. I thank God, Mr. Possnett, that I adopt a higher tone. I elect to stand on a loftier level than yours. I do not talk of legality, but of spirituality."

"You cannot evade your responsibility by harping on words or phrases, Priscilla. In any question of marriage one cannot express too rigid an adherence to what is legal and what is illegal."

"In that case, then, surely we shall be able to obtain a divorce in a court of law——"

"There is no such thing as divorce."

Mr. Possnett had unwittingly walked into the trap laid for his feet by a young woman who had for years been acquainted with his individual views respecting the dissolution by a court of law of a marriage celebrated in a church of God.

"There is no such thing as divorce," he said. "I refuse to recognize the validity of a so-called decree of divorce. I would think it my duty to refuse to perform the service of marriage between two persons either of whom had been divorced. Having once said the words, 'Whom God hath joined together, let no man put asunder!'"

"But surely divorce is perfectly legal, Mr. Possnett?" said Priscilla.

"I care nothing for that."

"But you said just now that in all questions of marriage one must be bound down by what is legal and what is illegal; and now you tell me that you refuse to be bound down to a legal decree of divorce. Oh, Mr. Possnett, you cannot blow both hot and cold in the same breath."

"In all matters but this—but our Church permits a priest to hold his own opinion, if it be formed on conscientious grounds. It is not like the Church of Rome; it recognizes the imperative nature of the call of religious scruples on the part of an individual priest."

"And the Church does well. Let the priest follow the example of his Church, and recognize the spiritual exigencies of a poor woman who loved a man and married him in all honesty of purpose and in all good faith."

"Talk not to me of such things; the fact remains—the terrible truth—that man is not your husband. Priscilla, this is, I know, a great trial; but you know whence it comes. I have taught you ill all these years if you fail to acknowledge the Hand—the Hand—you know that it comes from God."

"That is the reflection which prevents me from being overwhelmed, Mr. Possnett. I try to feel that it all comes from God—that it is meant to try our faith, and I cannot doubt that its effect will be to draw us closer together, my dear husband and myself—nay, I have felt that it has done so already. Our faith in each other has been strengthened—it has indeed."

"That is not the object of the trial. Trial is sent to purify the soul, as gold is tried by fire; the furnace of affliction is meant to cleanse, not to strengthen one's persistence in a course of sin."

"I have never doubted it, Mr. Possnett, nor can I doubt that this burden, though it is hard to bear, will but strengthen our characters—strengthen all those qualities which go to build up into one life the life of a man and a woman who love each other, and whose faith in each other has been proved under the stress of adversity."

The Reverend Osney Possnett felt that he was now being subjected to a greater trial of patience than he could bear. Here was this young woman, the daughter of his own churchwarden, facing him and turning and twisting his words to suit her own pernicious views! He could almost fancy that she was mocking him. He could scarcely believe that such a trial should be included among those of celestial origin.

"Priscilla, I, your priest, tell you that you are living in sin with this man who is not your husband, and I command you to forsake this life and to forsake that man who, I doubt not, has tempted you by the allurements of a higher position in life than that for which you were intended by God, to be false to your Church, false to the teaching of its priest, false to your own better nature. Leave him, Priscilla; leave him before it is too late!"

Again she laughed; but this time it was with a different expression.

"I cannot say '*Retro me?*' because I am not resisting any temptation," she said. "You have shown that you do not understand in the least how I feel in regard to my position—you could not possibly understand me if I were to refer to the church in which you preach as a house of sin."

"Priscilla, for God's sake, pause—pause——"

"I have not called it a house of sin; God forbid that I should be so foolish! but it was made the means of my committing the greatest sin of my life—the abandonment of myself—myself—at the bidding of my parents. All that has happened since, you have assured me as a delegate, is to be part of a great trial sent for the purification of my heart, my soul, whatever you please. Well, I told you that I accepted that view and that I hoped I should come away from it purified and strengthened. But I cannot get away altogether from the thought that perhaps it may be a judgment on myself for being untrue to myself when I entered your church at the bidding of my father and my mother to say words that I knew to be false—that they knew to be false—to make promises that I knew it would be a crime to keep."

"I care nothing about that, Priscilla. All that concerns me is that you were joined to a man according to the rites of the Holy Church, and that, he being still alive you are now wife to him and to no other."

"And you would have me now go to him and live with him as his wife according to God's holy ordinance, and to keep those promises which I made in your church?"

"I solemnly affirm that such is your duty."

"You say that, knowing the man, and knowing that he is a criminal—that he married me to save himself from the consequences of his crime—you can tell me that I should worship him with my body, that I should love, honour, and obey him till death us do part? Knowing that I have never had any love for him, you tell me that my place is by his side?"

"Your place is by his side. The words of the Prayer-book are there; no Christian priest has any option in the matter. The mystic words have been said. 'The twain shall be one flesh.'"

"Ah, there is the difference between us—the flesh. You will insist on looking at the fleshly side of marriage, whereas I look on the spiritual. Don't you think that there may be something to be said in favour of the spiritual aspect of marriage—the marriage voice which says, not, 'The twain shall be one flesh,' but 'The twain shall be one spirit'? What, Mr. Possnett, will you say that marriage is solely a condition of the flesh?"

"I refuse to answer any question put to me in this spirit by a woman who is living in sin with a man who is not her husband."

"You will admit that the trial to which I have been subjected has influenced me for good—making me patient and forbearing in the face of a repeated insult such as I would not have tolerated from any human being a week ago. I have listened to you, and I have even brought myself to pay you the compliment of discussing with you a matter which concerns only my husband and myself, but you have not even thought it worth your while to be polite to me—to treat me as an erring sister. You come with open insults—with an assumption of authority—to pronounce one thing sin and another thing duty. But your authority is a mockery—as great a mockery as the enquiry in the marriage service, 'Who giveth this woman to be married to this man?' when you know that the pew-cleaner will be accepted by the priest as the one who possesses that authority. Your authority is a mockery, and your counsel is worth no more than that of any other man of some education, of abilities which have the lowest market value of those required for any profession, and experiences of the most limited character."

"Woman—Priscilla, you forget yourself!"

The Reverend Osney Possnett, who had never had a chance in his life of reaching a point of declamation beyond what was necessary for the adequate reproof of a ploughman for neglecting to attend Divine service, and who had never been addressed except with respect bordering upon awe since the days of his curacy, found himself in a mental condition for which the word flabbergasted was invented by a philologist in the lumber trade. When he had told Priscilla that she was forgetting herself he forgot himself. He forgot his part. He had come to the Manor House, on the invitation of his churchwarden, Farmer Wadhurst, to administer a severe rebuke to Farmer Wadhurst's self-willed daughter, whose early religious instruction he had superintended, and who, he saw no reason to doubt, would be at once amenable to his ministration; but he found himself forced not only to enter into something of an argument with her—a course of action which was very distasteful to him—but also to be reproved by her for a sensualist, looking at the fleshly side of marriage instead of the spiritual—to be told by her that his opinion was of no greater value than that of an ordinary man who had never been granted the distinction of holy orders, which the whole world recognizes as a proof of the possession of the highest culture, pagan as well as Christian, the most virile human intellect, and an intuitive knowledge of mankind, such as ordinary people can only gain by experience!

He had come to be letter-perfect in the part which he had meant to play in her presence, and with a good working knowledge of the "business" of the part; but she had failed to act up to him. She had disregarded the cues which he waited for from her, and the result was naturally the confusion that now confronted him—that now overwhelmed him. He had in his mind actually, if unconsciously, the feeling that it was her failure in regard to her cues which had put him out, when he cried:

"Priscilla, you forget yourself."

"No, you do not quite mean that," she said, with a disconcerting readiness; "you do not quite mean that; you mean that I forget that for years I sat Sunday after Sunday under your pulpit listening to your preaching—that for years and years you gave your opinion, which was followed without question, to my father and mother on the subject of my bringing up; that until now I was submissive to you, with all the members of the household. That is what you had on your mind just now, and I do not wonder at it. I have amazed you. I don't doubt it; I have amazed myself. The troubles which I have had during the past eighteen months—you call them trials, and that is the right word—have been the means of showing me myself—showing me what I am as an individual: that I am not merely as a single grain of sand running down with a million other grains in the hour-glass only to mark time till the whole are swallowed up. I thank God for those trials which have made me what I am to-day. I can even thank God for the present trial, terrible though it seems, because I have faith in God's way of working to bring out all that is best in man and woman; and I know that we shall come out of it with our love for each other strengthened and our belief in God strengthened. That is what you forgot when you came here to-day, Mr. Possnett; you forgot the power that there is in suffering to develop the character, the nature, the individuality, the human feeling and the Divine love of every one who experiences it. That was your mistake: you did not make allowance for God's purpose in suffering. You thought that I should be the same to-day that I was eighteen months ago.

You have much to learn, both of God and man, Mr. Possnett. So have I. I am learning daily."

The Reverend Osney Possnett lifted up his hands—the attitude was that of Moses blessing the congregation; but by a sudden increase of emphasis and a tightening of the hands into fists it became the attitude of Balak the son of Zippor reproving Balaam the Prophet for having betrayed the confidence reposed in him as an agent of commination. He was not a man of any intelligence worth speaking of, and with so limited an experience of the world that the least departure from the usual found him without resources for meeting it. Such men are unwise if they make the attempt to play the usual against the unusual. They are wisest in avoiding it.

The Reverend Osney Possnett showed that he was not without wisdom by his retreat. Sorrow and not indignation was the lubricant of his farewell. His prayer was that she might be brought to see in what direction the truth lay before it should be too late.

And that was just the prayer to which Priscilla could say "Amen!" with all her heart.

CHAPTER XXXI

Two days later the papers were full of the news of the reappearance of Marcus Blaydon.

Jack Wingfield had been very impatient of the delay. Every morning that he opened the newspapers, and drew them blank, he swore at the man. What the mischief was he waiting for? Was he such an idiot as to fancy that he, Jack Wingfield, was likely to give a more promising reply to his demands than he had already given him? Did he hope to gain anything by merely menacing him in regard to the publication of his story?

Priscilla was clever enough to see that the man had hoped much from the visit which her father had paid her, and perhaps even more from that of the Vicar of Athalsdean. She felt sure that she saw what was the sort of game he meant to play when he returned to England. He had meant to try the familiar game of blackmail in the first instance, being idiot enough to think that Priscilla would jump at the chance of being allowed to pay over some thousands of pounds for his promise to clear out of the country and tell no human being that he was her husband. Failing, however, to convince her or Wingfield that their position would be to any extent improved by the acceptance of his terms, he had gone to her father, knowing that he had a sheet-anchor in the enormous respectability of Farmer Wadhurst. He did not want Priscilla—if he had wanted her he would have hurried to her the moment he found himself free, if only to tell her that he meant to start life afresh, in order that he might win her love and redeem the past—no; he did not want her; but he was well aware of the fact that her father was a moderately wealthy man, and that Priscilla was his only child. These were the possibilities that appealed to him. Perhaps the father might show his readiness to pay a respectable price for the preservation untarnished of the respectability of the family; but failing that, he might still be able to make a good thing out of the connection, for his father-in-law would stand by him, could he be made to see that it would be for the good of the family to stand by him. But her father's mission and the mission of the Reverend Osney Possnett having failed, the man had no further reason for delay in making public the romantic incidents in which he had taken a prominent part.

These represented the surmises of Priscilla and Jack, and they were not erroneous in substance, though in some particulars not absolutely accurate, as they afterwards found out.

What Jack confessed his inability to account for was the flight of the man across the Atlantic, when he had such good prospects opening before him as the husband of Priscilla, the daughter of that prosperous agriculturist, Mr. Wadhurst. To be sure, it was just on this point that he had allowed his imagination some play when he had that conversation with Marcus Blaydon. He had suggested that the fellow had gone across the Atlantic in order to be with some woman whom he had known before; but Jack was scarcely inclined to give the man credit for a disinterested attachment such as this, when he had such good prospects at home as the lawful husband of a beautiful young woman, whose society (post-nuptial) he had had but a very restricted opportunity of enjoying.

That was a matter which, he saw, required some explanation; but he felt sure that the explanation would come in good time; and it would be his, Jack Wingfield's, aim to expedite its arrival; and he knew that the success of the nullity suit depended on his finding out all about that unaccountable attachment which had forced a mercenary trickster into an unaccountable position.

But here were the newspapers at last containing the information that Marcus Blaydon, who had been placed in the early part of the summer in the forefront of the rank of maritime heroes—by far the most picturesque of all heroic phalanxes—had returned to England, none the less a hero because he had by a miracle (described in detail) escaped the consequences of his heroism; and engaged—also without prejudice to the claims made on his behalf when his name was last before the eyes of the public—in the discharge of a duty so painful as to cause him to feel that it would have been better if he had perished among the rocks where he had lain insensible for many hours after doing his best to rescue his messmates from a watery grave, than to have survived that terrible night.

That is what the announcements in some of the newspapers came to. But they had the tone of the preliminary announcements of a matter which is supposed to contain certain elements of interest to the public later on, if the public will only have the kindness to keep an eye upon the papers. Some of the phrases—including that important one about the "watery grave," appeared in all the accounts of the matter; but in a few cases the news did not occupy a greater space than an ordinary paragraph, while in others the attention of casual readers was drawn to it by the adventitious aid of some startling headlines—two of these introducing the name of Enoch Arden. Not once, however, in any newspaper, was the name of Mr. Wingfield introduced.

"They read like a rangefinder," remarked Mr. Wingfield, when he had gone through every line of the paragraphs. "That is what the fellow is doing—he is trying to find out our position."

But there was no need for the invention of such a theory to account for the guarded omissions in the paragraphs, the truth being simply that the professional correspondent of the Press agency who had handled the item understood his business. He had no wish to drag the name of a member of Parliament into a piece of news offered to him by a man whose trial for embezzlement he had attended professionally the previous year. In addition, he perceived how it was possible for him to nurse the information, if it stood the test of enquiry, until it should yield to him a small fortune. He understood his business, and his business was to understand the palate of newspaper readers.

And that was how it came that Mr. Wingfield was waited on by a well-dressed and very polite literary gentleman that same day, and invited to make any statement which he would have no objection to read in print the next morning on the subject of the return of the heroic Marcus Blaydon.

"The man told you, I suppose, that his trying mission to England was to claim the lady from whom he was parted at the church door after their marriage, and whom I married a short time ago," said Mr. Wingfield, M.P.

"That is the substance of the statement which he made to me yesterday, sir," said his visitor. "I hesitated to transmit it to my agency at London, not wishing, on the authority of a man of his antecedents, even though endorsed by Mr. Wadhurst, to publish a single line that might possibly— possibly——"

"Be made the subject of a libel action—is that what is on your mind?" said Mr. Wingfield.

"Of course—but in the back of my mind, Mr. Wingfield," replied the other. "What I was really anxious to avoid was saying anything calculated to give pain to——"

"I appreciate your consideration," said Jack pleasantly; "but I know that omelettes cannot be made without breaking eggs."

"Yes, sir; but I should like to avoid a bad egg."

"Then you would do well to avoid Marcus Blaydon."

The gentleman laughed, and shook his head.

"A bad egg, beyond doubt, Mr. Wingfield; but good enough for some culinary operations," said the skilful paragraphist. "It is true, then, that he was really married to the lady whom you subsequently—" Jack saw the word "espoused" trembling on his lips, and he hastened to save him from the remorse which he would be certain to feel when he should awaken at nights, and remember that he had employed that word solely to save his repeating the word "married."

"I believe that to be the truth," he said at once. "The man came here and claimed the lady as his wife, but she declined to admit his claim, pending the result of her appeal to the proper quarter for the annulment of her marriage with him."

The gentleman whipped out his note-book in a moment, and made with the rapidity of lightning some hundreds of outline drawings of gulls flying, and miniature arches, and many-toed crabs, and trophies of antlers, interspersed with dots and monkeys' tails, variously twisted, and Imperial moustaches similarly treated.

"Mrs.—Wingfield—" the gentleman had infinite tact and taste—"Mrs. Wingfield is making such an application? Messrs. Liscomb and Liscomb, I suppose?"

"Messrs. Liscomb and Liscomb."

"With Sir Edward retained, of course?"

"With Sir Edward. You seem pretty well acquainted with the procedure."

The gentleman smiled.

"I have been connected with the Press for fifteen years, sir," he said. "May I ask one more question, Mr. Wingfield? Is it the intention of the—of Mrs. Wingfield to remain at the Manor House pending the result of the litigation?"

"You may take it from me that she will run no risks," said Jack. "She will not change her present domicile for any other, so long as Marcus Blaydon remains out of gaol."

The visitor made some more lightning drawings in outline, and then became thoughtful.

"May I venture to express the hope that Mrs. Wingfield is in good health, sir?" he said—"in good health, and confident of the result of her application for a pronouncement of nullity?" he added, after a hesitating moment.

"She is in excellent health and spirits, thank you," replied Jack. "Of course, in matters of law one must always expect delay, and in such a point as that upon which we await a decision, it is natural that one should become impatient. However, we know that there is nothing for it but to sit tight for a month or two."

"I'm extremely obliged to you for this interview, Mr. Wingfield," said the gentleman, turning over a new leaf of his note-book, and looking up with his pencil ready. "Now, if there is anything whatever that you would like to be made public in this connection——"

"I don't know that I have anything in my mind beyond what I have just told you," said Mr. Wingfield. "Of course, you can easily understand that we would greatly prefer that nothing should appear in the newspapers about us or our lawsuits until they are actually before the courts, but we know that that would be to expect too much."

"If I am not taking too great a liberty, sir, I would say that, unpleasant though it may appear from some standpoints to have the particulars published, you will find that in the long run it will be advantageous to you. Public sympathy is better to have with one than against one."

"I suppose it is second only to having the law on one's side."

"Public sympathy is superior to the law, Mr. Wingfield; and they are beginning to find that out on the other side of the Atlantic. This case is certain to attract a large amount of attention. You see, we are just entering on the month of August. Upon my word, I shouldn't wonder if it became the Topic of the Autumn—I shouldn't indeed, Mr. Wingfield. Well, I'm extremely obliged to you, sir; and I won't take up any more of your time. Good morning."

"Good morning. Any time that you want any information that you think I can give you, don't hesitate to come to me."

"You are very kind, sir. I should be sorry to intrude."

So the representative of the Press went his ways, congratulating himself on having, after a Diogenes-search lasting, for several years, come upon a sensible man and a straightforward man, devoid of frills. Most men who had attained, by the exertions of their forefathers, to the position of landed proprietors, he had found to be not easy to approach on matters which they called private matters, but which newspaper men called public matters. Mr. Wingfield, however, so far from resenting an interview on a subject which required to be handled with extreme delicacy, had actually given him encouragement to repeat his visit.

He was determined that Mr. Wingfield and the cause which he had at heart should not suffer by his display of a most unusual courtesy.

The next day all England was discussing the case of the new Enoch Arden. They would have discussed the case throughout the length and breadth of the land simply on account of the romantic elements that it contained, even if the lady who played so important a part in it had been an ordinary young person; but as she was a lady whose achievements during the last byelection had been directly under the eye of the public, the interest in the romance was immeasurably increased. The representative of the Press agency who had the handling of the story from the first, had not found it necessary to embellish in any way the account of his interview with Marcus Blaydon in the morning or with Mr. Wingfield in the afternoon. After alluding to the mystery suggested by Mr. Blaydon's remark, published in connection with his reappearance in the land of the living the previous day, he described how he had waited upon Mr. Blaydon to try to convince him that the painful matters which had necessitated his making a voyage to England could scarcely fail to be of interest to newspaper readers; and how he had succeeded in convincing Mr. Blaydon of the correctness of his contention. Mr. Blaydon had then described the incidents associated with his escape from destruction; how he had been cast upon the rocks in his attempt to carry a line ashore, and how he had lain there for some days, with practically nothing to eat, and apparently suffering from such internal injuries as prevented him from reaching the house where those of his messmates who had survived the terrible night were being so hospitably treated.

Then, according to his own account, it occurred to Mr. Blaydon that the chance of his life had come—such a chance as comes but too rarely to an unfortunate man who has acted foolishly, but is anxious to redeem the past—the chance of beginning life over again. He was well aware, he said, that he would be reported as dead, and that was just what he wished for: to be dead to all the world, so that he might have another chance of succeeding in life without being handicapped by his unhappy past.

So Mr. Blaydon's story went on, telling how he had just made a start in this new life of his, when by chance he came upon an English newspaper, referring to the fact that the gentleman who had agreed to contest the Nuttingford division of Nethershire at the by-election had just married the daughter of Mr. Wadhurst of Athalsdean Farm. Then, and only then, did he, the narrator, perceive that he would have acted more wisely if he had written to the lady who believed herself to be his widow, apprising her of the fact of his being alive, and endeavouring to make for himself a name that she might bear without a blush. (Mr. Blaydon was well acquainted, it appeared, with the phraseology of the repentant sinner of the Drury Lane autumn drama.)

"What was my duty when I heard that my wife had gone through the ceremony of marriage with another man?" That was the question which perplexed Mr. Blaydon, as a conscientious man anxious not to diverge a hair's breadth from the line of Duty—strict duty. Well, perhaps some people might blame him; but he confessed that the thought of his dear wife—the girl whom he had wooed and won very little more than a year before—going to another man and living with him believing herself to be his wife, was too much for him. He made up his mind that so shocking a situation could not be allowed to continue, and he had made his way back to her side, only, alas! to be repulsed and turned out of her house with contempt, though the fact that her father had received him with the open arms of a father in welcoming the return of the prodigal, proved that even in these days, etc., etc.

Stripped of all emotional verbiage, Mr. Blaydon's statements simply amounted to a declaration of his intention to apply to the court to make an order to restore to him his conjugal rights in respect of the lady who was incontestably his lawful wife.

Following this was the account of an interview with Mr. Wingfield, M.P., who, it appeared, had already taken action in the matter on behalf of the lady referred to by Mr. Blaydon. The interviewer succeeded in conveying to a reader something of what he termed the "breezy colloquial style" of Mr. Wingfield, in the latter's references to the Enoch Ardenism of Mr. Blaydon; but very little appeared in the account of the interview that had not actually taken place at the interview itself. Readers of the newspapers were made fully acquainted with the fact that Messrs. Liscomb and Liscomb had already made a move in the case, and that the invaluable services of Sir Edward had been retained for the lady, and also that the lady was living at Overdean Manor House, which chanced to be the residence of Mr. Wingfield, M.P., and that it was her intention to remain there for a period that was not defined by the writer. He refrained from even the suggestion that the period might be "till the case is decided by the court."

The remainder of the column was occupied by a pleasant description of Overdean Manor Park in early August, with a quotation from the "Highways and Byways" series, and a brief account of the Wingfield family.

Of course, in addition to these particulars which appeared in most of the newspapers, the illustrated dailies contained a reproduction of the recently-used "blocks" of Mr. and Mrs. Wingfield on their now celebrated election campaign, as well as some entirely new photographs of the Manor House, and Athalsdean Farm, the birthplace of "Mrs. Wingfield"—nearly all the newspapers referred to Priscilla as Mrs. Wingfield, inside quotation marks; but three or four omitted the quotation marks, and an equal number, who were sticklers for strict accuracy, called her Mrs. Blaydon, though one of them half apologised for its accuracy by adding "as we suppose we must call the unfortunate lady."

The comments on the romantic features of the case which were to be read in different type in the columns devoted to the leading articles, were all of that character which is usually described as "guarded." The writers excused their want of definiteness on the ground that it would be grossly improper for anyone to offer such a comment as might tend to prejudice a judge or jury in the suits which would occupy the attention of the law courts during the Michaelmas sittings. It was quite enough for the writers to point out some of the remarkable features of the whole romance, beginning with the arrest of Marcus Blaydon when in the act of leaving the church where the wedding had taken place—most of the articles dealt very tenderly with this episode—and going on to refer to the impression produced on the court by the appeal for mercy to the judge made by Marcus Blay-don's counsel on the ground of his recent marriage to a charming and accomplished girl to whom he was devoted, and who would certainly suffer far more than the prisoner himself by his incarceration—an appeal which the judge admitted had influenced him in pronouncing his very mild sentence of imprisonment.

These were some of the nasty bits of publicity which Jack Wingfield had foreseen. Priscilla had reddened a good deal reading them, but she had not shrunk from their perusal. She accepted everything as part of the ordeal which she had to face. She even smiled when, a few days later, there appeared in one of the papers a letter signed "A Dissatisfied Elector," affirming that, as the election for the Nuttingford division had to all intents and purposes been won for Mr. John Wingfield by a lady who was not his lawful wife, the seat should be declared vacant.

Jack also smiled—after an interval—and threw the paper into the basket reserved for such rubbish.

CHAPTER XXXII

And then began the persecution which everyone must expect who is unfortunate enough to attain to a position of fame or its modern equivalent, notoriety.

The month was August, and no war worth the salary of a special correspondent was going on, so the newspapers were only too pleased to open their columns to the communications of the usual autumnal faddists, and the greatest of these is the marriage faddist. "The Curious Case" formed the comprehensive heading to a daily page in one paper, containing letter after letter, from "A Spinster," "One Who Was Deceived," "Once Bitten Twice Shy," "True Marriage," "I Forbid the Banns," and the rest of them. Without actually commenting on the case, these distinguished writers pointed out day by day how the various points in the curious case of Marcus Blaydon and Priscilla Wadhurst bore out the various contentions of the various faddists. Now this would not have mattered so much but for the fact that it was the most ridiculous of these letters which, after a column's advocacy of the principles of free love or some other form of profligacy, such as the "Spiritual Union," or the "Soul to Soul" wedding, invariably wound up by a declaration that "all honour should be given to that brave little woman, who has thrown in her lot with the man she loves, to stand or fall by the principles which she has so fearlessly advocated"—these principles being, of course, the very principles whose enunciation formed the foundation of the ridiculous letter.

The most senseless of all these letters was signed "Two Souls with but a Single Thought;" and the superscription seemed an appropriate one, for the writers did not seem to have more than a single thought between them, and this one was erroneous.

Of course, after a time Priscilla became almost reconciled to the position of being the Topic of the holiday season, though earlier she found it very hard to bear. At first she had boldly faced the newspapers; but soon she found that the thought of what she had read during the day was interfering with her rest at night. She quickly became aware of the fact that persecution is hydra-headed, and every heading is in large capitals. She made up her mind that she would never open another newspaper, and it was as well that she adhered to this resolution; for after some days the American organs, as yellow as jaundice and as nasty, began to arrive, and Jack saw that they were quite dreadful. They commented freely upon the "case," being outside the jurisdiction of the English courts, and they commented largely upon incidents which they themselves had invented to bear out their own very frankly expressed views regarding the shameless profligacy of the landed gentry of England, and the steadily increasing immorality of the English House of Commons. On the showing of these newspapers, Mr. John Wingfield was typical of both; he had succeeded in combining the profligacy of the one with the immorality of the other; and he certainly could not but admit that the stories of his life which they invented and offered to their readers, fully bore out their contention, that, if the public life of the States was a whirlpool, that of England was a cesspool.

It was only natural that the accredited representative of so much old-world iniquity should feel rather acutely the responsibilities of the position to which he was assigned; but he had been through the States more than once and he had also been in the Malay Archipelago, and had found how closely assimilated were the offensive elements in the weapons of the two countries. The stinkpot of the Malays had its equivalent in the Yellow Press of the United States; but neither of the two did much actual harm to the person against whom they were directed. If a man has only enough strength of mind to disregard the stinkpot he does not find himself greatly demoralised by his experience of its nastiness, and if he only ignores the "pus" of the Yellow Press no one else will pay any attention to its discharges.

He burned the papers, having taken care that Priscilla never had a chance of looking at any one of the batch. He was in no way sensitive; but now and again he felt tempted to rush off with Priscilla to some place where they could escape for ever from this horror of publicity which was besetting them. He did not mind being made the subject of leading articles, if it was his incapacity as an orator or his ignorance of the political standpoint that was being assailed; but this intrusion upon his private life was as distasteful to him as it would be for anyone to see one's dressing-room operations made the subject of a cinematograph display.

How could he feel otherwise, when almost daily he could espy strangers—men with knapsacks and women with veils (mostly green), all of them carrying walking sticks—coming halfway up the avenue and exchanging opinions as to the best point from which the house could be snapshotted? Such strangers were no more infrequent than the visits of men on motors—all sorts of motors, from the obsolete tri-car to the 60 h.p. F.I.A.T. He was obliged to give orders at the lodge gates that on no pretence was a motor to be allowed to pass on to the avenue, and that bicycling strangers, as well as pedestrians with kodaks, were also to be excluded. But in spite of these orders, scarcely a day went by without bringing a contingent of outsiders to the park; he believed that excursion trains were run to Framsby solely to give the curious a chance of catching a glimpse of the lady who figured as the heroine of "The Curious Case" column of the great daily paper.

But as far as Framsby itself was concerned, it did not contribute largely to the material of the nuisance. The truth was that the "sets" of Framsby, who had for some days made the road to the Manor suggest a picture of the retreat of the French from Moscow, owing to their anxiety to leave cards upon the young couple, now stood aghast at the information conveyed to them by the newspapers that Mrs. Jack Wingfield was not really Mrs. Jack Wingfield. They stood aghast, and held up their hands as if they were obeying the imperative order of a highwayman rather than the righteous impulse of outraged propriety. Some of them, who, through the strain put upon the livery stables, had been compelled to postpone their visit until a more convenient season, now affirmed that they had had their doubts respecting the marriage all along. There was some consultation among the "sets" as to the possibility of having their visits cancelled, as now and again a presentation at Court was cancelled. Would it not be possible to get back their cards? they wondered. The baser sort had thoughts of sending in the livery stables bill to Mr. Jack Wingfield.

But before a fortnight had passed it became plain to Jack and Priscilla that they were not going to remain without sympathetic visitors. Priscilla got a letter from Mrs. Bowlby-Sutherst—a vivacious letter, and a delightfully worldly one into the bargain. The writer stated her intention of coming to lunch at the Manor House the next day, and of bringing a fire escape with her to allow of her getting in by one of the windows if she were refused admission by the door. And when she came and was admitted without the need for the display of any ingenuity on her part, she proved a most amusing visitor, showing no reticence whatever in regard to the "case," and ridiculing the claims of Marcus Blaydon to conjugal rights, after the way he had behaved. Of course everyone with any sense acknowledged, she affirmed, that the marriage was between Jack and Priscilla.

When she had gone away Priscilla wondered if there was anything in what she had said on this point; and Jack replied that he was afraid that Mrs. Bowlby-Sutherst was too notorious as a patron of notoriety for her opinion to have much weight. But as things turned out, that was just where he was wrong, for within the week several other ladies of considerable importance—county importance—called at the Manor, and were admitted. These were people who owned London houses and had a premonition that next season Mrs. Wingfield—they were sure that she would be Mrs. Wingfield by then—would be looked on as the most interesting figure in the world of drawing-rooms; and Priscilla found them very nice indeed, referring to her "case" as if it were one of the most amusing jests of the autumn season. They showed no reluctance in talking about its funniest features—its funniest features were just those which a rigid disciplinarian would have called its most serious features—and they promised faithfully that when she should appear in the court they would be present to offer her their support—their moral support. They seemed quite downhearted when she explained to them how it was her hope that the arbitrament of the Divorce Division would be avoided by a decree of a judge on the question of nullity. They had quite set their hearts on the Divorce Court, and had in their eye a toilet scheme which they felt sure would be in sympathy with the *entourage* of that apartment, and to which they thought they might be trusted to do justice.

But as the social position of these visitors was among the highest in the county, Priscilla began to feel that there was no chance of her becoming isolated even at the Manor House. The reasonableness of her attitude appealed, she saw, to some reasonable people. She had great hopes that it would appeal as well to one or more of His Majesty's judges when the time came.

And she was not neglected by her dear friend Rosa Cafifyn; but this young woman came to her unaccompanied by her mother. The Caffyn household was divided against itself on this vexed subject of Priscilla's attitude. Mrs. Caffyn, who had never encouraged her daughter's friendship for Priscilla Wadhurst, was aghast at the publicity which her daughter's friend had achieved.

"She was always getting herself talked about," she remarked. "First there was that affair with the prince; everyone was talking about her speaking to him in French—in French, mind—for more than an hour." (Mrs. Caffyn seemed to have acquired the impression that a conversation in French could scarcely fail to possess some of the elements of the dialogue in a French vaudeville, and she had heard enough about that form of composition to make her distrustful of its improving qualities.) "And then," she went on, "there came all that horrid business about her marriage—the arrest of the man, you know, and all that. The next thing was the trial, where her name was mentioned in the hearing of all the common people—witnesses and people of that class—in the court. Later on there was the heroic drowning of the man, and then her marriage to Mr. Wingfield within a few months, and the electioneering business—I really think that she should have been more discreet than to get herself talked about so frequently. As for her present escapade, I can only say that it seems to me to be the crowning indiscretion of her life."

But the Reverend Mr. Caffyn, who had been talking to his patroness, Mrs. Bowlby-Sutherst, about Priscilla, was disposed to take the view of an easy-going looker-on at the world and its ways from a lesser altitude than that of his pulpit; and he smiled at Priscilla's resolution to remain at the Manor. He did not think that it mattered much just then. Had she not married young Wingfield in good faith, and had they not been going about together ever since? he asked. He had in his mind, though his wife did not know it, the saying of the wicked witty Frenchwoman who had accepted the legend of the King's making quite a promenade when deprived of his head, on the plea that, after all *"c'est le premier pas qui coûte."* And so his daughter had no hesitation in paying her visit to the Manor.

It was when she was going through the gates that she recollected how Priscilla had talked to her upon that morning long ago at this same place. What had she said? Was it not that if she were to love a man truly she would not allow any considerations of morality or any other convention to keep her apart from him?

Rosa wondered if there really was anything in the theory which was held by some people, to the effect that sometimes a judgment followed hard upon the utterance of a thoughtless phrase. She wondered if the publicity in which Priscilla was now moving had been sent to her as a punishment for her impulsive words.

Perhaps it was the atmospheric envelope, so to speak, of this thought which remained hanging about her in the house and prevented her visit to her dear friend from being all that she expected it to be. It was of course a delightful reunion; but somehow Priscilla did not seem to be just the same as she had been long ago.

With these variations of visitors and with plenty to occupy her mind and her hands Priscilla found the weeks to go by rapidly enough. She took care to be constantly occupied, by undertaking the reorganization of the dairy in connection with the home farm, and she had no difficulty in reviving Jack's interest in the scheme for introducing electric power for the lighting of the house and for the lightening of labour in whatever department of the household labour was employed. An expert on dynamos was summoned from Manchester, and his opinion bore out all that Priscilla had said to Jack on this interesting enterprise; and before a fortnight had passed the details of the scheme had been decided on and estimates were being prepared for the carrying out of the work.

In addition to her obvious duties Priscilla was making herself indispensable to Jack's mother in her long and tedious illness, reading to her and sitting with her for hours every day. It was, however, when Jack was alone with his mother one evening that she laid her hand on his, saying:

"My dear boy, I had my fears at one time for the step you were taking; but now I can only thank you with all my heart for having given me a daughter after my own heart. I have, as you know, always longed for a daughter, and my longing is now fulfilled with a completeness that I never looked for. She is the best woman in the world, Jack—the best woman for you."

"I hope that I shall be able to make her as happy as she has made me," said he.

"Ah, that is the very point on which I wished to speak to you," said the mother. "I wonder if you have noticed——if you have thought that she is quite as happy as we could wish her to be. A shadow—no, not quite so much as a shadow, but still something—have I been alone in noticing it?—something like a shadow upon her now and then."

Jack was slightly startled. He had taken good care that no newspaper containing an allusion to the "curious case" which was exciting the attention of all England and calling for immediate attention on the other side of the Atlantic as well, should get into his mother's hands; but now that she was approaching convalescence, he knew that however vigilant he might be in this respect, an unlucky chance would make her aware of all that had happened since the beginning of the attack that had prostrated her. He had been living in dread of such a catastrophe all the previous week, and now he perceived that it was imminent. Priscilla had not been able to play her part so perfectly as to prevent the quick feeling—the motherly apprehension—of the elder lady from suggesting something to her.

"It would be the worst day of my life if any cloud were to come over her path," he said. "I hope that if anything of the sort were to happen, it would only be a temporary thing—something that we should look back upon, wondering that it should ever have disturbed our peace."

"What!" she cried. "You have noticed it?—there is something!—you know what it is?"

"Oh, yes," he said, with an affectation of carelessness "there has been something—a trifle really—nothing of the nature of a difference between Priscilla and myself, but——"

"I am glad you can assure me of that—that it is not the result of any difference between you," said she. "I know that the first few months of married life are usually the most trying to both the man and the woman; but you can assure me that it is not——"

"I can give you such an assurance," he replied. "There has not been so much as a suspicion of difference between us in thought since she entered this house—in fact, since she became my wife."

"What is the matter, then? May I not know, Jack? Don't tell me if it is anything which concerns Priscilla and you only."

"Dearest mother, there is nothing that can concern us without being a matter of concern to you. Still, this one thing—of course you must know it; but what I am afraid of is that you will attach too much importance to it—that you will not see how it may be easily cleared away."

"You will tell me all about it, Jack, and I promise you not to think of it except in the way you say I should."

"It really is quite a simple thing—five minutes should clear it away for ever; and so far from its standing between Priscilla and myself, it will, I am sure, only draw us closer to each other."

He was not an adept in the art of "breaking it gently"; he had never had need to practise it. He felt that this, his first attempt, was but an indifferent success; he could see that so far from soothing her, his preliminary ambling around the subject was exciting her. And yet he feared to come out with a bare statement of the facts. He was snipping the end off a cigar; somehow he was clumsy over the operation; he could not understand why until he found that he was trying to force into the chamfered cutter the wrong end.

And his mother was noticing his confusion and becoming unduly excited.

Fortunately at this moment Priscilla entered the room—it was Mrs. Wingfield's boudoir, a pretty apartment for an invalid, the windows overlooking a garden of roses. Never did Jack so welcome her approach. The moment she passed the door she knew what was before her.

"Oh, by the way, Priscilla," said he, "you may as well tell mother just now all there is to be told about this disagreeable business. I have said that it is unlikely to take up more than a few minutes of the judge's time. You can best do it alone, I know."

He bolted.

His mother smiled, and Priscilla laughed outright; it was so like a man—each knew that that was just what the other was thinking—"so like a man!"

The elder lady's smile was still on her face when Priscilla said:

"There's really very little to be told about this disagreeable affair; but it must be faced. The fact is that we are applying to a judge to have my first marriage—that shocking mockery of a marriage—annulled, and everybody says that there will be no difficulty whatever about it."

"I don't suppose that there should be any difficulty, my dear," said Mrs. Wingfield. "But what would be the good of it?"

"Something has happened which makes it absolutely necessary," replied Priscilla. "But it is really the case that what has happened will make it very much easier for the judge. The wretch who, with a charge of fraud hanging over him, did not hesitate to make the attempt to involve me in his ruin, went straight from the gaol to America."

Mrs. Wingfield nodded.

"Don't trouble yourself, dear," she said. "I know all the story; it is not all squalid; you must not forget that he died trying to save the others."

"That was his lie," cried Priscilla. "He managed to get safely to the shore and he turned up here trying to get money out of us to buy him off. Jack showed him the door pretty quickly; so now you can understand how necessary it is that we should have the marriage nullified. A judge can do it in five minutes. Jack has been to Liscomb and Liscomb, and they told him so." (She was not now giving evidence in a court of law.) "Oh, yes; they had the opinion of Sir Edward upon it—five minutes! But in the meantime——"

"That's it—in the meantime," said Mrs. Wingfield slowly. She seemed trying to think out some point of great difficulty which had presented itself to her mind.

"In the meantime," she repeated. "Am I right, Priscilla, in the meantime you—you——"

"In the meantime, my dearest mother, if Jack were to die, and in his will refer to me as his wife, the judge of the Probate Court would decide that I should get whatever that will left to me. Is there anyone who will say that I am not Jack's wife? You will not say it, and you are Jack's mother."

"I certainly will not say it, Priscilla; but still—there are some who would say it, and—in the meantime—oh, it is terrible! my poor child; it is no wonder that there was a shadow cast upon your life. What you must have suffered—what you must still suffer! and how bravely you bore your burden in front of me!"

Priscilla had flung herself on her knees beside the sofa, and put her face down to the cushion on which the mother's head was resting; but her tears were not bitter, and her sobs were soft.

So she lay, her right arm about the shoulders of the other, for a long time, in complete silence.

At last she raised her head from the cushion, and then bowed it down to the pale face that was there until their tears mingled.

"I know what you are thinking, dearest," she whispered. "You are thinking that in the meantime I should not be in this house. Is not that so? Oh, I knew that that was your thought; but it will not be your thought when I tell you that...."

Her whisper dwindled away into nothing—it was not louder than the breathing of a baby when asleep.

But the elder woman caught every word. She gave a little cry of happiness, and held Jack's wife close to her, kissing her again and again.

"Dearest," she said, "you are right; your place is here—here—in the meantime."

CHAPTER XXXIII

In spite of the very good case which Priscilla had made out for herself to Jack's mother, without deviating from strict accuracy more widely than could easily be pardoned by even the severest moralist, and in spite also of the still better case which was made out for her by some of the contributors to that holiday page of the newspapers, she felt that she had considerable cause for uneasiness as the weeks went by and Messrs. Liscomb and Liscomb, having returned from Scotland or Homburg, were busying themselves about the nullity suit. Incidentally, they were concerned in two very dainty divorce suits and three libel actions which they hoped to get on the list before Christmas. They let Jack know that a defence had been entered to the nullity suit by Mr. Marcus Blaydon, so that the petitioner should not have a walk-over, whatever might happen; and they urged on Mr. Wingfield the necessity for finding out whether all that Captain Lyman knew would be in favour of Priscilla or of Marcus Blaydon.

It was apparent that what Captain Lyman knew would be an important factor in the case; but what he did know he had no chance of revealing, for it seemed as if Captain Lyman was lost. His name was in the registry of certificated mariners, but it was there as the master of the barque *Kingsdale*, and the owners of that ill-fated craft, on being communicated with by Messrs. Liscomb and Liscomb, stated that he was no longer in their service, nor did they know whose employment he had entered after the loss of his vessel. During the whole of the month of August the solicitors had, through their agents, been endeavouring to trace Lyman, but they had met with no success. The barque *Kingsdale* had been owned in Quebec, and he had been seen in that city in the month of June, but since then his whereabouts had been vague; and the clerk who was ready to rush off at a moment's notice in search of him, and to fathom the mystery of what he knew, began to feel that he stood a very good chance of being deprived of his excursion.

Messrs. Liscomb and Liscomb were beginning to write rather grave letters, They reminded Jack that they had absolutely no evidence to show that Blaydon had gone away from the English gaol to meet another woman than his wife; and as this was an important fact to establish both in the nullity suit and the possible divorce suit, and as, apparently, no one but Captain Lyman could give evidence on this point—a question which had not yet been answered—they thought no stone should be left unturned in order to find him and learn from his own lips what it was that he knew, and how much of it he did actually know, and whether his knowledge should take the form of an affidavit, or be carefully suppressed.

As a matter of fact Messrs. Liscomb and Liscomb gave Mr. Wingfield to understand that the success of their case would be seriously jeopardized unless they could place some evidence before the judge bearing upon the object of that trip made by Marcus Blaydon across the Atlantic.

Jack did not question the accuracy of their opinion in this matter; but what was he to do to provide them with the evidence they required? It was all very well for them to write about the necessity for leaving no stone unturned in order to find the extent of Captain Lyman's knowledge; but how could he, Jack Wingfield, travel through the world during the next couple of months, turning over stones to see if Captain Lyman was concealed beneath one of them?

He felt greatly disappointed, but he took good care that Priscilla remained in ignorance of the purport of Messrs. Liscomb and Liscomb's letters, and every day made it harder for him to keep her in this condition.

One afternoon he drove with her into Framsby, and their carriage stopped at a shop almost exactly opposite to the Corn Exchange, just when the frequenters of that institution were standing in groups along the pavement on the one day of the week when the Exchange was open. Business had been exceptionally good that day, and most of the farmers and millers were in a good humour. As soon as the rumour went round that the handsome lady in the carriage was the daughter of Farmer Wadhurst who was "standing up for her rights"—that was the *precis* that reached them of the "curious case" of the newspaper page—they took off their hats and gave her a hearty cheer.

This was not the first time that Priscilla had been so greeted in Framsby; but such proofs of the position she occupied in the hearts of the people, though gratifying, when considered from one standpoint, did not throw the light that was needed upon the question of what stone would, when turned, reveal the form of Captain Lyman ready to make an affidavit that should have weight with a judge. So while Priscilla drove home gratified by the kindly spirit shown by her sympathisers, Jack could not help feeling that he would gladly have exchanged it all for a single statement, made in the presence of a commissioner for taking oaths, bearing out the admission of Marcus Blaydon in regard to that woman on the other side of the Atlantic.

Of course Priscilla quickly perceived that he was becoming uneasy, and equally as a matter of course she found out the cause of the uneasiness. He told her something of what Messrs. Liscomb and Liscomb had communicated to him, though he did not go so far as to let her know that they considered the absent evidence to be vital to the success of the petition.

She took his explanation without saying more than a word or two.

"If Captain Lyman is not to be found we cannot have his evidence, whether for us or against us," she said. "And that being so, we shall have to do our best without it. I have great faith in Sir Edward's power of cross-examining. If he puts that man in the witness-box he should be able to get him to confess as much as he did to you."

Jack did not tell her that Messrs. Liscomb and Liscomb had explained to him that perhaps Marcus Blaydon might be prevented from going into the box by his own advisers, who might think it advisable to let the judge say whether or not she had succeeded in establishing her petition when she had been examined before him. It was well known that a very strong case indeed required to be made out in favour of pronouncing a marriage null and void before a judge would make such a pronouncement. So Messrs. Liscomb and Liscomb had told him; but he kept this information to himself.

It was with that phrase about leaving no stone unturned ringing in his mind, as if it were Messrs. Liscomb and Liscomb's telephone bell, that he sent off to the governor of the prison where Marcus Blaydon had been incarcerated the postcard which contained upon its gummy surface the imprint of the finger-tips of the man who had visited the Manor claiming Priscilla as his wife. In spite of the absolute certainty of Priscilla that he was Marcus Blaydon, Jack thought that there was just a chance that he was an impostor. Even within his experience there had been cases of men impersonating others with a view to blackmail or to an inheritance. There was just a chance that this man was not the real Marcus Blaydon, but a scoundrel of a slightly different pattern.

He sent the card in a small box, enclosing with it a letter asking the governor to be good enough to let him know if the finger-prints that it bore were those of Marcus Blaydon, who had been incarcerated in the prison for over a year.

With the lapse of only a few posts he received a communication from the acting-governor of the prison stating that he had sent on the card to the Criminal Investigation Department, and that the reply had been that the prints were those of Marcus Blaydon.

He told Priscilla what he had done, and what was the result, and she shook her head and smiled.

"It was very clever of you to get the finger-prints as you did," she said. "But I knew that I could not be mistaken in the man."

"There was only the ghost of a chance that the man was an impostor," said Jack; "but I felt bound to leave no stone—oh, there's that phrase buzzing about me again!"

"You were quite right, dear Jack," she said. "No stone should be left unturned in digging the foundation for our case."

Nothing further passed between them on this point; but two days later Jack received a private letter from the governor of the prison, stating that he had just resumed his duty after taking his annual leave, and that he had seen the letter which his deputy had answered.

"I can easily understand that you should be interested in an enquiry of the nature of that suggested by your communication," he added; "and though the reply which was sent to you may not have been just the one for which you hoped, yet I think it possible that it may be in my power to give you some assistance in any investigation you or your lawyers may be making in regard to Marcus Blaydon. It would not be regular to do so by letter, but if you could make it convenient to pay me a visit I might be able to place you in possession of one or two interesting—perhaps they may even turn out to be important—facts which came to my knowledge respecting the man when he was in my charge.

"When I read in the English newspapers, which I received in Switzerland, the particulars of the case in which Marcus Blaydon played so sinister a part, I made up my mind to place myself in communication with you; and I would have done so even if your letters had not been put into my hands on my return."

"It may mean a great deal or it may mean nothing," remarked Jack, passing this communication on to Priscilla.

Of course, Priscilla felt inclined, on a first reading of the note, to attribute a great deal of importance to it. "Why should the prison official take the trouble to write asking you to meet him if he was not sure that what he had to say was vital?" she asked Jack. But a second reading caused her to be less sanguine.

"It is just as you say it is: the man is guarded in his words; they may mean a great deal or they may mean very little," she said. "But he is in an official position, and no doubt he has had experience of curious cases and of everything that has a bearing upon them; and I can't think that he would have taken the trouble to write to you or to ask you to visit him unless he had something important to tell you."

"He says it may turn out to be important," said Jack; "but just now he thinks that it is only interesting. I am inclined to believe that it will never get beyond that qualification. You see, if he himself had thought that what he knew was vital to our interests he would have telegraphed to us the moment the first newspapers came into his hands."

"Yes, that is so, I can see plainly; but anyhow, you'll go, will you not?" said Priscilla. She could see plainly that Jack was a little annoyed because nothing had come of his cleverly-contrived trap in obtaining the man's finger-prints. He was not disposed to have any extravagant hopes of important information coming from a quarter that had failed him before. She knew that he was unreasonable; but she also knew that it was quite natural for him to be affected as he was by the failure of the authorities to say that the finger-prints were those of some man other than Marcus Blaydon.

"Great Gloriana! Of course I shall go to see him, and you will come with me," cried Jack. "No matter what he has to say to us, I feel that no stone——"

Priscilla clapt her hands upon her ears and rushed out of the room.

The county gaol to which Marcus Blaydon had been committed was a long way from Framsby. To reach it necessitated a journey to London, and thence into the heart of the Midlands. Passing through London they called upon Messrs. Liscomb and Liscomb to tell them of their mission, and the junior partner, who was acquainted with Major Crosbie, the governor of the prison, became greatly interested in the letter which he had written to Jack—so interested, indeed, that if the duty had not been laid upon him of receiving professional visits from two most promising prospective co-respondents and three defendants of newspaper libel actions, to say nothing of sundry uncompromising plaintiffs, he would, he declared, accompany his clients into the very presence of Major Crosbie.

"Whatever he may have to communicate, you may be sure that it will have a bearing upon the case," he said. "He will put you on the track of evidence—real evidence—not merely what somebody said that somebody told somebody else. You know where we are deficient in this particular."

"Yes," said Jack quickly, being afraid that he might go on to express himself strongly in Priscilla's presence regarding the need for evidence on the object of Blaydon's trip across the Atlantic. "Yes, we know pretty well how we stand. Any proof that Blaydon was a blackguard will be received with gratitude."

"That's it," said Mr. Liscomb.

"I thought Sir Edward's cross-examination might be expected to do great things for us in this way," said Priscilla.

"It may do something, but not a great deal," said Liscomb. "Judges are fond of facts; they don't care much about cross-examinations, however brilliant the newspapers may call them. You can easily see how the fellow, now that he has been put on his guard by your hint that you mean to try to connect his voyage with a woman, will be careful to have a story ready to account for all his movements, and he has only to stick to it to pull through, however Sir Edward may browbeat him. If you can bring the woman into court we shall have him in the cart."

That was all that Mr. Liscomb had to say to them, and they began to feel that they might as well have gone on direct to the gaol instead of calling upon him. And that was exactly what Mr. Liscomb himself thought. The honour and glory of being associated with the "curious case" were not inordinately estimated by him; the firm had been so closely connected with such a number of other curious cases ever since he had become a partner.

They found Major Crosbie waiting for them in a private room at the governor's house. As he was somewhat irregular in offering them the information of which he was possessed, he was too strict a disciplinarian to receive them in an official apartment. Within the precincts of his private residence he felt himself at liberty to talk as he pleased. A conscience capable of such reasonable differentiation is most valuable in an official.

He waved aside in a graceful way Mr. Wingfield's expression of gratitude for the invitation to this interview.

"There is no need to say a word on this point, Mr. Wingfield," he said. "Your case is a most curious one."

Jack confessed that he had heard it so described.

"A very curious one. It had been for nearly a week in the papers before I had a chance of hearing anything about it; but when I heard the name Marcus Blaydon I at once recollected some particulars which had come under my notice officially in connection with that man Blaydon. You are aware that it is part of my duty to read not only those letters which the prisoners in my charge write to persons outside, but also those which are received for themselves. Now, Blaydon received while in this prison four letters, all of which had been addressed to him at Prangborough, where, as you doubtless know, he lived."

Priscilla assented. Prangborough was the town in which her Aunt Emily lived.

"They had been addressed to him at Prangborough, and from there were forwarded to the prison. I find by reference to my official diary that three of them came from apparently the same correspondent and were posted at the same place—London in Canada; they were signed 'Lucy.' The fourth was from a man, evidently a captain in the merchant service, named Horace Lyman. It had been posted at Sunderland, and was received by me a short time before the expiration of the man's term of imprisonment."

"That is the letter which would be of importance to us if it told us what is the present address of Captain Lyman," said Jack.

Major Crosbie shook his head.

"You cannot expect a letter written nearly seven months ago to state positively what is the writer's address to-day," said he with a laugh. "But the contents of that letter made it clear that the writer and his correspondent were not on the best terms; and that the reason of this was the ill-treatment by Blaydon of the writer's sister, whose name was Lucy."

"And the woman's letters—did they make anything clear?"

"The woman's three letters made a good deal clear. The one of the earliest date suggested very clearly that she was the man's wife."

"What, Blaydon's wife!" cried Jack. "That would be the best possible news for us."

"So it occurred to me," said Major Crosbie. "If the man had been married—as the letters suggested he was—some years before he came under my notice—under our notice, I should say—and if his wife was alive, as she must have been when those letters of hers were written, the curious case becomes a very simple case indeed."

"And the letters suggested marriage?" said Priscilla, interrogatively.

"They undoubtedly suggested marriage—at least, they would have done so to someone with a smaller experience than I have had of such correspondence. But from what I know I should say that to assume that because a woman addresses a man as 'My own husband,' she is that man's lawful wife, would be a very unwise thing to do. Such a form of address, I have learnt by experience, comes quite naturally to the woman who is not married to the man but who should be on the grounds of the most elementary morality. It is the form used by the woman who has been deserted by the man, but who hopes to get back to her former place in his affection. She seems to think, poor thing, that if she assumes the title of wife whenever she has the chance, she will in time come to feel that she is his wife. I am not sure if you recognize the—the—what shall I call it?—the naturalness of all this."

He glanced first at Jack and then at Priscilla, and paused as if for their acquiescence in his suggestion.

They acquiesced. Jack nodded and muttered "Quite so." Priscilla said:

"I am sure it is natural—it is quite plausible. But it might be possible, might it not? to gather from the rest of the letters whether the woman was trying to bring back a husband or a lover."

"It is sometimes a good deal more difficult to do so than you could imagine," replied the Governor. "I used to think that I could determine this point by the character of the letters; the most earnest letters—those that were the most loving—the most full of endearment—were written by the woman to her lover; the tamest—the most formal, with a touch of nasty upbraiding, came from the legal wife to her legal husband. That was the general principle on which I drew my conclusions; but I soon found out how easy it was to make a mistake by building on such foundations only. You see, women differ so amazingly in temper and in temperament, leaving education and 'the complete letter-writer' out of the question altogether, that a wife who is not quite a wife may be carried away by her feelings of the moment, and say something so bitter that you could only believe it to come from a true wife, and the true wife may be really in love with her husband, and ready to condone his lapses without a word of reproach. That is how it is quite easy for one to make a mistake in trying to differentiate on the basis of correspondence only."

"Quite so," muttered Jack.

"I can quite believe that," said Priscilla. "But about these particular letters?"

She thought it quite as well to bring back Major Crosbie from his consideration of the abstract to that of the concrete. She could see that Jack was becoming slightly impatient at the somewhat cynical expression of the Governor's experiences.

"I was just returning to the letters written to Marcus Blaydon," said he. "It was necessary for me to state to you the difficulty which I find in the way of coming to any legitimate conclusion on the point which concerns you most, in order to prevent you from falling into the mistake of believing that you are quite safe, when investigation may prove that you have assumed too much."

"Of course—quite right," said Jack. "But you believe that the woman was his wife?"

The Governor caressed his chin with a neat forefinger.

"I think, after going very carefully once more over the copy of the letters, that there would be sufficient in any one of them to allow a Grand Jury to bring in a true bill," he replied.

Jack saw that the man described very neatly what was in his mind. But Priscilla had never served on a Grand Jury. She required further explanation.

"What I mean to say," resumed Major Crosbie, "is that the letters suggest a relationship which may prove on investigation to be a legal union contracted three years ago in Canada. You observe how cautious I am?"

"I do indeed," replied Priscilla, and she did not acquiesce merely out of politeness.

"I should be reluctant to say one word that might lead you to expect too much," said he. "My experience leads me to look for the worst and not the best in men; but I should be reluctant to say that the letters signed 'Lucy' did not come from a woman who was the legal wife of Marcus Blaydon."

"That is so much, at any rate," said Jack; "and now if you can give us any clue as to how it would be possible to be brought in touch with Horace Lyman, we will be evermore indebted to you."

"The woman is his sister—so much I gathered," said the Governor. "And I learned that he was waiting for Blaydon at the prison gate when Blaydon was released. That is all I know. But the sister's address is, as I mentioned just now, London, in Canada—at least, that was her address when she was in communication with Blaydon. Her letters were not illiterate, though of course they were not carefully written. They showed what critics would possibly call an ill-balanced mind—extremes of blandishments on one page, and threats of the wildest nature on the next. I can give you copies if you would care to see them."

Priscilla shook her head. She could not see herself sitting down to read the confidential letters of the poor woman.

"I am quite willing to accept your judgment on them, Major Crosbie," she said.

"I think that you are right to do so," said he. "If you were to read them they would certainly convey more to you, who have fortunately had no experience of this form of correspondence, than would be good for your future peace of mind. You would say at once when you saw the address 'My dearest husband,' and the reiteration of the same word, 'husband' with various vehement adjectives—you would undoubtedly feel confident that the pair were married, but you must think of that possibility with great suspicion."

"You have suggested it, at any rate, and for that you have our heartiest thanks," said Jack. "Why, only to be able to put that name 'Lucy Lyman' on Sir Edward's brief means an enormous gain to us."

"But you will, of course, send someone out to Canada to make the thing sure," said Crosbie. "You may be able to find the woman herself, and to bring her to England to confront the man. Whether she's his wife or not, that will be a help to your case."

"I should rather think that it will be a help," cried Jack. "If it can be shown that the man went straight from this place to the side of that woman in Canada, I don't see how any judge could refuse us a verdict. I shall start for Canada to-morrow."

"For Heaven's sake consult with your solicitors first," said Crosbie. "They may think that one of their own agents is the best person to pursue the necessary enquiry in Canada. And now that we have gone as far as we are likely to go into this matter, even though we should confer together for a week, we shall have lunch. My wife and daughter are unfortunately still in Paris—I left them starting on a round of shops—but you will make allowances for a household run for the present *en garçon*." The lunch was, however, so excellent as to leave no need for any allowance to be made by either of the visitors; and when it was over their host offered, as they expected he would, to show them over the prison. Jack knew that governors of prisons, as well as commanders of cruisers and vergers of cathedrals and superintendents of lunatic asylums, take it for granted that every visitor is burning to be "shown over the place"; and he felt too deeply indebted to Major Crosbie not to afford him an opportunity of exhibiting his hobby at this time. So for the next hour and a half he and Priscilla gave themselves up to this form of entertainment. The Governor spared them none of the interesting horrors of the "system." They were shown the handsome young bank clerk who, on a salary of one hundred and twenty pounds a year, had managed to keep a motor and to go to a music hall every night of his life for three years without once arousing the suspicion of the directorate; the ex-Lord Mayor (not of London) who had made a fortune by insuring people's lives (in an American office) and then encouraging them to drink themselves to death; the soldier who, after winning the Victoria Cross twice over, and saving two batteries of field artillery, had taken to beating women in Bermondsey, and had one day gone a little too far in this way; the great financier who had done his best to save the life of the King by standing by in his 300-ton yacht when his Majesty was in no danger, and had a little later been sentenced at the Old Bailey for another audacious fraud; the young man of "superior education" who had done several very neat forgeries, and was now making pants in the tailor's shop; the ex-officer of Engineers who had lived in a mansion on the

Cromwell Road for several years on the profits of writing begging letters, and was now, by the irony of Fate, engaged in sewing canvas, mail-bags in which probably, when he came to be relieved of this obligation, his own compositions would be conveyed to their destination—all of these interesting persons the visitors saw, with many others of equal distinction. And they went away fully satisfied, and with a consciousness of having cancelled a good portion of whatever debt they owed to the Governor.

"Funny!" said Priscilla suddenly, when they were sitting opposite to each other in the dining-car a few hours later. "Funny, isn't it, that that man with the reddish hair who was working out his sentence for forgery should be the Reverend Sylvanus Purview, who read the marriage service between Marcus Blaydon and myself!"

"Great Gloriana! Are you positive?" cried Jack.

"As positive as I was about the other," said Priscilla. "And what's stranger still, he recognized me the moment we entered the tailor's shop. I saw as much by his face, though I had not recognized him in his prison clothes. He was a temporary hand taken on by Mr. Possnett to do his duty when he was absent on his holiday. He lodged in Mrs. Bowman's cottage, and went away without paying her. It created rather a scandal in our respectable neighbourhood."

"The rascal! I suppose he'll lose his frock, now," said Jack.

"Mr. Possnett wrote to the Bishop about him; but he had left the diocese, and no one knew what had become of him," said Priscilla.

"Well, we know now. I wonder what it was he forged. He was clearly a bad egg from the first. How did you feel when you recognized him?"

"Delighted," cried Priscilla. "I felt as if I were paying him back in full the grudge that I owed him." Jack laughed.

CHAPTER XXXIV

They remained in London that night, in order that they might tell Mr. Liscomb how they had fared on their visit to the prison. They had a good deal to discuss between themselves in the meantime. Upon one point they were in complete agreement, and this was with regard to Major Crosbie's belief in the relationship existing between Marcus Blaydon and the woman who had signed herself 'Lucy.' He had endeavoured to be very cautious in all that he had said on this important point in their presence. He had been extremely careful not to commit himself in any way, or to leave them any chance of reproaching him afterwards for leading them to have false hopes that the marriage of Blaydon with Priscilla was a bigamous one. But in spite of his intelligent caution, the impression which he had produced upon them was that he at least was a firm believer that Blaydon and his Lucy were man and wife.

They tried to reconstruct the whole of Blaydon's story so far as Priscilla was concerned. It was quite plausible that, after marrying his Lucy in Canada and living with her for some years, they had quarrelled—had not Major Crosbie said that the letters betray a very ill-balanced temperament—one page showing her going into an extreme of affection and the next flying into an excess of abuse? This was eminently the sort of woman with whom a husband would quarrel, and from whom he would eventually fly.

And then fancying that he had escaped from her, and being led to commit those frauds for which he was afterwards sentenced to imprisonment, was not his wooing of Priscilla just what might be looked for from such an unprincipled man? He had an idea, no doubt, that he would be able to squeeze a fortune out of her father, and when he had made his position secure, he would have cleared off, perhaps leaving Priscilla a message that he was not her husband.

They had no trouble whatever in piecing together such a story of fraud as was adapted, they felt sure, to the fraudulent tendencies of the man and the ill-balanced passions of the woman on the other side of the Atlantic—Priscilla could see her quite clearly—a tall, darkhaired and dark-skinned creature—a termagant—the sort of woman that a sort of man would love fiercely and desert with joy when the dust of the ashes of his passion began to make his eyes smart and to irritate his nostrils. And as she pictured her, this woman was not the one to let a man wrong her and remain unpunished. She would not be such a fool as to allow a man to approach her unless he meant marriage; and she would certainly be able to hold him captive until he was ready to marry her.

But while Priscilla believed what she wanted to believe—namely, that the man and the woman had been husband and wife before he had left her, she would have been sorry to allow herself to be so carried away by that impression as to believe that Marcus Blaydon might not have behaved to that woman as the scoundrel he had shown himself to be in regard to herself. She would have been sorry to think that he was not capable of deceiving his Lucy and running away from her; and being so obsessed by the certainty that the man was a villain, she could not feel so sure as she would have liked that he had actually married the woman who had been writing to him.

She and Jack agreed, however, that Major Crosbie, a man who had been associated with greater villains, and a greater number of them, than almost any living man, certainly believed that Blaydon and that woman were man and wife, and against the belief of a man so well qualified to judge, the impressions of ordinary people not moving in criminal circles must be held of small account. And Priscilla, feeling this, was quite satisfied to allow her belief in the persistent villainy of Marcus Blaydon to yield to such *force majeure*.

But these beliefs and impressions and speculations were, after all, of no importance in relation to the final issue of their visit to the prison, compared with what they had achieved in learning in what direction to begin their search for whatever Captain Lyman could tell them. When they had set out upon their journey to the prison, the only thing that they had before them was the discovery of the whereabouts of Captain Lyman, who might possibly be able to give them some information in regard to the woman whom Jack, with his acquaintance with the wickedness of men, had asserted, when face to face with Marcus Blaydon, that this same Blaydon had gone straight from gaol to meet. But from this rather indefinite quest they had come with some very definite information indeed, not respecting Captain Horace Lyman, but respecting the woman herself. They had no need of the help of Captain Lyman or the fulness of his knowledge just now. They were in a position to go direct to the woman, and then...

"We are going ahead a bit too fast," said Jack, when they had got so far in their review of all that they had gained by their visit to the prison. "We would do well not to go just yet beyond the point when we set out for Canada."

"*We?*" cried Priscilla. "Do you mean to say that you would take me with you?"

"I told you a long time ago that I meant to run no risks where you are concerned, and that's my situation still," replied Jack. "I do not intend to let you out of my sight until this business is settled. It is about time that you had a holiday, and there's no better place for holiday-making than Canada in the Fall."

She could not speak to acknowledge her appreciation of his care for her. She pulled his arm about her and nestled in its hollow.

"There is no such amazing sight—no such picture of colour in the whole world as the Canadian backwoods in the Fall," he continued. "It will amaze you. The sight of those leaves..."

Off he went, and for the rest of the evening they threw aside every consideration of the ostensible object of their trip to Canada and devoted themselves to their itinerary of the St. Lawrence, with excursions north and south, and a week at Niagara. Not another word did they say about the man or the woman, or the possible effect of producing the latter in the English courts to testify to the man's perfidy. They were going on a holiday together, and that was enough for them. They exchanged plans until bedtime.

Even at breakfast the next morning Priscilla returned to the topic, asking him what clothes she should take with her on her journey, and he replied that she couldn't do better than take the usual sort; an answer that sent her into a little fit of laughter which lasted until he had shaken his newspaper out of its folds and glanced at the first page. Then her laughter was stopped by his familiar exclamation:

"Great Gloriana! What's this?"

"What's what?" she asked.

He did not answer her.. His eyes were staring at the paper. He was reading something with an intensity that prevented his hearing her.

She waited patiently until he looked up in a puzzled way, and remarked once more:

"Great Gloriana!"

"What is it, Jack? What have you been reading there?" she said.

He gave a little start, as if he had not expected to see her beside him.

"I beg your pardon," he cried. "I was so—so—knocked—read it—the letter—there—farther down."

"Horace Lyman!" she cried. "What is this?"

The name that had been so much in their thoughts for all these weeks was there—printed in small capitals at the foot of a letter addressed to the editor: "Horace Lyman, master mariner."

It did not take her long to read every word that appeared above that signature.

The letter was headed "An Impostor," and between that heading and the signature she read the following:

"Sir,—A copy of your esteemed paper, dated the 2nd ult., having come into my hand, I learn that a man named Marcus Blaydon has been giving an account to your representatives of an incident which he describes as a miraculous escape from drowning when endeavouring to carry a line ashore from the wreck of the barque *Kingsdale*, off the coast of Nova Scotia, on the night of April the 9th. Sir, I fear that you have been hoaxed by an impostor in this matter; for it would be impossible to believe that any man who, when he reached the shore, had the heartlessness to free himself from the line, leaving his messmates to their fate—certain death, as he had every reason to believe it would be—and then to hurry away from the scene of the disaster, would have the effrontery to face men and women—and *women*, I repeat—in a Christian land.

"Sir, I am prepared to prove every word that I say, and what I do say and affirm solemnly and before my Maker, is that Marcus Blaydon cast off the line which he had carried ashore, leaving us to our fate, and walked away from the coast inland without making any enquiry and without making any attempt to procure help for us in our extremity from some of the fishing population of that coast. With his further movements ashore I am also fully acquainted up to a certain point; but I still say that I refuse to believe that even so inhuman a wretch would presume to have the impudence to face Christian people in a Christian country."

That was the letter, written by the hand of a sailor-man all unaccustomed to that elegance of diction which marks the sentences of a newspaper correspondent, but at the same time quite practised in the art of striking out straight from the shoulder, regardless of pleonasms in composition.

"That is Horace Lyman, and that is Marcus Blaydon," said Priscilla without emotion.

"Look for a leader," cried Jack, turning over the pages of the newspaper. "I shouldn't wonder if there was a leader or something on this letter. A man would need to convince the newspaper people pretty completely of his rights in this matter before' he could induce them to print such a libel. By the nine gods, here it is!"

And there, sure enough, was a short editorial note calling attention to Captain's Lyman's letter and stating that Captain Lyman had proved to the satisfaction of the editor that he could, if given an opportunity, substantiate every word of the serious charges which he had brought against Marcus Blaydon, a man whose name the public had acclaimed as that of a hero in the Spring, but who, it would now appear, so far from being a hero, was a paltry adventurer, without any of those better qualities which are occasionally found associated with adventurers.

The newspaper was one which had made a name for itself by reason of its fearlessness in exposing fraud and for its persistence in following up a clue to an imposition, no matter by whom attempted.

Jack read the editorial comment and laughed.

"I'm afraid there will be no trip to Canada, Priscilla," he said.

"On our part, no," she said.

He looked at her enquiringly.

"On our part? Do you suggest that—that—he———"

"I think that he will go to Canada—to London, Canada," said she.

"Even though her brother has shown him to be such a skunk?"

"*Because* her brother has done so."

"Is that woman?"

"Yes, that is woman."

"I'm learning. And she is married to him, you still think?"

"No; I don't believe now that she is. However, we'll soon learn the truth. We shall have no difficulty in getting in touch with Captain Lyman now. The newspaper people will be certain to have his address in case of accidents. They would not care to be saddled with a libel action unless they could lay a hand on Captain Lyman at a moment's notice."

"I'm certain of that; they'll give us his address fast enough at the newspaper office. We shall call for it when we have seen Reggie Liscomb."

They had agreed with Mr. Liscomb to call upon him on their return from their visit to Major Crosbie, to acquaint him with the result of their interview with that officer; and when they entered the private room of the junior partner, they found him with a copy of the newspaper which they had just been reading, on the desk in front of him.

"You have seen it?" said Jack. "Captain Lyman's letter?"

"I have gone one better. I have seen Captain Lyman himself," said Mr. Liscomb.

"Then you know his present address and we need not send for it to the paper?" said Priscilla.

"You certainly need not be at that trouble. His address just at this present moment is 'Waiting-room, 3, Bishop's Place.'"

He touched a bell.

"Send in the gentleman who went last into the room," he said to the messenger, and before Jack or Priscilla had recovered from their surprise, a black-bearded, well-built man, wearing a jacket and carrying a tall hat of an obsolete pattern that had been called in several years before, entered the room, and gave a fine quarterdeck bow all round.

"Captain Lyman," said Mr. Liscomb, "this is the lady and gentleman about whom we had our chat just now."

"Proud, ma'am—proud, sir," said Captain Lyman, bowing once more.

"Captain Lyman," said Priscilla quickly. "Was your sister Lucy ever married to Marcus Blaydon?"

"Never, ma'am, never; and never will be if I can help it," was the reply.

CHAPTER XXXV

There was a long silence in the room when that quick answer had been given to Priscilla's quick question.

Captain Lyman looked first at Priscilla, then at Jack, and lastly at Mr. Liscomb. He seemed not to understand quite why he had been asked that question, but as it had been asked, he was ready to reply to any other that might be put to him. But no one seemed to have a question ready.

It was Mr. Liscomb who broke the silence. He looked up from the newspaper which he had been reading and said:

"Captain Lyman, I should like to ask you how it came that you allowed that report of the man's being drowned to be published in the papers when you were aware of his being alive, and why you allowed him to be written about as a hero when you knew from the first that he had cast off the line, leaving you and your shipmates to your fate, as you say in this letter? That's a question which people will be pretty sure to ask, and you may as well be prepared for it."

"I'm quite prepared for it, sir," replied Lyman. "I cooked the report for the benefit of my sister, who was—but it's a long story, sir, and there's not much in it that you haven't heard before, of a woman without wisdom and a man without a conscience."

"It's the oldest story in the world—and the newest; but every variation of it is interesting—in fact, nobody cares about any other sort of story," said Mr. Liscomb.

"I'll cut this particular variation as short as I can," said the mariner. "I have a sister, and she fell in love with Blaydon, it must be six years ago. There was no reason why they should not have married, for he had a good billet and she had a trifle of her own; but the marriage didn't come off, and the man behaved badly—she told me so when I returned after a voyage—if I had been at home I'd ha' taken damgood care that the marriage did come off. But it didn't, and the next I hear is that he has borrowed money from her and cleared off. It was near about three years before I got wind of him, for you see I'd been knocking about the world, first in one ship and then in another. I had put into Sunderland in the barque *Kingsdale*, and there I found a letter waiting for me from my sister, telling me that the man was in gaol but would be out in a week or two, and that I was to write to him and then wait for him at the prison gate, and not lose sight of him until I brought him to her. I was able to do what she told me, for the barque was in the graving-dock for a month. I met him the moment he got his freedom, and we sailed the next day. He wasn't very willing to come with me, but he never said a word about having been married the year before until we were pretty far out of soundings, and then he showed me the paper with accounts of his arrest outside the church, and of his trial, when he was let off light by reason of the jawing of the lawyer about the poor young wife that was waiting for him to turn his erring feet into the straight path, *et cetera*—you know the sort of stuff lawyers talk, sir!"

"I do—I do; I do it myself," said Mr. Liscomb. "Never mind the lawyers and their tricks; go on with your story."

"I ask your pardon, sir. Well, of course, when I saw that he was married already I had no further use for him. All I could do was to give him a sound hiding with a rope's end; and a sounder one man never got, though I say it that shouldn't."

"We'll pardon your boast, Captain," said Mr. Liscomb.

"Oh, certainly," acquiesced Mr. Wingfield, heartily.

"Thank you, gentlemen. I did my best, and no man can do more. Well, nothing happened until the barque ran on the rocks, and then he came to me and said he was a good swimmer and he would like to try to make up for his wickedness by carrying a line ashore for us. I was fool enough to be taken in by him. He got the line ashore, but then he cast it adrift—when we hauled it in we found that the knot had been properly loosed——"

"It couldn't have become unfastened by the action of the waves?" suggested the lawyer.

The Captain smiled grimly.

"No knot that I tie is of that description, sir," he said. "No, the rascal slackened the bight and then walked away without saying a word to anyone until he came to a house nine miles from the coast, where he was able to loan a suit of clothes—he had his pockets full of money—and the next day he caught a train for the town where a friend of his lived, and there he lay till he caught sight of a newspaper that told him that his wife had married again, and he came to England to see if there wasn't some money in it for him."

"That's quite clear; but you haven't said why you allowed the reports of his heroic death to be printed, when you knew the truth," said Mr. Liscomb.

"I'm sure the lady will see that I did it because I wanted to let my poor sister down gently," said Captain Lyman. "I wanted her to believe that the man was drowned, and I wanted her to think the best of herself—to feel for the rest of her life that, after all, she had loved a man that showed himself to be a man in the way of his death. But when I landed in England a week ago, and came across the papers with that 'curious case' in them, I saw that Lucy was bound to know all; and having picked up with a newspaper young gentleman, he took me, as I told you just now, sir, when we were alone, to the office of his paper and, after a talk with the head boss, I wrote that letter. It was the same gentleman that told me to call on you, sir."

"You did the right thing, and you'll never regret it," said Mr. Liscomb.

"No, I don't think I'll regret it, if it puts a spoke in that blackguard's wheel," said Captain Lyman, brushing the cylinder of his silk hat with his sleeve. "You have my address, sir, in case you need me at any time," he added when at the door.

"And I think we shall need you," said Mr. Liscomb. When Jack and Priscilla were left alone with the man of the law he questioned them as to the result of their interview with the Governor of the prison, mentioning how he had led them to believe what he certainly believed himself—that Marcus Blaydon and the woman who had written to him were man and wife.

"And how do we stand now?" asked Jack. "Are we anything the better for Lyman's visit?"

"Not a great deal up to the present," said Mr. Liscomb. "What I now fear is that Blaydon will clear off without waiting to oppose the petition for nullity."

"Then all will be plain sailing," cried Jack.

"Anything but that," said Liscomb, shaking his head. "There's nothing that the judge is more cautious about than collusion. If a case like this is not opposed, he begins to suspect that the opposition has been bought off. We shall have to make the whole thing very clear to him."

"And that is more difficult now than it was before," said Priscilla; "for we cannot now say that he went straight away from the prison to the woman in Canada. As a matter of fact, he was taken away from England practically by main force; and the woman in Canada was the last person whom he wished to be near."

"I am glad that you appreciate the difficulties of the case," said the lawyer. "The sacredness of the ceremony of marriage is cherished by the people of England very much more scrupulously than are its obligations. A judge feels that his responsibility in a question of pronouncing a marriage null and void is almost greater than he can bear. I believe that one of them never could be induced to believe that he had the power to pronounce such a decree. It all comes from those foolish words in the marriage service, 'Whom God hath joined together let no man put asunder.' The old powers of the Church survive in that sentence. The marriage was not a civil contract, but a sacrament of the Church, and some nice hanky-panky tricks the Church played in the same connection. And now when the ceremony in the church is only kept on as an excuse for a display of the *dernier cri* of fashion, and when the civil contract part—the only part that is according to the law of the land—is made the centre of some beautiful but absolutely useless embroidery of words and phrases, the final aweinspiring sentence, 'Whom God hath joined together let no man put asunder' is supposed to be the motto on the seal of a sacred bond. But it is really nothing more than the ordinary phrase of a parson addressing his congregation, unless you wish to assume, which for obvious reasons I don't, that the civil laws of England have the same Divine origin as the Ten Commandments."

Priscilla smiled. How much plainer he had expressed what she had often tried to express, was what she was thinking at that moment.

Jack was becoming uneasy. If Priscilla and that lawyer were to begin to exchange opinions and compare views on the great marriage question, they might easily remain in that stuffy office for another hour or two. But as usual, Priscilla's extraordinary capacity for keeping silence came to his aid. She smiled, but said not a word.

"Then how do we stand just now?" asked Jack, picking up his hat.

"Well," said Mr. Liscomb. "I am bound to say that I am disappointed, but by no means surprised——"

But at this point he must certainly have been surprised; for he sprang from his chair with an exclamation.

It was not to be wondered at; for with a bang and a rush, the man who had just left the room returned to it. He had a paper in his hand—the first edition of an evening paper.

"She has killed him!" cried Captain Lyman. "Lucy has killed him—my sister—there it is—and I didn't know that she was in England. She must have read about the case and come across! Oh, my God! she has killed him, and I remember her when she was a little girl with golden hair lying in her cot—as innocent as a lamb. Oh, damn him! but he's in hell now—thank God there's a hell for him—thank——"

The room was not big enough for the curses that welled up in the big heart of the sailor. The atmosphere became impregnated in a moment with the smell of turpentine and bilge-water, and a freshly opened consignment of flour of sulphur.

Mr. Liscomb had snatched the paper from him. Jack glanced over his shoulder while he read. Priscilla sat down. Her face had become deathly pale. She watched Captain Lyman weeping into a large handkerchief of the bandana variety. She felt as if she were taking part in a tableau.

Then the door opened, and the senior partner entered with another newspaper in his hand.

"Good heavens! you have seen it also?" he cried. "A terrible thing!—a shocking thing!—the best thing that could have happened! Good-morning, Mrs. Wingfield. Don't allow yourself to be upset. Let me get you a glass of wine—brandy perhaps would be better."

"There is no need," said Priscilla. "You see, I don't know what has happened. Please don't try to break it gently to me, Mr. Liscomb."

"A kiddie with curls as fair as flax, ma'am," cried Captain Lyman, waving his handkerchief in the direction of the lady.

The senior partner stared at him.

"This is Captain Lyman," said Priscilla.

"Lucy she was called at her christening, and she was as innocent as a lamb before he got hold of her. But she killed him—killed him dead—it's all in that paper—and I didn't even know that she was in this country, sir. She didn't come across to kill him; I'll swear that she didn't. But maybe it would have been better if I'd told her the truth."

"The truth is—ah—sometimes justifiable," said Mr. Liscomb. "This, however, is a clear case of self-defence. She will not be imprisoned for a day."

"But she loved him, sir," said Captain Lyman. "What is it makes women love a man like that; can you tell me?"

"Self-defence," came the voice of the junior partner. "He was following her with a revolver. He had fired three shots, one of them grazed her shoulder. There were two witnesses—she seized the first weapon that came to her hand—he ran upon the prongs."

"Justifiable, oh, of course," said the senior partner. He glanced towards Priscilla. "Bad taste to congratulate her," he whispered to his brother Reggie. "Get them out of this as soon as possible; and send me in a copy of the writ in Farraget's case. Get rid of the sailor. He's no credit to the office."

"I can't forget her—fair hair and such sweet blue eyes," resumed Captain Lyman.

"Come along with us, Captain Lyman," said Priscilla. "Thank heaven we've got rid of them so easily," said the senior Liscomb.

"The woman did the best job for the Wingfields that ever was done for them," said the junior. "As the case stood, I doubt very much if Sir Gabriel would have given us a decree, and there was no evidence for a divorce. They can get married to-morrow."

The next edition of the evening papers contained a full account of the opportune killing of Marcus Blaydon by Lucy Lyman. It happened the previous evening in the strawyard of Athalsdean Farm, where Marcus Blaydon was staying with Mr. Wadhurst. Three of the yardmen saw the woman enter and enquire for Mr. Blaydon; and she had gone, according to their direction, into one of the outhouses where he had been superintending some work, for it seemed that Farmer Wadhurst did not allow him to eat the bread of idleness. The men shortly afterwards heard the sound as of an altercation, and then of a shot. The woman rushed out shrieking, and Blaydon came after her, with a revolver, from which he fired two more shots at her. He was overtaking her when she picked up one of the two-pronged forks with which the bundles of straw were tossed from the carts, and turned upon him with it. He was in the act of rushing at her, but he never reached her; he rushed upon the two prongs of the fork and fell dead at her feet.

That was the whole story; for although the woman was arrested and admitted that she had produced the revolver in the presence of the man in order to terrify him and force him to go away with her, it was perfectly plain that he had got possession of the weapon, and had endeavoured to take her life, his efforts being only frustrated by the accident of the strawyard fork lying in her way when she was trying to escape.

"Justifiable homicide"—that was the phrase which was in everybody's mouth during the next few days; and everyone who spoke the words added that he or she supposed that Mr. Wingfield and Priscilla would now get married in proper form.

But that was not Priscilla's intention at all. She meant to have the contract between herself and Marcus Blaydon pronounced null and void in a court of law, and she expressed herself to this effect to Jack. She thought that she would have some trouble in inducing him to see that it would not be just the same thing if they got married the next day; but she found that he was with her on all points in this matter. Messrs. Liscomb and Liscomb were instructed to proceed with the case; and a good many people, when they heard this—including Messrs. Liscomb and Liscomb—said that Mr. Wingfield and Priscilla were a pair of fools.

And that was exactly what the judge said when he was appealed to a couple of months later in the form of a petition by Priscilla. "A pair of young fools!" This was when he was driving home from the court. When he had had a sleep and a game of whist at the *Athenaeum*, and a chat with his wife, he said again, "A pair of young fools!"

The next day he granted the petition.

It so happened, however, that there was another scene in this matrimonial comedy; for on the very morning after the return of the Wingfields, the Reverend Osney Possnett called upon Priscilla.

"He is come to tout for a job," was the comment of Mr. Wingfield upon this incident. "Tell him to send in his estimate, and we'll consider it with the others. Like his cheek to write '*Most important*' on his card."

"I cannot understand what he means," said Priscilla. "Surely he does not hope to persuade me that a judge of a civil court has no authority to pronounce a decree of nullity!"

"You never can tell," said Jack.

And then the clergyman entered. He was in a state of great agitation, and Priscilla believed that tears were in his eyes.

He went toward her with both hands extended.

"My poor girl—my poor Priscilla!" he cried. "I am to blame—I only am to blame. Such a thing has happened before, but only once, I believe, during the past twenty years."

"What has happened, Mr. Possnett?" she enquired. "Are you quite sure that you are to blame?"

"Yes, that's the question," said Jack, who did not know when to keep silent.

"No, no; it was my fault. I should have made more ample enquiries; but I was in a hurry, and I never dreamt that he was not all right," cried Mr. Possnett.

"Do you mean about Mr. Sylvanus Purview?" said Priscilla. "If so, we know all about him; he is in prison. We saw him there some time ago."

"What, you are aware that he was an impostor—that he had forged his ordination papers—that he had never been a priest in holy orders?"

"We heard nothing of that," said Priscilla. "Major Crosbie heard nothing of it either, I'm sure. He told us that the man was of superior education, and had been sentenced to imprisonment for forgery, but it was in connection with a bond."

"No one could have told you about his fraud upon me, for he only confessed to me yesterday," said Mr. Possnett. "He had expressed a desire to the chaplain to see me, and the Governor wrote to me—a cautious letter—mentioning this fact. Of course I went to the prison, and I saw the unfortunate man. He seemed to me to be truly contrite—the chaplain is well known for a zealous preacher. The man's right name is Samuel Prosser, and he lived in Australia. He was at Melbourne College, and he had a remarkable career in New South Wales. He came to me from a London agency, bearing, as I thought, satisfactory credentials for a *locum tenens*. He had forged every one of them. He confessed it to me. I believe he would have done so even if he had not seen you at the prison, and heard your story from the chaplain. But I shall never forgive myself—never! Happily yours was the only marriage he celebrated. The usual procedure in such a case is to take legal steps to have all marriages celebrated by a man who, though unqualified, is accepted *bona fide* by the contracting parties as an authorized clergyman, pronounced valid—it has been resorted to more than once; but in this case——"

"I don't think we'll go to that expense," said Jack. "At least, my wife and I will talk the matter over first."

"Ah, just so. But my dear Pris—Mrs. Wingfield, can you ever forgive my want of care in this matter? Oh, it will be a warning to me in future—culpable want of care—can you ever forgive me?"

"Well, yes, I think I can," said Priscilla.

And there is every reason to believe that she did—freely.

"My dear Priscilla, after all you were the most unmarried woman of all the world when you came to me," said Jack.

"And now I believe that I am the most married," said she.

And all Framsby left cards the next day.

THE END.

Milton Keynes UK
Ingram Content Group UK Ltd.
UKHW030622061024
449204UK00004B/397